Unlock the secrets to who you and your friends *really* are through the language of birthdays!

THE SECRET LANGUAGE OF
BIRTHDAYS

teen edition

ALICIA THOMPSON

OVER ONE MILLION COPIES SOLD OF THE ORIGINAL!

Based on the original by Gary Goldschneider and Joost Elffers

The Secret Language of Birthdays, Teen Edition

RAZORBILL

Published by the Penguin Group
Penguin Young Readers Group
345 Hudson Street, New York, New York 10014, U.S.A.
Penguin Group (USA) Inc., 375 Hudson Street, New York, New York 10014, U.S.A.
Penguin Group (Canada), 90 Eglinton Avenue East, Suite 700, Toronto, Ontario, Canada M4P 2Y3 (a division of Pearson Penguin Canada Inc.)
Penguin Books Ltd, 80 Strand, London WC2R 0RL, England
Penguin Ireland, 25 St Stephen's Green, Dublin 2, Ireland (a division of Penguin Books Ltd)
Penguin Group (Australia), 250 Camberwell Road, Camberwell, Victoria 3124, Australia
(a division of Pearson Australia Group Pty Ltd)
Penguin Books India Pvt Ltd, 11 Community Centre, Panchsheel Park, New Delhi—110 017, India
Penguin Group (NZ), 67 Apollo Drive, Rosedale, North Shore 0632, New Zealand
(a division of Pearson New Zealand Ltd.)

Penguin Books (South Africa) (Pty) Ltd, 24 Sturdee Avenue, Rosebank,
Johannesburg 2196, South Africa

Penguin Books Ltd, Registered Offices: 80 Strand, London WC2R 0RL, England

10 9 8 7 6 5 4 3 2 1

LIBRARY OF CONGRESS CATALOGING-IN-PUBLICATION DATA
Thompson, Alicia.
p. cm.
ISBN: 978-1-59514-232-0
[1. Birthdays--Miscellanea. I. Title
BF1729.B45 T46 2009
133.5/4042 22

2008040083

Printed in the United States of America

Introduction

· ·

No one knows how, no one knows why, but birthdays often have a surprising way of revealing truths about people. There's a belief known as *personology,* which explores the idea that personalities are cyclical. According to personology, those born on the same day of the year—regardless of what year it is—will have certain characteristics in common. People who share a birthday may also have similar strengths and weaknesses, similar tendencies and predilections, likes and dislikes. So you can *discover a lot about yourself* and your own potential—for good and for bad—by learning more about your birthday. You can also find out secrets to understanding your friends and family based on the days *they* were born.

So welcome to The Secret Language of Birthdays— Teen Edition! This is an adaptation of *The Secret Language of Birthdays* by astrology, numerology, and tarot experts Gary Goldschneider and Joost Elffers. The birthday descriptions listed in this book begin with March 21st (Aries), following the zodiac year and ending on March 20th (Pisces). *On every page* are symbols indicating special details about that personality. You can find *the keys* to those symbols on the next few pages. Each sign of the zodiac has its own separate section, as listed in the table of contents. At the beginning of each of those sections, you will find an explanation of that sign. Also, there are *quizzes throughout,* specially designed to explore different elements of personality!

What are you waiting for?
Find out what your birthday has to say
about you!

THE SECRET LANGUAGE OF
BIRTHDAYS

teen edition

ALICIA THOMPSON

Table of Contents

Here are the KEYS to unlocking your birthday symbols!

What will they say about you?

Best Hobby

From yoga to eavesdropping, this is the activity
that defines your spirit!

Style Inspiration

Whether a famous fashion icon (Sarah Jessica Parker),
a place to shop (H&M), or just a certain piece of clothing
(adorable bandeau bikini), this is the look that suits you best.

Best Pet

You may share a special connection with this kind of
animal—or maybe it would just look really cute at the end of your leash.

Best Accessory

Anything from a remote control to a fedora to your school backpack,
this is one thing you'd go nowhere without.

Power Color

Whether okra, sapphire, or charcoal, this is the hue
that's oh-so-YOU

Star Match

A famous person who shares your birthday.

Best Date

Looking for something to do with that special someone?
This should give you an idea of how you can have the most fun,
from parasailing to Parcheesi.

Theme Song

Careful not to get it stuck in your head!

Best Job

Toungue-tied on career day? This info
will impress even the grouchiest of guidance counselors.

Best Vacation Spot

This could be the place that will change your life forever,
or simply where you need to go to get away from it all.

Strengths / Weaknesses

Face it: We *all* have areas we need to work on.
These are yours, so tune in and take notes.

Aries Girls
are all about new beginnings

They experiment more often than a science lab, trying out new roles, new hobbies, and new friends. They are lively, energetic, social, open, and honest. Their "take me as I am" attitude can also make them seem selfish and stubborn.

• •

Most likely to be training for a
10k in platform heels.

Beverage they most resemble: Cherry Coke.
Tons of flavor and totally unique.

Strengths to play on: Leading people,
knowing what they want.

Pitfalls to avoid: Leading people ON,
refusing to compromise.

Aries

March 21 –
April 20

Element: Fire

Ruler: Mars

Motto: "Shut up and dance."

March 21

If you were makeup, you would be clear lip gloss: You're all about total transparency. Born on the official first day of spring, when the days start getting longer, your personality is guided by the idea of light and clarity: you're always honest, you say exactly what you think, and you are exactly what you seem. Even though you always tell the bare-naked truth, sometimes you feel misunderstood because you're not making an effort to fit in.

$ Radio personality

Kate Moss

Indie tea shop

+/− It is really great that you are so expressive about your feelings, but your tell-it-like-it-is attitude can hurt your friendships. (Did your BFF *really* need to know about the pimple on her left shoulder?) There's a saying: Every rose has its thorn. In your case, it's true, so learn to keep the seriously stinging statements to yourself.

LET THE TULIPS OF THE WORLD CROWD TOGETHER; YOU'LL MAKE LIKE AN ORCHID AND STAND OUT ON YOUR OWN.

love match

A class-clown Pisces boy has a not-so-funny way of showing his affection; all that criticism is just his way of showing how much you intimidate him. Dig a little deeper, and you'll find an individualistic spirit that's a perfect mirror of your own.

friend match

When it comes to friends, you've got a take-it-or-leave-it outlook. But be careful that you're not shutting people out because deep down you fear that they might reject you. A sweet and sensitive Scorpio will stick by your side.

March 22

You have got a lot more voltage than a tanning salon, and you're just as sunny. You know what you want and you know how to get it, from an extension on your English term paper to that expensive pair of chandelier earrings. (Thanks, Daddy!) You believe you have an all-access pass to all that life has to offer—complete with bonuses and rewards—and your friends look up to you for your up-front, all-on-the-line attitude. But it's definitely not all sunshine and light with you: If something doesn't go your way, you're likely to throw a tornado-worthy tantrum, so learn to control your temper before it does some serious damage.

friend match

A summer-born buddy does a pretty decent job keeping up with you, both mentally and when you're booking it down the school hallway, but more importantly, she can help you take a breath once in a while.

love match

A Scorpio slacker in your math class seems way too laid-back to be right for you, but he'll always let you do what you do best: lead. Show him how to plot out x and y, and you'll find many points of intersection.

Sneakers

Skydiving

Reese Witherspoon

+/− Your energy is impressive, but it does not hurt to slow down a bit every once in a while. Juggling swim-team, homework, yearbook, gymnastics, friends and family will suck the life force out of anybody, so give yourself time to chill out before you wind up seriously fried.

March 23

Nonfiction writer

Keri Russell

Grunge

Inquisitive, Versatile, Caring

It's a good thing you're not feline, 'cuz curiosity would have quickly put an end to each and every one of your nine lives. You're always looking for answers, big and small—from which conditioner works best to de-frizz to how we *really* got here. As a result, you excel in the sciences and your super-attentiveness to the ups and downs in other people's lives means you've got a loyal following of friends. Just make sure you don't stick your nose where it doesn't belong. Sometimes it's best to make like a bee and mind your own *bzzzz-ness.*

+/— Your trusting nature makes it easy for people to rip you off. (Case-in-point: the $30 bottle of miracle shine hair serum in your bathroom that did nothing but make your scalp burn.) So if something smells fishy, channel your inner cat and skedaddle.

friend match

A protective Libra who likes to act as your personal bodyguard can stop you from getting stabbed in the back by a very jealous Sagittarius, who resents the fact that you always seem to have the secret 411.

love match

A Gemini crush has really got you chattering, but careful before you spoil your chances with too much idle talk. Air signs like to walk the walk, so your best bet is a little less conversation, a little more action.

You're the cotton white tee of the zodiac: totally simple and absolutely adored. You avoid drama like you avoid elastic-waist jeans and are living proof that you really can catch more flies with honey: Your friendliness, sweetness, and your spontaneity have people lining up to get a sample. You're not asking for attention, though; in fact, you're just as happy to be by yourself, reading a book or surfing your favorite blogs.

Volunteering at a soup kitchen

Brussels griffon

Alyson Hannigan

March 24

Positive, Open, Affectionate

+/− You always see the best in people, but the truth is that not everyone deserves your vote of confidence. Some of the people buzzing around you (like the "friend" who's always "complimenting" your cute round stomach) are just making noise, so kick the negativity to the curb before it sours your sunny outlook.

friend match

A Saturn-ruled friend can be stand-offish, which is why she depends on you to help her break out of her comfort zone. Only she can truly understand your dual need for both sociability and alone time, which makes you the true definition of BFFs.

love match

Fire signs have a reputation for passion, but you don't give your heart away that easily. Self-protection is not a bad thing at all, particularly if you come up against Tauruses and Cancers. Leos are always a solid and reliable match for you.

March 25

If life is a dance floor, you're the Deejay: You spin your own beats and jam to your own rhythm; you inspire people to get up and shake it; and even when you're not center stage, your upbeat attitude ensures the party rocks 24/7. Full of energy and not likely to let other people's opinions try to cramp your style, you nonetheless have an excellent radar for how the people around you are feeling. That's partly why everyone is drawn to you.

> YOU'RE ALWAYS SPINNING YOUR PEOPLE'S FAVORITE SONGS.

friend match

You do not like to be ignored, so a Capricorn who's always stealing the spotlight is seriously starting to get on your nerves. A mischievous Aquarius bestie will be more than happy to share center stage with you.

Film critic

Sarah Jessica Parker

Cancun

+/– You're raring to go round-the-clock, but there's another element of you that doesn't take a rest either: your constant criticism of yourself and other people. Having high standards is one thing, but setting yourself up to be disappointed is something else. Save the critiquing for your English essays.

love match

Your sky-high standards make it hard for anybody to break through your outer wall. But your 24/7 critiquing means you risk missing out on an awesome Libra who has a sense of humor and an absolute dedication to fun that make him the perfect date to bring to a plus-one party.

March 26

If you were an ice cream flavor, you would be vanilla: simple, loved, and an all-time original. You like to keep life as free of stress as possible and would much rather be rocking flip-flops and jeans than wedge heels and micro-minis. Similarly, because you have no fear of alone time, you're more likely to hit the park with a book than the mall with a crowd. That doesn't mean you don't have a loyal following of friends, though. You and your BFFs are like apple pie and ice cream: a perfect match.

friend match

An energetic Libra is perfect for getting you out of the house and onto the beach (or into the mall). She's not a girlie girl, like you, but she's social enough to introduce you to a broader group.

★ ★ ★ ★ ★ ★

A beaten-up copy of your favorite novel

Keira Knightley

"Put Your Records On" —Corinne Bailey Rae

love match

You need someone as laid-back and laissez-faire as you, like a totally chilled out Gemini. Stay away from a certain Scorpio—no matter how melt-worthy his eyes are. His seriousness will seriously stress you out.

★ ★ ★ ★ ★ ★

+/− Your religiously relaxed attitude is great for keeping things mellow, but sometimes the slow-and-steady thing means you get left in the dust. If you want something, it pays to get a jump on it, particularly if other people are competing for the same prize (like a certain cute boy). Hanging back 24/7 means golden opportunities are going to pass you by.

March 27

Debate team

Mariah Carey

"I Don't Want to Be" —Gavin DeGraw

Independent, Realistic, Innovative

Like the vegetable aisle in a grocery store, you always tend to keep things fresh. Whether you are putting together your unique ensembles (only you could turn an old scarf into a bandeau top), experimenting in the kitchen (scallop-and-apple soufflé, anyone?), or working on an art project, you have a strong vision and don't let other people's opinions cloud your point of view. And though you're very passionate, on the outside you stay as cool as a cucumber.

+/− Let's face it: sometimes your call-it-like-you-see-it attitude can come off as overly critical. (So your BFF is more pop-wreck than pop-star—if it makes her happy, let her sing.) Too much negativity will spoil even your closest relationships, so keep a lid on the catty comments.

YOU SEE THINGS IN BLACK AND WHITE AND WILL ALWAYS FIGHT FOR WHAT YOU BELIEVE.

love match

A Taurus b-baller with an overinflated ego is in constant conflict with you; neither of you can concede in an argument. But you actually respect a guy who can give as good as he gets, so set your sights on an opinionated and intelligent Leo.

friend match

A Neptune-ruled girl with a fierce sense of humor and a love for new things is your perfect friend match, though you often choose to hang out by yourself. It's not that you're a loner—you just need time to power down and reload.

9

You're like a gold-sequined minidress: no accessories needed. You work best on your own and often go long periods of time by yourself. When your close friends seek advice about their latest dramas, you take your advice from the sign on your older sib's door: KEEP OUT! It's not that you're not sensitive to your BFFs feelings—you are—it's that you know the value of minding your own business. You do make it a point to avoid clingy people, though, and when you feel like someone's trying to rope you into long-term commitment, you often give that person the slip. You and neediness are like big plaids and floral prints: You just don't mix.

iPod

Rabbit

Julia Stiles

March 28

Autonomous, Diligent, Serene

+/− If you really feel like a friend's cramping your style, it's okay to ask for some space—but it's not okay to ditch him or her out of the blue. Just because you've got emotional strength to spare, doesn't mean everyone's so hardy, so make sure you learn a nicer way of saying, "Back off.!" (No, "Go away!" doesn't count.)

love match

A Sagittarius guy will stick closer to you than glue and will leave you feeling icky. You need a self-directed and independent boy, like a Leo or a Libra, with passions and interests all his own.

friend match

An outgoing air sign is always feuding with your more serious earth-sign friend, and you always feel like you're stuck in the middle. Fortunately, your natural independence means you can hang out by your lonesome while they cool off.

March 29

If you had a superhero power, it would definitely be X-ray vision: You don't want anything to get by you. You'd rather be the spectator than up on the stage, but that doesn't mean you aren't active; your ability to get things done behind the scenes (like organizing your school's winter formal or planning your BF's birthday party) ensures that you always get A-list billing among your circle of friends. Because you're always paying attention, you always have a jump on the newest gossip and the hottest trends. Just recognize that some things don't need commentary (like your friend's hilarious tan lines), or you'll soon discover why every superhero has a super-arch nemesis.

The latest Marc Jacobs bag

Silver

TV network executive

+/− You know what you like (and more importantly, what you don't). But everyone is entitled to an opinion, so stop acting like Mussolini and dictating all the time. Does it really matter whether mushrooms or black olives make a better pizza topping?

friend match

You're very loyal; when you make friends, you keep them. But a back-stabbing Gemini may not be worth all your time and effort. Stick close to a Libra, who will never play Brutus to your Caesar.

love match

A gorgeous, fun-loving Capricorn will appreciate your quirks and still be strong enough to stand up for what he believes in. (Absolutely no anchovies, for one thing.)

March 30

Your motto is "My way or the highway," and over the years, you've kicked a lot of people to the curb. You're super-driven and have more energy than a twelve-pack of Red Bull (getting up at 5 a.m. to jog before school? No problem!), making it hard for your friends to keep up. And though you have original ideas, you deeply value other people's opinions. Don't let other people's criticism stand in the way of your dreams. When you take the road less traveled, as you do, there will always be people trying to get you back on the straight and narrow.

friend match

A loyal Pisces will never resent being your cheerleader, and she appreciates your unique outlook. Deeply connected to the world around her, a Pisces can help you build more lasting connections with the people you meet.

love match

An easygoing earth sign can help balance out your high-maintenance attitude, but a Uranus-ruled guy—with very strong ideas about how things should be done—may be the challenge you need.

National Honor
Society

"We Used to
Be Friends"
—The Dandy
Warhols

Semester abroad
in Australia

+/− It's okay to have your own way of doing things (who says you can't put jam on top of ice cream?), but sometimes the most popular route is also the easiest. Listen to older siblings and friends—they have valuable advice and can keep you from running up against roadblocks. (They know not to wear white to an all-school barbecue—they've made that mistake before!)

March 31

René Descartes, famous for the words: "I think, therefore I am."

Red

Triple-shot Venti Mocha Frappuccino

Clear-thinking, Logical, Spunky

If you were a body part, you'd be the fingernails, because you're all about hanging in there (and, let's face it, clawing your way to the top), Dominated by themes of strength and perseverance, when the going gets tough, you get tougher.

+/− You know what you want—and you want it now. But your single-direction focus makes a one-way street look open-ended: Learn to listen to other people's opinions and try to be more open to new ideas.

YOUR DRIVE MAKES YOU A FIERCE COMPETITOR AND A NATURAL LEADER.

love match

You tend to follow your head, but there's no math formula that will lead you to ever-lasting happiness with Prince Charming. Instead, let an intuitive Libra school you in matters of the heart.

friend match

You're not exactly the warm and fuzzy type, but you need to feel the love just like everybody else. A zany Gemini or an über-expressive Aquarius can help de-freeze your emotional core.

You are the One who is most like a set of fingers: You always have a feel for what's really going on, and you can always be counted on. Hardworking and successful, you love to master difficult tasks (from knitting your friends matching skull caps for Christmas to julienning carrots for a kick-ass stir-fry). People forget how young you are because you always keep it together, but sometimes it's okay to loosen up those buttons and act your age.

Teal

Professional

Greek Islands

April 1

Dignified, Sincere, Skilful

+/− You're a teacher's favorite: You do all of your work and never bust out a lame excuse for why your homework is late. (No sushi-and-soy-sauce incidents for you.) But you definitely need extra help on your social life, which gets a solid D—for Dead. Make time for your friends, or you risk getting left behind.

love match

When it comes to guys, you're supershy, so it's hard for you to even talk to your crushes. But there's one Scorpio sweetie in your class who makes it a lot easier. And if even the thought of having a boyfriend causes you to break out into a cold sweat, just enjoy his friendship for now.

friend match

Sometimes you need some help breaking out of your shell, so look to a fun-loving, carefree Mars BFF to help you kick back and let loose.

April 2

If you were a Broadway musical, you'd have to be *Annie*: You really do believe that the sun will come out tomorrow (admit it—you know you belt the sound track in the shower). You're full of ideas about ways to improve everything, from your school cafeteria (sushi bar and make-your-own-sundae buffet, anyone?) to the world at large (your motto is "Go Green.") You're 100 percent honest and assume everyone else is, too, which can get you in trouble. Some people are like storm clouds: They can ruin even the sunniest day.

Megaphone

Nighttime picnic

Environmental lawyer

+/− Your glass is more than half-full when it comes to the things you believe in: it's overflowing. Your listening skills, on the other hand, are totally stopped up. Your friends have opinions, too, and you need to learn to respect them.

friend match

You view things in black and white, which is why you need your more intuitive Neptune-ruled pal to help you with the shades of gray. Sometimes you get caught up in your ideas about what you think is going on—luckily, seeing the big picture is kind of her specialty!

love match

To you, a boyfriend is a mythical creature, like a unicorn. Maybe it's because you're a romantic fire sign, but the sloppy, immature boys at your school just aren't very inspiring. Look to a soulful Libra to give you a whole new outlook.

If you ever work on a movie, you'll definitely be the director, You love organizing (all of your clothes are arranged by color, fabric, and season), and when you get assigned a group project, you naturally assume the leadership role. You don't have to struggle to get your way, either; when you have a vision, it's not hard for you to get others to see eye to eye. You have a tendency to focus a lot on what you want, though. Every once in a while, it pays to give up creative control, so let your friends choose the movie at least part of the time—when it comes to your role as BFF, you don't want to end up on the cutting-room floor.

friend match

You and your Gemini pal love to talk and talk and talk. Good thing she can count on you to keep all her secrets, including her mini-crush on one of your teachers last year. (Thankfully, she's moved on to someone her own age!)

love match

As outgoing as you can be, you often clam up around guys. But remember, guys understand subtlety as much as you understand Russian (a.k.a. not at all!), so if you want your Spring-born crush to know you like him, you have to tell him!

+/− It's great to be social, but depending on other people to help you feel good about yourself will just lead to a big, fat flop. You're writing the script here, so pencil in some more self-confidence: Remember, you need to be your own biggest fan.

Blackberry

Show dog

Amanda Bynes

April 4

The latest issue of *Vogue*

Advertising executive

Where else? L.A.

Innovative, Lively, Ambitious

If you were a card game, you would be Uno, because you always have to be Number One. When the dance floor's empty at homecoming, you're the first to step out and shake it; you were the first to rock skinny jeans and the first to ditch them for wide legs. You love anything new and are obsessed with staying one step ahead of the game, though sometimes all that enthusiasm can actually trip you up. Sometimes what the team really needs is a closer to bring it all home, so it's important that you learn to commit and focus.

+/— Sharing your feelings is an important element to any relationship, but when your BFF asks you whether her butt looks big in her new jeans, she doesn't really want to know. Your mouth gets you in trouble a lot, so learn the rules of the game: Get a clue and learn to say sorry, or next time you'll get no Get-Out-of-Jail-Free card.

love match

You pride yourself on not spending any time worrying about who likes you, but a certain Sagittarius sweetie keeps looking in your direction. So ask yourself this: Are you really "above" love, or were you just not paying attention?

friend match

Even your fellow Uranus-ruled BFF has a tough time changing your mind once it's made up. Then again, she's the same way, so you'll just have to agree to disagree. At least things are never boring when you're together!

Red carpets of the world, watch out: You've got serious star power. No matter what you love or how you choose to channel your energies (and regardless of whether a reading light or the limelight is more your thing), you'll always be on the A-list, getting recognized for your dedication and talent. Once you've found a passion, you stick with it for life, although the same can't be said of your friends and relationships, which change faster than a pop star's hair colors.

Scarlet

Student council

Bette Davis

April 5

Consistent, Hard-Working, Successful

+/− You are like a busy bee! Giving up gives you the hives. But sometimes quitters *do* win: Don't feel you need to waste time on activities you don't enjoy. So don't stick with the Botany Club just because your mom signed you up for it. Go ahead and branch out!

love match

Your Mercury crush seems to change his mind about girls all the time, but you've been hopelessly devoted since the first day of middle school, despite all the other guys you've flirted with since then. Look for someone who's got a little less flake, like a Taurus or a Leo.

friend match

You work hard, but you know how to play hard, too! Fellow fire signs tend to keep things exciting, so you and your Leo BFF love to hit the mall on the weekends together.

April 6

If you were a subject in school, you'd be science, because you're all about experimenting. Even if your originality shows up more in your wardrobe selection (leg warmers as a scarf—why not?) than it does in your abilities with a Bunsen burner (it's not your fault those two chemicals cause an explosion when mixed!), the fact is you're always trying something new. You want to get the skinny on everything, from the mystery meat in the cafeteria to the new girl in school, and sometimes your friends feel like they're rolling with their own personal private investigator. You always get to the bottom of things.

Ice-skating in the park

Travel writer

Hedgehog

+/− Wanting to uncover the truth is one thing; digging for dirt is another. You don't need to dish on other people's secrets, so lay down that shovel before you dig yourself into a hole.

friend match

Your summer-born BFF is the opposite of you: totally gullible and very innocent. You help protect her from scam artists and jacked-up cell phone plans, and she keeps you from being such a skeptic: If a cutie in the mall says you look adorable in your new jeans, he's probably into you.

love match

While you are very busy conducting experiments in your science class, your Virgo lab partner is feeling some serious chemistry for you! He may not be your usual type, but sometimes the only way to discover something new is to mix it up.

You are more upbeat than a drum set: You keep a positive attitude no matter what difficulties face you, and your optimism is as hard to resist as a techno beat. (No surprise: At school dances—even the lame ones—you're often the one to get your friends grooving.) With all your enthusiasm, it's no wonder your friends look to you to be their cheerleader, and in general you're always ready to give them a boost when they're low. But when you're disappointed, you rapidly change your tune, and your infamous temper tantrums are an all-time party foul.

friend match

Mean people suck, and you don't tolerate any rudeness or unkindness. You stick up for your autumn-born best friend all the time, and she returns the favor by keeping you cool, calm, and collected whenever you're about to blow your top.

love match

You're super supportive, so if your Capricorn crush wants to try out for the football team, you'll be the loudest one cheering from the bleachers. Don't think your rah-rah spirit goes unnoticed—there's nothing like a bright smile to catch someone's attention!

Hot pink

"Girls Just Want to Have Fun" —Cyndi Lauper

Spring break in Mexico

+/− It's wonderful that you have ideals, but if you expect perfection 24/7, you're bound to be in for a rude awakening. Nobody's perfect—not your friends, parents, teachers (definitely not them), or coaches—so cut the people in your life some slack. Being so high-strung will just lead to a big ol' SNAP.

Miniature golfing with the guy of your dreams

Tutoring

Adopted tabby

April 8

Ethical, Giving, Responsible

You play Jiminy Cricket to your best friend's Pinnochio: You're the voice of conscience. (And you can always tell when she's lying.) Whether you're giving up your time at the local animal shelter or giving up your fave dress because one of your friends needs to borrow it, you're always doling out handouts. Naturally shy, you prefer hanging in the background and tend to stay away from high-profile pursuits like theater. No matter what you get involved in, your competence and maturity mean that before long you'll be pulling the strings.

+/− Your generosity is admirable, but sometimes you need to get yours. Unless you like the smell of feet, there's no point in playing doormat. So when your friend asks you to help with her math homework, make sure she pays you back by helping you conjugate those Spanish verbs.

love match

You're a sucker for the underdog, so you have a crush on the geeky earth sign who sits in the front of your history class. His loyalty and ability to honor commitments make him excellent boyfriend material.

friend match

When you're protesting the cafeteria's questionable lunch meat, your fiery sun-ruled friend is right by your side—and she can get you to loosen up when you're in danger of sacrificing yet another Friday night to homework. Remember, the cause that really needs attention right now is your social life!

Whoever said, "Moderation in all things" forgot to CC you on the memo: You never do anything halfway. If you fall in love with a new band, you're suddenly the Number One fan, and your soccer coach knows he can count on you to give 110 percent every time. Your energy and enthusiasm spread to your friends like a bad case of the measles (but without the ugly spots, thank God), and you often find yourself in a position of leadership. Just be careful not to fill their heads with Spam: In some things (like chocolate and back talk), a little really does go a long way.

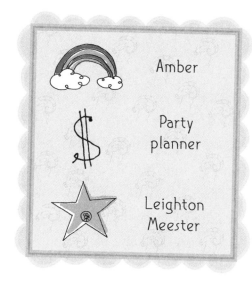

Amber

Party planner

Leighton Meester

April 9

Strong-Minded, Persuasive, Progressive

+/− Though many people think it's a value never to give up, in truth it pays to know when to stop. Not every rule (like traffic laws!) was made to be broken, so give your walk on the wild side some much-needed bed rest.

love match

One minute you like that Aquarius charmer in your history class, and the next minute you think he's an obnoxious jerk. It must be tiring to ride that roller-coaster ride of emotions, so maybe you should stick with that solid, smoldering Scorpio, who will help you stay on an even keel.

friend match

You're not the type of girl who'll spill her guts in Truth or Dare, so it takes a lot more to get something out of you. An air-sign pal of yours is a top-notch listener, so she's the one you'll go to when you need advice or just want to talk without any kind of gimmicks or games.

April 10

When it's time to play
Truth or Dare with you, there's no way anyone's getting your dirt: You're always down for the dare, no matter how crazy. (Streaking down your street ring a bell?) But as crazy as some of your choices might seem, you're not actually a dare devil; most of the time, you do a good job of evaluating the risk (you knew your neighbors were on vacation) and staying out of trouble. In fact, though you're never afraid to strike out on your own, your common sense ensures that your plans rarely backfire—and that's the truth.

friend match

At first, you and your now-BFF Virgo were at each other's throats, but after being forced to work together for a group project, you realized you had a lot in common after all, like loyalty and a mutual obsession with fashion. What's Even better? Her "innocent" act helps the two of you get away with murder.

Treo

Rock climbing

Mandy Moore

+/− Sometimes people just need to vent. It's great that rationality is your strong suit, but don't expect others to stay as calm as you. So if your best friend is having a bad day, don't lecture her about how she should feel, just lend a shoulder and acknowledge how she does feel.

love match

You've got a thing for a blond golden boy in your class, but should you really take that gamble? You're the kind of girl who'll give anything a chance, but because you and he are both influenced by the Sun, it's possible you could get burned.

You should have your own Secret Service, because you're always playing president. You lay down the law (no metallic leggings, ever!) and dole out advice (your BFF owes her new haircut entirely to you). When it comes to your style of leadership, you're definitely more democracy than dictatorship—you never make your friends feel stupid—and your inner circle is happy to let you be head-of-state. Mature, confident, and excellent at winning people over to your point of view, your approval ratings are always sky-high.

friend match

When it comes to group situations, you're a true diplomat, but skirmishes may arise one-on-one. So if your bud born on the 15th is miffed about something you've done, try using one of your most trustworthy tactics—saying sorry.

love match

A Mercury-ruled skater boy has got you wondering, are you or aren't you going out? Don't look to the dictionary for a definition of your relationship. Try asking him, and if he can't give you a straight answer, that is your answer.

Bodyguard
(The cutie in your class counts!)

Gold

Jackie O

+/− Generally, you've got a good idea of what's best for those you care about. But minds are like umbrellas—they have to be open to do any good—so don't blind yourself to other solutions just because you think you've already found the perfect one.

April 12

Unlimited minutes cell-phone plan

Labrador retriever

Claire Danes

+/− You have the dirt on so many people you could open your own gardening center, but not everyone thinks it's cute that you're always spilling their secrets. Learn to keep your mouth shut sometimes or you'll wind up buried!

Social, Articulate, Knowledgeable

You may not be a doctor, but you always have your finger on the pulse. Whenever something goes down (breakup, hookup, breakdown), you're always the first to know, and there's nothing you like more than holding a pre-school news session with your BFF (with you as the star anchor, of course). You love being surrounded by people—you thrive at parties, malls, and social events—and sitting still drives you crazy. But don't let other people's opinion of you make your confidence flatline; you need to feel good in your own skin.

love match

You want a guy who actually listens, so that self-centered sun-ruled dude isn't going to cut it. Not only does he totally ignore what you have to say, but he'd much rather talk about the stupid reality TV he likes to watch. Change the channel, and try a sensitive water-ruled boy instead.

friend match

You're always speaking up for your shy Pisces friend—what are BFFs for after all? She definitely appreciates it, but she's not as sensitive as you might think. Give her the chance, and she'll show you how strong she can be!

You're like a made-to-order couture dress: totally one of a kind. You never play Follow the Leader and always strike out on your own, whether you're pioneering a new trend (you totally started the skirts-over-skinny-jeans thing) or experimenting with new cuisine. (Sea urchin, anyone?) You have trouble with authority—you've had more than a few blowups when your parents tried to tell you what to do—and are totally fearless. Just know that butting heads all the time will lead to one big headache (and possibly detention!).

Lime green

Boho chic

Christina Aguilera

April 13

● ● ● ● ● ● ● ● ● ● ● ● ● ● ● ● ●

Stubborn, Pioneering, Outspoken

+/− You've got no problem with conflict, so you'll let a flare-up turn into a wildfire. You have to learn to pick your battles—is the fact that your BFF wants pizza instead of Chinese really that big a deal?—or you'll burn through more than a few friendships.

love match

True, a Cancer beach bum in your Spanish Class is hotter than Puerto Rico in August, but watch out: He's totally taken! Until he ditches the girl, you're going to have to admire this hottie from afar. But once she's out of the picture, feel free to turn up the heat.

friend match

Your born-on-the-30th BFF might raise her eyebrows at your latest getup but you know she'll always support even your wildest ideas. And because she's not as much of a risk taker as you are, she can keep you from getting too out of control.

April 14

If you were a dessert, you would definitely be the Thanksgiving pumpkin pie: extra sweet and totally traditional. You're very close to your family and you're all about rituals: Friday night sleepovers, Sunday pancake breakfasts, hot chocolate and gossip on Wednesday afternoons. In fact, you hate the idea of change and don't even like to switch up your breakfast (toasted sesame bagel with veggie cream cheese, thank you very much). Fortunately, once you pick your friends, they are in for life (and you've got plenty to choose from): Your sweetness, loyalty, and generosity mean people flock to you like ants to a holiday picnic. Just remember, taking risks can lead to amazing surprises! Don't be so afraid of the unknown.

Dinner and a movie

Sarah Michelle Gellar

Summer house in the Hamptons

+/− Certain things are fine to hold onto: friendships, family heirlooms, your first teddy bear. But bad habits need to be given the boot. Next time you give up on nixing the nail biting before you even try, remember that another word for change is growth.

friend match

You and your Gemini BFF have been inseparable since the first day of third grade. You love how she's not afraid to speak her mind, and she respects you for your loyalty and dedication.

love match

You can't stand drama of any kind, so look for an earth-sign cutie in your science class to keep things balanced. He's low-key but never boring—exactly like you!

April 15

Sometimes you act just like an alley cat, always sniffing around in other people's junk. Minding your own business is not something you do well—you're obsessed with knowing the Who, What, and Where. (Who was he kissing? What was he thinking? His hand was where?!) You have a naturally scientific mind, so you're an excellent planner of everything from birthday parties to fabulous outfits, but because you're super-social, your curiosity applies mostly to people, not things—sometimes your friends feel like they're part of a focus group.

friend match

From picking out next year's classes to buying a new lava lamp for her room, you like to be kept in the loop about everything your fellow spring-born BFF is up to. But don't be offended if she needs quiet time once in a while.

Folding telescope

School newspaper

Emma Watson

love match

A love-struck Libra who sits behind you in English has it bad. But you're beyond school romance, and you'd much rather curl up in front of your DVD player than go out with someone you barely know. Be sure to let him down gently— he might turn out to be a friend.

+/− Nobody needs to remind you what curiosity did to the cat. Some messes are best left undisturbed, so if your BFF says she doesn't want to talk about her problems, back off until she's ready. Otherwise you'll get the rep of a plain old pest.

April 16

- Smile
- Puggle
- Low-key, hoodie-and-flip-flops kind of girl

Generous, Funny, Accepting

If you were a movie, there's no doubt you'd be a comedy. Any downtime with you is bound to have your friends ROTFL, but you've got much more to offer than a 24/7 stand-up routine. You are super-generous, always lending clothes and homework help, and extremely sensitive to other people's feelings. But don't let people take advantage of you (like a certain lab partner who always seems to take credit for work you've done). There's nothing funny about getting walked on.

+/− It's great to use humor to cheer up your friends or lighten an awkward situation, but not everything needs to be turned into a punch line. Sometimes your friends need a shoulder to cry on, not a one-woman laugh factory, so make sure you use humor to deal, not deny . . . otherwise you might get booed off stage for good.

Tissue

love match

If you're looking for something steady, look for a rock-solid Sagittarius, who can appreciate your sense of humor but keep you from bouncing off the walls. But if you want something short-term, a Mars-ruled bad boy might be just the ticket.

friend match

You've been friends with that moon-ruled chick for a LONG time, so it's not like you two have never had rocky times. It'd be so easy to refuse to let go of that time she borrowed your shirt and spilled mustard all over it, but you don't sweat the small stuff—friendship is way too important.

You only need a few letters of the alphabet, but they spell one big word: R-E-S-P-E-C-T. When you speak you expect people to listen, even if you never raise your voice. (And let's face it: you don't need to.) Smart, capable, and mature, you've got the logic skills of a lawyer and are great at bringing people over to your point of view. But you can also be very critical of yourself and others, so give the trash-talking a rest before your friends feel like they really are on trial.

$ CEO

Victoria Beckham

Chateau in Paris

April 17

Grounded, Strong-Willed, Responsible

+/– No wonder you're friends with that Venus-ruled chica in your science class . . . she's only the most popular girl in school. But unlike the super-snarky popular kids in movies, you two keep it real. How do you think you got to be so well-liked in the first place?

love match

It's super-tempting to take that born-on-the-22nd boy up on his offer to go to the movies, but you're not sure you're compatible. Chemistry is like one of your little sister's tantrums—you just can't ignore it, no matter how hard you try—so wait until you feel that spark with someone.

friend match

An outgoing air sign is always feuding with your more serious earth-sign friend, and you always feel like you're stuck in the middle. Fortunately, you are naturally independent, which means you can hang out all alone and still have a good time.

April 18

You should be a lawyer, because you are always defending somebody. You have a strong sense of right and wrong and aren't afraid to hold court on your opinions. Whenever there's a competition you are the one rooting for the underdog, and you go to bat for your friends whenever they're treated unfairly.

Kudos on getting your BFF's curfew kicked back to 10:30—9:00 was just cruel Just make sure all those closing arguments aren't putting you on the defensive.

> YOU CAN BE WAY TOO SENSITIVE TO OTHER PEOPLE'S REMARKS.

friend match

You do not like to be ignored, so a Capricorn who's always stealing the spotlight is seriously starting to get on your nerves. A mischievous Aquarius bestie will be more than happy to share center stage with you.

Prada messenger bag

Use those debating skills in Mock Trial

Coco Chanel

+/− If you hear so much as a peep about your Scorpio BFF's new hairdo, you'll be defending her loud and clear for everyone to hear. (Okay, so the bangs may have been a mistake . . . but you're not about to let other people say it!) In return, she'll be the shoulder you lean on whenever you're feeling down.

love match

There may be a cute, arty Pisces who comes off a little too pushy, but give him a chance. You could grow to like him as much as he clearly likes you, and he might help shake up your boring old routine.

You're just like superglue: You're all about keeping it together. You plan everything in detail, from your outfits to your schedule to the menu for your sleepover (chicken quesadillas and veggie tamales). Nothing drives you crazier than being out of control—even though you don't even have your license, you're still a backseat driver—and you love to be in positions of power (captain of your swim team, senior editor of the yearbook). But sometimes your power trips make your friends and family want to say *hasta*, so save the remote control for your TiVo.

friend match

You should take out an ad: Aries girl seeking full-time BFF. You've got a ton of friends already, but what you really need is someone you can count on 24/7. Be warned: Pair up with a Taurus and you'll be bumping heads so often you'll have a 24/7 headache.

Platinum

"Glamorous"
—Fergie

Italian villa

love match

There's a boy whose b-day adds up to 6 who's impressed with a lot more than your science skills. Next time he asks you to pair up for a class assignment, step up the game and ask him to your friend's pool party.

+/− You're drawn to people with lots of influence, but just because someone acts like Little Ms. Thang doesn't mean she's the best person to hang out with. Don't let the glitter of power blind you to the real traits you should be looking for in your friends, like honesty and loyalty.

April 20

Aviators from the army surplus store

Movie producer

Preppy

+/− You're not on trial for anything, so why do you always feel like you have to prove something? Have some faith: Your accomplishments speak for themselves, so you don't have to run your mouth about them.

Powerful, Exciting, Private

When you were little, your favorite game was Follow the Leader—and you were always the one blazing the trail. You don't mind the twists in the road, either. Challenges that would make other people make a U-turn just spur you on to go further. You fall easily into leadership positions, from bunk head at camp to stage manager of the school play, and you have a reputation for being extremely social. But you're actually very private. Sometimes you forget that your friends are more than just your supporters, so switch it up once in a while and let them take the lead.

love match

You're right on the cusp of fire sign and earth sign, so you can be a little touchy when it comes to love. That mischievous Mars-ruled boy only teases you because it always gets a reaction, so ignore him if you want him to stop. Or be honest with yourself and admit how much you love it.

friend match

It's not that you don't love hanging out with your born-on-the-8th BFF, it's just that you also like to keep your options open. So you might hit up thrift stores with her or go to the zoo with your crush. . . . Who knows?

What kind of FRIEND are you?

For Halloween, you and your BFF dress up as

a. Miley Cyrus. *Well, you're Miley, and your BFF is one of her adoring fans.*

b. Aly and AJ. *Best friends who sing—cute!*

c. Conjoined identical twins. *You even glued your arms together.*

Your BFF's boyfriend dumps her. You show up at her house to cheer her up with

a. Your tap shoes, a gym mat, and your iPod. *Once she sees your hilarious new gymdancetics routine, she'll be ROTFL.*

b. A box of tissues and your best listening face.

c. The scrapbooks *detailing all of the amazing times you and your BFF have had since third grade—just the two of you! Boyfriends are so overrated.*

If you had to describe yourself in one word, it would be

a. Fabulous.

b. Optimistic.

c. Shy.

On a typical Friday night, you and your friends will be

a. Shooting a short film in your basement. Your best friend is a natural with the camera—and you're a natural in front of it! Scarlett Johansson, stand back.

b. Hitting a movie, swinging by the mall, maybe just vegging on the couch and ordering Thai. It depends on what everyone is in the mood for.

c. Sausage-and-mushroom pizza at 7:30 and then repeated screenings of your fave Disney movies (especially *Finding Nemo*). Routine hasn't changed in four years!

QUIZ!

Pick a favorite pairing

a. Whipped cream with a cherry on top.

b. Peanut butter and jelly.

c. Chocolate-smothered pretzel.

When you play soccer in gym class, what position does your coach put you in?

a. Striker. *You like running ahead of the pack and you're not afraid to go for the goal.*

b. Goalie. *Coach knows you can be trusted not to let your team down.*

c. Defense. *You prefer to hang back. Not a big fan of balls flying at your face, either.*

Your best friend gets invited to a party, but you didn't score an invite. Coping strategy?

a. Throw a competing blowout on the exact same night. *You know your BFF will make the right choice.*

b. Help her choose her outfit in advance, then hang with other friends on the night of the party. *No big deal—that's why you run with a big crew.*

c. Cry hysterically. Self-loathe. Repeat.

The one time you and your BFF had a major fight, what was it about?

a. To be honest, you're not exactly sure. *You love the girl and everything but have a teensy habit of zoning out when she speaks. It was something about "blah blah blah, never listen, blah blah. . . ."*

b. A total misunderstanding. *She thought she wasn't invited to your pool party, when really her evite had just gotten caught in the spam filter.*

c. To be honest, you're not exactly sure. *You think she may have asked for "space," but you immediately blacked out from the trauma.*

An Army of One

"I" is your favorite letter of the alphabet and "me" is your favorite note on the scale. You're so busy social climbing, you make a StairMaster look like a slacker. You always speak your mind, and you've gotten in more than a little trouble for being insensitive. It's not all bad, though—you're fun, spontaneous, outgoing, and creative, and you can always be counted on for a laugh. Once a week do; something your best friend wants to do; she'll appreciate the gesture. Look for a confident Gemini or Capricorn who won't be threatened by your solo act.

A Two-Way Street

You're the world's perfect BFF. Like a pair of relaxed fit broken-in jeans, you're low maintenance (and always look good). Laid-back most of the time, you know how to throw down when it's time to party, and you're quick to get your shoulder soggy if one of your friends needs a cry. Just remember to cut yourself a break once in a while: You don't need to be all things for all people. You can't please—or appease—everybody.

Static Cling

You've got more attachment issues than superglue. Your cell-phone bill is sky-high because you need to know exactly what your BFF is up to every single second, and your biggest fear is walking into a party/restaurant/bathroom by yourself. But be careful: BFFs aren't adhesives. It's natural to need space, distance—and other friends! Just remember any girl would be lucky to have you in her life, and a true friend won't leave you in the lurch. Look for superloyal signs who value friendships as much as you do, like a faithful Leo or a Taurus.

QUIZ!

Taurus Girls

are loyal, observant, and dependable

Taurus is the first earth sign of the astrological year, which means Taurus girls are grounded, practical thinkers. Despite their tendency to be stubborn, they seek harmony and security, typically keeping the same friends and habits for a long time. Just like a kindergarten drop-out, though, they have difficulty sharing and aren't the best team players.

Most likely to be: At the mall racking up credit-card debt.

Pantry staple they most resemble: Olive oil and vinegar. Simple and reliable, impossible to mix.

Strengths to play on: Patience, independence.

Pitfalls to avoid: Procrastination, ignoring others.

Taurus

April 21 – May 21

Element: Earth

Ruler: Venus

Motto: "My way or my running shoe in your face."

Sailing

Tropical fish

"Pocket Full of Sunshine"
—Natasha Bedingfield

April 21

Tasteful, Caring, Ethical

Put business before pleasure, but pleasure is your business. You love sleeping late, weekly mani-pedis, dark chocolate, and shopping. Your motto is "Why do today what you could put off until tomorrow?" But you've got a serious side too; when you commit to something you commit 100 percent (when you were a Girl Scout, you always sold the most cookies), and your word is more golden than the McDonalds arches. You can always be counted on. Beware of treating your friends like business associates. Love them for who they are, not what they can bring you.

+/— Don't let your love of the finer things lead you into trouble.

> SOME THINGS (LIKE SELF-TANNER AND DADDY'S CREDIT CARD) REALLY ARE BEST WHEN USED IN MODERATION.

love match

True, you'd LOVE to go out with that Cancer cutie in your class, but your BFF's already got her eyes on him. No worries. A smoldering Sagittarius is much more your style—serious enough to ground you, but not so serious that he can't kick back at Six Flags on the weekends.

friend match

You're the kind of intuitive girl who can read your summer-born pal like a book. But she might not be as body-language literate as you are, so you're gonna need to clue her in if you've got something major on your mind.

You and a recipe have one thing in common: Order matters. (Ever try to mix the pasta with the sauce *before* it's been cooked?) Maybe because you're naturally shy, you love to hang back—but that doesn't mean you're out of the picture. You live to organize and are always forming new clubs at your school and planning your friends' birthday parties. People look to you to take charge, but don't let it go to your head. No one likes a diva (not even one who can make a tea light out of a seashell).

That to-do list in your purse

Sapphire

Yearbook

April 22

BOSSINESS CAN MAKE FRIENDSHIPS GO SOUR.

Organized, Down-to-Earth, Imposing

+/− When you successfully pull off a new project, your head has a tendency to swell faster than a sprained ankle. So spend time with your old friends and family members to keep you grounded—otherwise you just might float away!

love match

Watching those chick flicks you love so much makes you want a boyfriend of your own, but you need a guy who will give you space to breathe. Your best bet is a sporty, laid-back Libra, who won't mind if you need your Friday nights with the girls.

friend match

Your confidence can be intimidating for some people, but your fire-sign pal will give as good as she gets. It's one of the things you love about her—she's always up for a good debate!

April 23

You're like a pale pink sweater-set combo: always appropriate and totally safe. Once you find something you like, you stick with it (you've had the same best friends since third grade and wouldn't dream of eating anything but a peanut butter bagel for breakfast), and you tend toward activities that have a built-in support system—no solo sports like swimming or track for you! Just make sure that you don't put the rut in routine—try a new haircut or a different kind of cuisine once in a while!

TRY TO DEVELOP
CONFIDENCE IN YOUR
OWN ABILITIES.

friend match

You and your Scorpio BFF share everything, but her tendency to put herself first—in line at the cafeteria, when scoping cute guys, and while dishing up the ice cream at your birthday party—can get on your nerves. Scorpios can be very self-centered; try to find balance with a sweet, generous Gemini.

Ivory

Cavalier
King Charles
spaniel

Shirley
Temple

+/− You're like bad news: You always travel in pairs. You've got a cell phone practically glued to your ear because you hate to be alone. But leaning on others all the time will just leave you feeling lopsided.

love match

There is an earthy musician who never seems to notice you. Really, he's just shy. If you make the first move, he may just change his tune.

You should be a bodyguard, because you're always trying to **keep the people you love safe.** Whether you're making sure your little bro wears his bike helmet or helping your BFF study, you're always on the lookout for your family and friends, and you make sure they know it. **Just make sure you don't put the *mother* in smothering: You have a tendency to treat your friends like children, and sooner or later they're bound to rebel.**

 YOUR HEART'S LIKE PLASTIC WRAP— TOTALLY TRANSPARENT.

friend match

Your Saturn-ruled BFF is so wild and crazy it's a full-time job for you just to keep her out of detention. You don't mind; you actually love to vibe off her zany energy, and she would be completely lost without your calming and practical presence.

Lavender

Therapist to the stars

Kelly Clarkson

love match

When your Aquarius crush has a problem, you're the first person he calls. But his laid-back attitude toward love means you might be in danger of swinging too far in the friend direction, so make a move before you end up in the "platonic pal" dead zone.

$+/-$ You have zero problems expressing your feelings: You're always blogging about your feelings, and you change your Facebook profile twenty-five times a day. Your mood swings so much it belongs on a playground, so remember: All that up-and-down will make you sick after a while. When life is stressing you out, take a deep breath before blowing up.

April 25

Supermodel boyfriend

Camping

Renée Zellweger

Vigorous, Steadfast, Dynamic

You should be a movie star, because you're always ready for the *action!* You've got a BIG personality; whenever you walk into a room, people *notice.* You'd much rather walk the walk than talk the talk—all that chatter just leaves your ears ringing. You love to be outside, so whether you're the first off the high board at the pool or taking a header during a soccer game, you're always diving headfirst into something.

+/− You've got a temper that matches your energy: It keeps going and going and going. If someone upsets you, it is okay to let them know, but if they apologize, accept it and move on.

love match

You need a guy who can match your energy and enthusiasm, so look for a certain Scorpio who has all the moves to keep up. Just be sure you take it slow; Scorpios fall fast and hard, and you don't want him confessing *love* before you're ready to commit to *like.*

friend match

You're not the kind of girl who'll choose a BFF lightly, but you find yourself gravitating toward other earth signs. It's no surprise: They'd much prefer to hit the pool than the mall, and they don't think sitting at home gossiping on the phone for five hours counts as quality time.

You could have a garden, because you love to watch things grow. (But the dirt and the worms? Not so much.) You're great at playing matchmaker—your BFF has you to thank for her adorable new boyfriend—and you're equally good at hooking up new projects and groups at school. (Organizing the end-of-the-school-year field trip to Six Flags? All you.) Ironically, though, you're kind of a wallflower.

YOU'D MUCH RATHER ROLL ALONE THAN WITH A CROWD.

Coral

Comedy club

Bohemian

April 26

Stalwart, Independent, Responsible

+/− *You never say die, and your persistence is usually a good thing,* but sometimes it pays to jump ship—like if you're in the middle of a dead-end argument. Kill the drama!

love match

Your closest peeps know you love to laugh, but when it comes to your autumn-born crush, you always keep a straight face. He might seem super-serious, but you have all the tools to get him to lighten up. Loosen up and act natural around him—you'll be rewarded with much more than smiles.

friend match

You're stubborn, but a logical Libra friend can always bring you around to her point of view. After all, you know if it's coming from *her*, it must be solid advice! In return, you help her branch out and meet new people.

April 27

If life were a concert, you'd be a solo performer: You love to work on your own. Actually, though, you're more likely to be found behind the scenes than stepping up in the spotlight. You excel in school and in the few extracurriculars you choose to get involved with, but you're not one to go around trumpeting your accomplishments. (Only your BFF knows you're a state-ranked equestrian.) Though you are a straight-A student, when it comes to speaking your mind, you definitely get a failing grade.

Stay in with rented movies and homemade s'mores.

Tennis

Bungalow on a small private island

+/− You're totally valued by the people you let into your life. So why not relax the strict door policy and let in a few stragglers once in a while? You never know who you'll meet.

love match

There's a boy born on the 2nd who's completely crushing on you, but you're so concentrated on your studies, you've been blind to all the wistful glances he's been casting your way. Remember that life isn't all about science homework and algebra and try out a new equation for once: U + Boyf = Distinct Possibility.

friend match

Your Pisces pal attracts people like honey attracts bees, while you prefer keeping a low profile. It's a perfect balance: She helps you get out (admit it, she had to practically drag you to the spring dance), and you help her stay grounded.

You have got more stamina than the Energizer Bunny: You really do keep going and going and going. Not only will you stick with your violin lessons, you'll make first chair. You'll run a track meet with a sprained ankle, and if you say you'll be your BF's date to a lame family party, not only will you show, you'll be laughing with Aunt Bebe and tearing up the dance floor with weirdo cousin Mark in ten minutes.

NO MATTER WHAT YOU WANT, YOU'LL GET
IT—NO MATTER HOW MANY OBSTACLES STAND IN YOUR WAY.

love match

Your Gemini crush is more up-and-down than a roller coaster, but he always reels you back in with his charm. Step back and reassess. You might be better suited to a more dependable Taurus, and you'll *definitely* feel less seasick.

friend match

It seems like your aggressive Mars-ruled pal is always getting into fights with everyone, from her mom to her snooty older sis to the lady behind the Chipotle counter. Good thing she can depend on you to help her pick her battles, otherwise it would be all-out war.

Starbucks
cup

"Get the
Party Started"
—Pink

Jessica
Alba

+/— If life were a musical scale, you'd get stuck on a single note: *me.* It's great that you have strong likes and dislikes, but let your friends pick a movie once in a while or you will have them whistling a new tune: bye, bye, bye.

April 29

Jade

Stylist

Uma Thurman

Reliable, Poised, Social

You're like a high-end digital camera: You're all about a quality image. Very focused on how others see you, you always try to put your best foot (and hair, and smile, and outfit) forward. Your MO? *Never let them see you sweat.* Just make sure that all the time you spend checking yourself out doesn't interfere with your time to check *in* with your friends.

YOUR FRIENDS AND FAMILY CAN RELY ON YOU IN ANY CRISIS, BIG OR SMALL (FROM A BROKEN HEEL TO A BROKEN HEART).

+/− Mirror, mirror, on the wall, who's the vainest one of all? It's okay to care how you come across to others, but being totally image-obsessed is a turnoff. If you want a fairy-tale ending, put down that mirror (and spoon and reflective cell-phone screen) once in a while.

love match

There's not much about you that a certain guitar-playing water sign doesn't notice, from your new bag to the fact that you snipped your bangs an extra half inch. But what makes you well matched is the fact that he sees beyond the flawless front—and likes you even more for it.

friend match

You can get kind of serious, but your playful BFF helps lighten you up. She's highly influenced by Neptune, which means she's got an awesome imagination—just what a pragmatic, goal-oriented girl like you needs.

If life were a closet, you'd be a safety pin: You're always on point and no matter what the crisis (broken bra strap, busted fly, lost button), you can be counted on in a pinch. Your parents can depend on you to help out your little sis, and your homework is always on time. When it comes to your obligations, you put the be-all-end-all in dependable. That's partly because you like to keep things tightly under your control. You like routine and stability and have had the same friends since you were five. Just make sure your resistance to change doesn't leave you stuck!

$ Surgeon

Thoroughbred horse

Kirsten Dunst

April 30

Protective, Dutiful, Resolute

+/−   You're a true Taurus: You have a hard time budging on your opinions, no matter how many people bump heads with you. But you don't want the reputation of an ox, so learn to stand down every once in a while.

love match

A winter-born guy in your class has you contemplating cuddling up by the fireplace. But careful before you get burned—he has a serious jealous streak and a temper that flare up without warning. A flexible water sign with a *seriously* funny streak can always be a better bet.

friend match

You can shrug off people's negativity, but you won't stand for anyone dissing your BFF. Her b-day adds up to 2, which means she's better in partnerships—good thing she has you!

May 1

You're a human blog post:
You've always got something to say about the world around you. You've usually got the exclusive on how your friends and family are feeling—you're the first to notice when your BFF's feeling low—and you've got an opinion on everything from the new Mexican restaurant in town (too greasy) to the new boy in school (too greasy). Your razor-sharp tongue means you're respected for your honesty but also feared for your bluntness. (Did you really have to tell your sister that her haircut makes her look like a walking popsicle?)

Crimson

Stand-up comedian

Puerto Vallarta

SOME PEOPLE ARE INTIMIDATED BY YOUR BLUNTNESS.

+/− Your motto is "It's better to be safe than sorry." But sometimes the only thing you'll regret is not taking the plunge, so if something (or *someone*) new seems appealing, go ahead and risk it.

love match

A slick Scorpio is keeping secrets from you, but don't get turned off to the possibilities of true love. Here's a hint about your one and only: He was born on the 21st, and he has a scathing sense of humor that matches yours.

friend match

A spring-born BFF will stick with you no matter what you say—plus, her Pollyanna attitude will balance out your tendency to get negative. Be sure to show her the same patience she shows you.

If you were an item of clothing, you'd be a bra: Supporting
People is your raison d'être. You're fascinated by psychology and are always trying to pick your friends' brains. (If *only* your parents had let you move a couch into your bedroom.) You're quick to spot a liar and are the go-to girl when your friends need advice about their love life. But all that ESP means you're occasionally tempted to do a little too much gossiping. Nobody likes a girl who spills secrets, so keep your lips zipped.

EVERY SO OFTEN, TRY TURNING THE ANALYSIS INWARD.

love match

On the surface, you seem like a no-nonsense kind of girl, but a guy whose birthday adds up to 8 will bring out the romantic in you. He'll find your stubbornness charming.

Freud's Interpretation of Dreams

Donatella Versace

Paris

friend match

Your best friend, a Gemini, can be very gullible. Luckily she has you: You can see through fakeness like you have X-ray vision and have a spot-on sense of when someone spells bad news.

+/− For all the time you spend observing other people, it's not often you turn the lens on yourself. You've got your own bad habits—like a tendency to be Little Miss Princess when it comes to getting your way.

May 3

Red
Bull

Golden
retriever

"No Sleep
Tonight"
—The Faders

+/− You are a social butterfly when it comes to large groups, but when it comes to guys? More like a wallflower. Don't be afraid to put yourself out there.

Insightful, Clever, Charming

You're like a Boeing 747: You're all about mobilizing the masses. You love to get people moving, and whether you're launching a new fashion trend (armbands?) or starting up a new extracurricular activity (competitive double Dutch, anyone?), you always know which direction your peeps should be heading. You're super-practical but never boring; you love making your friends laugh and having a good time, and your people know that when they're riding with you, they'll be living the high life.

love match

You're ruled by the number 3, which means you are an independent girl. You may love to flirt, but it will take more than some chiseled abs to get you to commit—like a certain sensitive Capricorn with a winning smile.

friend match

You and a Scorpio BFF are a match made in detention heaven, guaranteed to have a blast (and get into trouble) wherever you go. A laid-back Libra could help balance out the trio.

If you were a shirt, you'd be a tank top with a built-in shelf bra: You're totally practical and always ready for action. Your friends know they can lean on you when they're having a crisis, big or small. (No more sesame bagels! Ripped homecoming dress!) But just because you love to give other people a boost, doesn't mean you're a pushover; you can be very stubborn, too.

Double-date with your BFF and her boyfriend

Varsity volleyball captain

Audrey Hepburn

YOU EXCEL AT TEAM SPORTS AND IN GENERAL ARE HAPPIEST WHEN YOU'RE IN THE MIDDLE OF A GROUP

May 4

Caring, Stable, Warm-Hearted

+/− You get obsessive about what other people think of you, but you can't live your whole life courting other people's good opinions. You've got a lot of people who love you no matter what, so don't stress the haters.

love match

You are a lover of beauty, so it is no wonder you are drawn to an Aquarius so good-looking he makes Adonis look quite schlubby. Careful: His vanity is as swollen as his pecs. A funny and even-tempered Libra will mirror your own easygoing attitude well.

friend match

Most people adore you, but a moon-ruled girl's moods are threatening to rain on your parade. She resents your optimism; stay positive by sticking close to a happy-go-lucky Capricorn.

May 5

If knowledge is power, you ought to be the dictator of a small country. (And, yes, the cafeteria *does* count.) You've got more know-how than Wikipedia. You're all about teaching others: From tutoring French to your language-challenged best friend, to showing your little bro how to kick a soccer ball. But you can't be right 24/7, so before you spout off, check your facts.

Peer counselor

Life coach

"We're All in This Together" —Ben Lee

LEARN TO SAY "JE SUIS DÉSOLÉE" (A.K.A. I'M SORRY) WHEN YOU'RE WRONG.

+/− You want to share your experience with others, but occasionally you need to back off and let people make their own mistakes. Sometimes the only way for them to learn to stay away from a hot stove is to get burned! Besides, it can be a fine line between "bossy" and a certain other "b" word...

love match

A Cancer cutie is always butting heads with you, but his way of flirting is to play devil's advocate. If you get tired of sparring, look for a type A Aries whose views are aligned with your own.

friend match

Though you succeed in most things, you definitely need help when it comes to learning to laugh off your disappointments. A giggly Gemini can help you keep things in perspective.

If you were a book genre, you would definitely be fantasy: Not because you are obsessed with dragons or swords, but because you are extremely imaginative and see the *possible* where others see the *im*possible. You're inclined toward theater and the arts and dream of being famous, and your natural sensitivity means you have a sixth sense for what other people are feeling. It also means that negative vibes can seriously damage your mojo, **so be careful about who you let into your life.**

friend match

You're an excellent listener, which your Virgo BFF—who has an opinion on almost everything—really appreciates. Just make sure she upholds her end of the bargain and provides a shoulder to lean on when *you* need support.

love match

A Mercury-ruled hottie has your moods making like a seesaw: up-and-down, up-and-down. It's not good for you to be influenced by so much volatility, so stick with one of the more stable earth signs, like a fellow Taurus.

Indigo

Ballet

Betsy Johnson

TRY NOT TO BE SUCH
AN OPEN BOOK.

+/− You can get hurt easily because your emotions are so close to the surface. It's great that you feel things deeply, but you've got to protect yourself.

May 7

Royal blue

Wandering around the local street fair

"Stand by Me" —Ben E. King

Dignified, Devoted, Artistic

If you were a pet, you'd be a golden retriever: totally devoted, 100 percent loyal, and completely adored. Your friends are like family to you (and actually, you've known your BFFs almost since birth, so they count), and when you get involved with a new activity or cause (like raising money for the families of hurricane victims), you dedicate yourself to it completely. You're super-generous when it comes to other people, but there's one thing you never give yourself: a break. Take it easy every once in a while.

+/— When you hit a stumbling block—like a failed math quiz or a first-day-of-school fashion disaster—you tend to obsess over it for years.

LEARN TO LET THE PAST GO.

love match

A super-devoted water sign is your perfect match, so try not to get distracted by a funny daredevil Sagittarius—*he puts the OMG in Big Trouble.*

friend match

Your Libra BFF has been by your side since day one of kindergarten and you are so loyal, you always stick up for her. But if she keeps ditching you and making other plans, it might be time for an upgrade. Friends are like underwear—you *need* to change them every so often.

You're a human megaphone: always broadcasting loud and clear. You've got an opinion on everything, from your mom's Thanksgiving menu (absolutely no brussels sprout) to your BFF's new bangs (ah-dorable), and you never shy away from calling it like you see it. Although sometimes your mouth can get you in trouble, the people who know you best respect you for your honesty. That's probably because one of the messages you're always relaying is how much you love your friends and family: You're supergood to your inner circle.

> MAKE LIKE A DIET SODA AND LIGHTEN UP ONCE IN A WHILE.

Extra tube of your BFF's lip gloss

Action flick then ice cream

Resort in Thailand

May 8

Prudent, Convincing, Caring

+/− It's okay to have strong opinions, but it's not okay to lecture all the time.

love match

Saturn's influence over you makes you seem overly serious sometimes, but a certain brown-eyed boy ruled by Mars is going to make you feel like smiling 24/7.

friend match

As a Taurus, you're super-dependable, so if you say you're going to meet your friends at the mall at noon, you'll be there at five till! A flaky Neptune-ruled friend may drive you crazy, but she'll also help you kick back and relax.

May 9

You and Judge Judy share something: You're totally committed to justice. Very mature and über-responsible, you have a strong sense of right and wrong and will fight for fairness in every situation, from baby-sitting wages (anything less than $8 an hour is a crime) to a longer lunch period. (How do they expect you to scarf a sandwich and reapply lip gloss and gossip with your BFFs in fifteen minutes?) But make sure that all that judging doesn't make your ratings plummet with your friends—everyone makes mistakes, so back off.

MAKE SURE YOU'RE NOT USING AVOIDANCE TACTICS BECAUSE YOU'RE SECRETLY AFRAID OF BEING HURT.

Copper

Op-ed columnist

Rosario Dawson

+/− You, of all people, should know that two wrongs don't make a right. Just because you're angry—even if it's for good reason—doesn't mean you have the right to blow up. Make like an ice cube and chill.

love match

You're so concerned with taking care of business, you forget to take care of the sad state of your romantic affairs. An air sign with an easy laugh is worth the risk. Just go for it!

friend match

A Pisces pal relies on you to stick up for her whenever someone teases her on the lunch line or tries to cheat off her homework. But you need support, too, so make sure she's in your corner when you need a come-from-behind victory.

May 10

You have tons of friends, but in your mind, you're definitely a solo act. You're a great leader and a *bad* enemy. (You know you've had your share of drama.) But striking out on the road less traveled so often means you're frequently caught in a less-than-safe neck of the woods, so it's important to think through the consequences of your actions.

YOU LIKE TO DO THINGS YOUR OWN WAY AND DON'T SWEAT IT
IF OTHER PEOPLE DISAGREE WITH YOU.

friend match

Don't worry if you've made a few enemies at school—powerful people have a way of doing that. A fellow Sun-ruled rival might just turn out to be your new BFF once you start talking, so make a truce.

love match

A Scorpio is attracted to your way of doing and saying whatever you want. He's just as outspoken, so when you two start talking, words—and sparks!—will definitely fly.

EVEN THE FIERCEST
PERFORMERS NEED BACKUP
SINGERS!

Morning hike

Jack Russell terrier

Bohemian

+/− You've got a fierce grip on what *you* need and want, but you could be more sensitive to other people's needs.

May 11

Vintage record player

Chameleon

"Colorful"
—Rocco Deluca

+/− It's great to fantasize, but sometimes you need to *focus*. If you want to pursue acting, sign up for the school play. If you want to be a veterinarian, volunteer at the local animal shelter.

LET YOUR MOTTO BE "JUST DO IT".

Imaginative, Fun-Loving, Creative

You're like a vintage pair of pink-tinted sunglasses: The world just looks different through your eyes, and you're completely irreplaceable. You believe that normal = boring, and you'd rather die than be part of the mainstream. Quick to speak your mind, you have a habit of surprising even the people closest to you with the strength of your opinions and the uniqueness of your habits. (Bronzing foam really *is* the best invention since sliced bread— and who says you can't have sushi for breakfast?) Be true to yourself; you're one of a kind.

love match

An autumn-born hottie may not be the free thinker you'd like him to be, and there's no way you could go out with someone who just wants you to conform. A totally outrageous and fun-loving Scorpio will be a better match.

friend match

A practical Capricorn BFF may seem like your polar opposite, but that's exactly what makes you a perfect pair. She can help you remember deadlines (and to wear a jacket in the winter!); you can get her to try sparkly blue eye shadow and to dance like a madwoman at the Spring Fling.

You are just like recess:
You're all about playing games. You love to have fun, and you're always punking your friends, but your infectious sense of humor means nobody can ever stay mad at you. You know tug-of-war's not just for the playground: You love to debate and often argue the opposite side just to stir things up at the dinner table. Because people naturally look up to you, there's one game that's absolutely your favorite: Follow the Leader.

Summer camp

Reality TV show host

Emily VanCamp

May 12

YOU'RE ALWAYS IN FRONT!

Talented,
Ironic,
Mischievous

+/− You're so funny you could be a stand-up comedian. But nobody wants to be turned into a punch line, so give that acid tongue of yours a rest.

love match

An Aries with a wicked sense of humor just might dish out a taste of your own medicine. Your relationship will no doubt be a barrel of laughs, but if you're looking for more than fun and games, stick with a more solid sign, like a Leo or a Taurus.

friend match

Your fave day of the year? Easy—April Fool's Day! A Jupiter-ruled pal is incredibly gullible, so you can count on her to always fall for one of your jokes.

May 13

You are like a pair of stilettos on a soft lawn: You always make an impression. Naturally social, you have a ton of friends and love to be surrounded by people (the mall is your favorite place), and no matter what you do (like wear your hair in a slicked-back high ponytail), pretty soon other people are following suit. High ponytail? Fine. Side ponytail? A no-no.

Lemon

Gwen Stefani

Trendy hotel in New York City

+/− It's okay to court your friends' approval, but don't let other people's opinions dictate how you feel about yourself. Some people are just like last year's platform clogs: Best tossed out and quickly forgotten.

BE SURE YOU USE YOUR POWER FOR GOOD, NOT EVIL.

friend match

A level-headed water sign will help you rein in your tendency to indulge in all the wrong things, like overpriced shoes and very bad boys. In return, you can get her to sample the finer things in life—like dark chocolate and blond surfers!

love match

A moody Virgo boy might seem totally wrong for you, but in this case opposites attract! Spending time with you will bring a smile to his face, and he'll help you develop some deeper interests (like yoga—*sooo* relaxing).

If life is a highway, you've got your pedal to the metal. Whether you're shuttling from school to gymnastics to choir to your best friend's barbecue or cramming in a study session before you have to hit the mall for a fall formal dress, you're always going full speed ahead. You're a total perfectionist, but you'll never get caught stressing about past fumbles.

YOUR MOTTO IS "ONWARDS AND UPWARDS."

friend match

You love being surrounded by people and going to parties, but a fellow earth sign is more grounded than you and often needs time to breathe and recharge. Follow her lead, and you'll have even MORE energy when it comes time to paint the town red. Or pink, as the case may be.

$ News anchor

Cate Blanchett

"Such Great Heights" —The Postal Service

love match

You're ruled by the quick-changing Mercury, so you're ready to make the jump from *friendship* to *relationship* before your crush can say "attack of the girlfriend." A Saturn-ruled boy will move too slowly for your tastes, so if you want to speed things up, look for a fiery Sagittarius ruled by the mutable Jupiter.

+/— You will do anything to get ahead, but don't step on the little people to get what you want. If your English teacher singles you out as doing an awesome job on your *Hamlet* group project, you should still give props to your pals.

May 15

Hazel

Art club

Simplicity, simplicity, simplicity!

+/− You keep many of your deepest hopes, dreams, and wishes to yourself. But you'll never feel totally fulfilled unless you clue someone in to the secret life of *you*, so try to be more open to your friends and family.

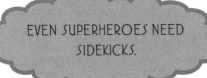

EVEN SUPERHEROES NEED SIDEKICKS.

Magnetic, Insightful, Enigmatic

You're the human equivalent of a Rubik's Cube: almost impossible to figure out. You draw people to you quicker than a magnet draws loose change. Ironically, though, you prefer to be on your own. Super-creative, you're always focused on a new project (building a dress out of bottle caps, experimenting with oil paints) and love to work solo. And like a busy bee, you are very organized, too.

love match

A tell-it-like-it-is Taurus will be frustrated that you seem to keep so many secrets. You're much better off with a sensitive Scorpio who also likes to spend time alone; even if you never verbalize everything you're thinking, he'll understand.

friend match

Few people get to hear you really speak from the heart, but you always share everything with a summer-born BFF. You know she'd never betray you by spilling your secrets or (gasp!) judging, and you show her a different way of looking at the world.

You are just like a hot pink leopard-spotted stiletto: totally outrageous and just for fun. You don't have a shy bone in your body and are all about putting on a show for anyone who will watch. From belting out "I Will Survive" on the bus to rocking a pink boa as a bandeau tank top, you're totally unafraid to express yourself. But sometimes your honesty is more like ho*nasty*; when you're about to throw a tantrum, take a deep breath and relax.

Karaoke machine

Janet Jackson

A cowboy hat with a sundress

May 16

Colorful, Uninhibited, Expressive

> YOU CAN'T STAND IT WHEN PEOPLE DON'T TELL YOU WHAT THEY'RE THINKING.

+/– Your hilarious outbursts in class sometimes lighten the mood, but they can also be a real downer (like when you get detention for disrupting a quiz). One of the most important things about humor is *timing*, so learn when you should tone it down.

love match

Romantic planet Venus is the ruler of Taurus, and you're also influenced by the dreamy qualities of Neptune, so it's no wonder that when you fall for a guy, you fall hard. A sensitive Libra is absolutely worth the plummet, so go ahead and take the plunge.

friend match

You can't stand it when people don't tell you what they're thinking, so stay away from moon-ruled friends: They tend to keep their troubles to themselves. Friends ruled by the sun, on the other hand, are just like your guidance counselor's door: always open.

May 17

You should be a CEO, because you're all about the bottom line. You like to keep things short and sweet, so whether you're giving it to your friends straight (that bikini puts the *oh no* in *oh no she didn't*) or breaking down math equations into easy-to-answer parts, you're always looking to find simple solutions to life's problems. You apply your less-is-more approach to your friends, too, preferring to stick close to a very small circle.

FBLA president

"Under Pressure" —Queen

Secluded spa with your BFFs

+/− Your motto is "Business before pleasure", but you know what they say about all work and no play.

HAVE SOME FUN OR YOU'RE HEADED FOR A MAJOR MELTDOWN.

love match

You're a not damsel-in-distress type, so you might blow off a more traditional Taurus who offers to carry your books or open a door for you. But even Joan of Arc needed help sometimes, so don't be afraid to show weakness. Every so often it's nice to have someone help you shoulder the burden.

friend match

You're not going to spill your guts (or your trade secrets) to just anyone, but a loyal autumn-born BFF will never betray your trust. She's just like you—you both expect people to prove their loyalty before you let them in the inner circle.

You're such a mover and a shaker, you could be an extra in a hip-hop video. But your talents are much more practical than that: You take care of *business,* which is why you always head up group projects and find yourself making decisions on behalf of your crew. You're always looking for ways to improve the status quo, so whether you're giving your older sis a much-needed makeover or redecorating your BFF's room, you're making the world a brighter place.

friend match

A Gemini friend might be tempted to use you as her personal assistant, but you're not a dog, so remind her you don't play fetch. Speak up about what *you* want, and if she can't provide you the support you need, a fun-loving Aries will always pull her weight in the friendship.

love match

A fire-sign hottie is so distracting you're tempted to let your grades slip. Instead, make a study date with a serious but oh-so-cute Virgo who will help you mix business *and* pleasure!

Emerald

Community outreach

Tina Fey

+/− Your friends and family can always count on you to help out in times of trouble, but you always forget to look out for yourself! If you always put aside personal goals, it will only add up to unhappiness, so remember to look out for Number One.

May 19

Orange

Rollerblading around town

All-inclusive in Turks and Caicos

Elemental, Energetic, Fair

You're just like the weather: unpredictable, so people have to make their plans around you. You've got a ton of energy and can be forceful when you want something; you find it easy to convince others to support you, whether your cause is better bagels in the cafeteria or disaster-aid-relief donations. But you never stay focused on any one goal for long, and your moods can go from in the clear to the end is near faster than you can say, "Run for cover."

+/− Even if you don't agree with all the choices your friends make, *it's no excuse to rain on their parade.* If your BFF wants to wear a muumuu to school, so what? It's her choice, so lay off the lecturing.

love match

A loyal Leo might try to pin you down, but you never stay interested in one guy for long. But what goes around comes around, so be prepared for a volatile Mercury-ruled boy born on the Virgo-Libra cusp to run away with your heart.

friend match

The changeability of your sign means you actually mix well with a large group of people. Careful, trying to get a water sign to mix with a Uranus-ruled friend is like trying to make a smoothie with the blender top off: messy!

You're just like Six Flags:
You're all about amusement. You need constant activity to keep you from snoozing and spend a lot of time listening to music, shopping, and chatting with your friends—and not so much time on homework (yawn). You have a tendency to get obsessed with things, so when you find a new band, food, or dress you like, you won't talk about anything else for days. Just make sure to take care of your obligations—flunking a quiz because you didn't make time to study is *never* fun.

Pinkberry cup

Professional athlete

Punk

May 20

Exciting,
Innovative,
Expressive

+/− Your mind is like a motor that's always running, and your mouth is connected to the same switch. Save the monologues for the stage and let other people speak up.

love match

Variety is the spice of life, and your life is plenty spicy with an Aries and an air-sign artist both vying for your heart. You're all about amusing yourself right now, but be sure that you're not playing too freely with other people's emotions—that's a game that nobody wins in the end.

friend match

A chill Jupiter friend can calm you down when your life is getting stormy (and your moods are turning black), but for someone with as much energy and passion as you, you need a drama-loving Cancer.

68

May 21

They say that hindsight is 20/20, but you have perfect vision looking backward *and* forward. You're quick to spot solutions to everyday problems—you were the one who turned your BFF's basement into an impromptu indoor beach party when her birthday barbecue was ruined by rain—and you don't mind if you have to hurdle some difficulties along the way. (Admit it, when you were little, you *loved* those 5,000-piece puzzles.)

SUPER-SOCIAL AND VERY FLIRTATIOUS, YOU ONLY FOCUS ON YOUR *OWN* GAME.

$ Film director

Tropical fish

Morocco

+/− It's fine to be confident, but if your head gets any bigger it's going to need its own zip code. Let *other* people sing your praises, or you may start getting permanent silent treatment from your friends.

love match

A mischievous Mercury-ruled guy has cultivated a bad reputation, but you're no stranger to breaking hearts, either—and you *never* listen to gossip. Go with your instinct (as though you wouldn't!), but don't be surprised if this fiery coupling goes up in flames. Oh, well. The fireworks will be worth it.

friend match

You see (and appreciate) that an anti-social Aquarius is really just defying the norm. You don't let yourself be ruled by what other people think is right, and she doesn't, either, making you a match made in rebel heaven.

What's your FLIRTING style?

About romance, you believe:

a. All's fair in love and war.

b. A smile is your best accessory.

c. Good things come to those who wait.

d. If it's meant to be, it will be.

You want your crush to think you are:

a. Drop dead gorgeous.

b. Fun.

c. Pretty and cute.

d. Funny.

You're invited to a party and you know your crush will be there. You wear:

a. Tiny BCBG black mini, *high-heeled wedges, a strapless tank—even in January.*

b. Your skinny jeans, *a cute halter top, your fave gold sandals.*

c. A flowered knee-length Anthropology dress, *a pink cardigan, ballet flats.*

d. Jeans, sneakers, and a T-shirt, *as usual. If you wore anything else, he'd know something was up—plus, you don't even own a skirt!*

QUIZ!

Your favorite thing about your crush is:

a. How popular he is. *Everyone loves him!*

b. His smile and sense of humor.

c. He doesn't make you feel dumb *when you forget your own name.*

d. How cute his butt looks *when he jogs on the track in front of you.*

Your ideal date is:

a. Hitting a pool party. *A perfect excuse to see and be seen . . . in a bikini!*

b. Grabbing dinner, *relaxing in the park, and talking.*

c. A movie. *As long as you don't have to make convo, you're Okay.*

d. A pick-up game of touch football. *Lots of excuses for "accidental" contact.*

Oh, no! Your crush is dating someone else. You:

a. Immediately launch a campaign to ruin her rep.

b. Start looking for a replacement ASAP. *Maybe his adorable soccer-playing friend?*

c. Sob hysterically for days; *stalk his new GF's Facebook page.*

d. Offer to drive the happy couple to the mall. *Who said three's a crowd?*

Why do your relationships usually end?

a. He begins avoiding you. *No matter how many times you call his house, he never seems to be at home.*

b. You finally kiss, *and he has a tongue that makes a rotor blade look lazy.*

c. He calls you by someone else's name.

d. He tells you he thinks of you as a friend.

The Invading Army

You've got one game plan when it comes to getting the guy you like: Overwhelm and conquer. Nothing's off-limits. (Even stalking.) It's great to be confident but not to be an attack dog—yikes! Back off a bit and let him come to you; trust that you're worth it.

The Good-Time Girl

Good flirtation requires a killer smile, confidence, and the ability to chill. You have the perfect zen attitude about dudes and dating: If you just kick back and do your own thing, the right guy will find you. You're also not afraid to invite him to go bowling with your crew if Mr. Right needs encouragement.

The Shrinking Violet

If confidence were a vitamin, you'd have a serious deficiency. News flash: Guys get shy just like you, and you're never going to make progress by daydreaming. Learn to be yourself around your crush, and you'll be surprised by the results.

The Buddy-Buddy

You're every guy's best friend, always down for an impromptu game of Ultimate Frisbee or a Guitar Hero marathon in the basement. But beware of the Platonic Friend trap; find subtle ways to remind him that you are not just one of the guys. Rock a skirt once in a while and suggest that the two of you hit a movie—alone.

QUIZ!

Gemini Girls
are social butterflies

Gemini ladies are lively, curious, and brainier than a Math League convention. A dual sign represented by the twins Geminis crave close connections and are super-outgoing. When it comes to making the rules, though, there's only a Numero Uno: Confident, outspoken, and free-spirited, Geminis definitely do their own thing.

Most likely to be: Arguing their
way out of a late pass.

Beverage they most resemble:
Red Bull. Sweet but strong, full of energy.

Strengths to play on: Intelligence,
sense of adventure.

Pitfalls to avoid: Restlessness,
senseless experimentation.

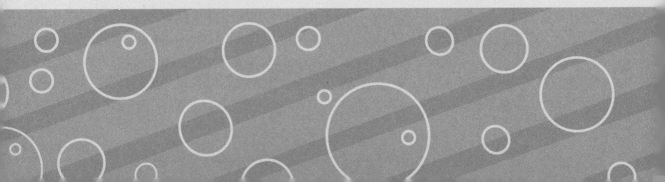

Gemini

May 22–June 21

Element: Air
Ruler: Mercury

Motto: "Minds are like underwear: Change often or perish."

School events coordinator

Museum curator

Ginnifer Goodwin

May 22

Persistent, Energetic, Productive

You and the tax man got something in common: Both of you just love to collect. Whether it is platform shoes, magazines, photos, or friends, you're a regular pack rat. You're very organized and prefer logic problems to English essays, which is why your friends look to you for help in math and science. It's not that you seek easy answers, though—in fact, you're very focused and can work on problems (like which boy to ask to the spring fling!) for months at a time. (Fess up. Will boys be your newest collection?)

+/− You like to be in control, **but** sometimes your tendency to obsess makes Martha Stewart seem like a slacker. Organizing your closet is one thing, but color coding every single item of clothing as well as cross-referencing by fabric? Flat-out scary.

☆ • ☆ • ☆ • ☆ • ☆

love match

You treat love like it's a soccer game: As soon as one guy's off the field, you've got another one subbing in. But a quiet and generous Aries will be the one to throw a wrench in all of your plans and leave you with one game plan only: Score him!

friend match

You have the same philosophy about friends that you do for everything else: It pays to collect them all. But you're so busy trying to make friends with everyone, you don't have time to cultivate close ties with anyone. Focus on your connection with a single BFF, like a logical and focused Sagittarius.

You're a human lightning bolt, always zapping energy around. (And your enemies know that to cross your path can burn.) Your enthusiasm for life is totally contagious, which is why your friends stick to you closer than a pin to a magnet; fortunately, your down-to-earth demeanor means you're always a positive influence. Happy to work in groups, you'd make a far better agent or promoter than you would a movie star. You are completely happy to work your magic in the background while other people shine.

Orchid

Jewel

"Smile
—Vitamin C"

May 23

Convincing,
Magnetic,
Quick-Witted

+/− You love to do good unto others, but all that positive energy straight fizzles when it comes to taking care of yourself. Next time you host a pool party, make sure you're having a good time before you worry about anyone else.

love match

You come across as über-confident, but the truth is you tend to clam up around guys. A Virgo with a killer sense of humor will never judge you negatively, so feel free to let your real self shine— you'll have a new Number One fan.

friend match

Your impressionable water-sign BFF definitely looks to you for guidance, and you're more than happy to provide it. Make sure the flow of info doesn't just go one way, though; she can teach you valuable lessons about sticking up for yourself.

May 24

Expressive, Social, Involved

You are like the zoom setting on a digital camera, always blowing things up for a clearer view. Not content with superficial answers, you're always digging deeper: Why does your crush act shady one second and super into you the next? How does your English teacher find foundation that exact shade of pasty white? You have a lot of opinions, and you are quick to express them. In fact, your honesty sometimes borders on abuse, as those who have been on the cutting end of one of your criticisms could tell you.

Journalist

Parrot

Swiss Alps

+/− You and a talk show have one thing in common: You have always got something to say. But every anchor needs a cohost, so try shutting your mouth once in a while and listening to what other people have to say.

friend match

A deep-thinking Scorpio is your natural friend match, because you can lose yourselves for hours in conversation on just about anything, from the offerings in the cafeteria to the secrets you're sure a certain Sagittarius soccer player is keeping. But you should reach out to a fun Capricorn who keeps you from taking yourself too seriously.

love match

You might be outspoken, but you are actually kind of shy one-on-one. Ironically, you are best suited to a guy who will take the lead in conversation (at least, at the beginning—nobody will keep your motormouth at rest for long!), like a smart and opinionated Leo.

If you were a font style, you would be bold and all caps. Whether you're protesting the use of trans fats in the cafeteria or pairing floral and stripes, you're always making a statement. Some people think you're all surface, because you rock a new hairstyle once a month and love to snap up the newest cell phones, but just like a bag of Doritos, you've got hidden depths.

friend match

You never compromise your principles, and you need support from a friend who will take your side when you're out crusading. A Virgo who doesn't care what anyone else thinks will back you up, whether the cause du jour is a denim miniskirt you think your parents should buy you or the disappearance of marine life. *Vive la révolution!*

Magenta

Horseback riding

Molly Sims

love match

Don't be scared off by smoldering and serious Capricorn. He will bring out a side of you that people rarely get to see. He'll discover that underneath all of the bells and whistles you can be quiet, loyal, and compassionate—just like him. And along with his intensity comes a whole lotta Chemistry!

+/− You're the opposite of a pooper-scooper: You don't take anyone's crap! Deep down, though, you're a total softie, so let your fam and friends know how much you care about them before you wind up in deep . . . you know.

May 26

Plum

Emo

"What Goes Around"
—Justin Timberlake

Protective, Passionate, Honorable

If you were a movie genre, you'd be an old-school Western, because (face it!) you're an outlaw at heart. Extremely opinionated, you have a my-way-or-the-highway attitude, which ironically makes people gravitate toward you, as any time spent in your company is bound to be more exciting than a roller-coaster ride at Six Flags. You have very strong beliefs (no leggings—ever!) and consider yourself as a very strong, moral person, but your no-holds-barred behavior is more rebel than responsible.

+/− You're quick to defend the people you care about, **but you're not a member of the Secret Service, so stop playing bodyguard. A friend may not appreciate your constant interference—she can stick up for herself, so let her.**

DESPITE THE FACT THAT YOU CAN SOMETIMES COME ACROSS AS AN ICE QUEEN, AT HEART YOU'RE TOASTY WARM.

love match

Be prepared for a sports-obsessed Taurus to make you melt; he's opinionated, fun, and generous, just like you.

friend match

Neither you or a Scorpio BFF is happy to walk the straight and narrow 24/7, but be careful that all of your trailblazing does not lead you down some dangerous roads. The practical-minded Capricorn in your life can be a positive influence.

You're just like a cell phone: all about communication. Outspoken and opinionated, whether your interests lie in the social realm (running for class VP) or are more personal (getting first chair in the county orchestra), your goal is always to share your accomplishments with others, and your outrageous sense of humor means that spending time with you is like being in a comedy club 24/7. Careful, though: You love people but aren't always the best at reading them, and some of your jokes might be falling flat due to very bad timing. Try to be more sensitive to your friends' feelings or you risk having no audience left.

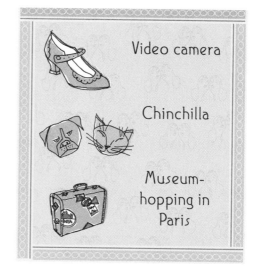

Video camera

Chinchilla

Museum-hopping in Paris

May 27

Humorous, Persistent, Sophisticated

+/− Sometimes you're just like one of those tiny video screens on an iPod nano: You've got a lot of trouble with the big picture. It's important to listen; try to get a broader perspective before you shut the door on other people's opinions.

friend match

A laid-back Cancer won't judge your occasionally out-there opinions, but she'll also keep you grounded whenever you're starting to spiral too far out into the stratosphere. In return, your enthusiasm and passion will be like a constant caffeine jolt to her often-unmotivated self.

love match

To balance out the influence of Mercury on your sign, you will need a practical optimist: someone who gets things done and believes the best about people. A sunny Leo—with a sense of humor equal to your own—will give you the support you need.

May 28

You're like a GPS system:
Always finding new trails, you work best when mapping out your own route. You not only come up with a ton of great ideas (such as a make-your-own-sundae bar at your next b-day party!), you make sure to turn them into reality, making you the go-to girl for parents, teachers, and friends who need a favor. Your creativity can bring you into conflict with people around you—like when your mom insists a miniskirt made out of bottle caps is not appropriate for winter weather. Try to listen to other people's perspectives before going haywire.

Sewing machine

Stage crew

Kylie Minogue

+/− You're the opposite of a bottle cap: You have tons of trouble sealing the deal! Although you get psyched to start a new project, crossing the finish line is a serious challenge. Before you launch into writing a new screenplay, finish the short film you started.

love match

You have a ton of energy, so your idea of an ideal date does not include lounging around reading poetry to your guy. A try-anything Libra will keep up with you and *keep* you interested—no poetry allowed.

friend match

You are extremely art-oriented, so math and science are not your favorite subjects. A Saturn-ruled friend can help you think logically, whether the equation you're solving is $2x + 7 = 15$ or you + a cute boy in gym class = possibility?

Daring, Expressive, Dynamic

May 29

If you were an event in the Olympics, you would be gymnastics, because you're all about the balancing act. You work extremely well in groups, always playing peacemaker when your friends are fighting and figuring out a compromise in even the most stressful situations. (Your BFF wants to hit the pool and you want to hit the movies. Solution? Shopping!) Ironically, you have a need to KIC (Keep It Cool) despite the fact that your own temper has more ups and downs than an escalator.

love match

There's nothing you like better than a sense of humor, so a hilarious (and hot) Cancer will have you swooning over his witty way with words. The moon's influence on him means he's actually kind of shy, so you'll have to make the first move.

friend match

You need to be surrounded by people and always keep a circle of friends close. Careful: Sometimes your crew feels like it's playing adoring audience to your one-woman show, so quit hogging the stage.

Turquoise

Miniature golf

Field hockey

+/− Sometimes you feel just like a can of Coca-Cola that's been recently shaken up: all bottled up and ready to explode. Controlling your anger is okay, but ignoring it isn't—it will only lead to a big, sticky mess later on. Try talking about your feelings.

May 30

Longchamp nylon tote

Platinum

"I'm Like a Bird"
—Nelly Furtado

+/− Free livin' is good in theory, but in practice it can get you in a lot of trouble with the people you care about. If you make a promise, keep it—otherwise you'll get the reputation of being flakier than dandruff.

Quick, Expansive, Skilful

Both you as well as the New Hampshire license plate have the exact same motto: "Live free or die." You hate being stuck in one place and dream of traveling: From Paris to Prague, swimming with the dolphins, dancing in Rio. You're full of energy and launch yourself easily into new projects, but you get bored so easily you don't your commitments through. Your need for *la liberté* extends to all areas of your life: You hate being enchained by other people's expectations of you and will dress, speak, and do exactly what you want. (*Oh la la.*)

love match

The free-spirited ways (read: Canceled plans and no phone calls) of a fire-sign guy will give you a taste of your own medicine. When you get tired of the drama, look for a sweet and solid Aquarius who won't leave you hanging.

friend match

You tend to make decisions on the fly without giving a lot of thought to the consequences. A super-serious Sagittarius may seem like your polar opposite (she color codes her school binders!), but the two of you are like the different parts of an Oreo cookie: much better when taken together.

You and Kate Moss could really be best friends (or at least, best frenemies): You are totally cool, cutting-edge, and always a step ahead of the trends. A lot of people find you intimidating, but really you're a total softie. In fact, the reason you strut your stuff is because you know you have to fake it till you make it, and your cool-as-a-cuke exterior conceals a lot of insecurities. Whenever you're feeling down, remember: You've got more star power than an issue of *Us Weekly*.

> YOU MAY NOT REALIZE IT, BUT YOU HAVE A LOT OF SECRET—OR NOT SO SECRET—ADMIRERS.

Club opening

Brooke Shields

Eurotrash

May 31

No-Nonsense, Capable, Adaptable

+/− When you're arguing about something, you're like a dog that's just dug up a bone: You won't let it go. It's fine to have strong beliefs, but your stubbornness makes you seem plain pigheaded. Let go of the drama before your life becomes a zoo.

love match

You might be attracted to a confident Taurus in your Spanish class, but a long-term coupling will be less of a match and more of a battle. An intuitive Virgo with a mind for compromise will be a positive—and mellowing—force in your life.

friend match

You need a BFF who is calm and laid-back to bring harmony to your life, like a take-it-as-it-comes Pisces, who will help you decompress when you're ready to flip your lid.

June 1

If you were a game, you would be I Spy: Totally fascinated by the world around you, you must be as aware and in-the-know as possible. But you follow the see-and-be-seen rule, too, and often claim the stage to be the center of attention. Your big secret? All that hamming is really just that—an act— and in some ways you're very private, keeping a lot to yourself.

Aqua

Gossip columnist

Marilyn Monroe

ALTHOUGH YOU SEEM TO BE SUPER-SOCIAL, YOU SOMETIMES FEEL LIKE THE ONLY GAME YOU'RE PLAYING IS SOLITAIRE.

+/− You spend a lot of time thinking about how you come across to others and not a whole lot of energy thinking about what makes you happy. Be clear about what you want, and you'll be much more likely to get it. Happiness comes from within, but you still have to work for it!

love match

You hate to be alone, so before your crush on a cute Aquarius has faded, you're pursuing a brooding poet who's ruled by hot-and-cold Mercury. You're not a frog, so quit all that jumping around. Focus on yourself for a while, and your love life will fall in line.

friend match

A perceptive Pisces friend will see past your posturing and understand what's really going on in your life. Whether you need a long talk, a sob fest, or a spa day, she'll be there.

If you were a kitchen utensil, you would be a blender, because you need to mix it up. You crave variety—softball one day, painting the next, soccer after that—and setbacks rarely get you down for long. (Curfews—who needs 'em?) In fact, those born on your birthday are natural problem solvers, and if your friends sometimes feel like you stir up drama just to smooth it out later, they're probably right. It's no surprise that your emotional life has got more highs and lows than a thermometer, so every so often make like a virgin piña colada and chill.

THERE'S NOTHING WORSE THAN BEING
YOUR OWN WORST FRENEMY.

+/− It is great that you know how to clear hurdles when they come up, but that doesn't mean you have to create problems for yourself. Keep your anger in check.

Pot-bellied pig

Boho

"New Shoes"
—Paolo Nutini

love match

A brooding bad boy born in November may be too complicated for some, but you're attracted to the challenge. If you don't mind hitting some low points, the thrill of the ride might be worth it.

friend match

A feet-on-the-ground Capricorn won't let the drama get her down. Ruled by Saturn, she has excellent focus and can help you keep things in perspective.

June 3

Auburn

Poetry slam at a small café

Lawyer

+/− There are some situations you cannot talk your way out of. If you dump Coca-Cola down your best friend's fave dress when it is on loan, can all the creative excuses and replace it.

Talkative, Convincing, Witty

Whoever said a picture is worth a thousand words obviously never heard you speak. Quick-witted, logical, and argumentative, you wax poetic on every subject, from the best variety of veggie burgers to the importance of (what else?) free speech. And though you are drawn to activities and extracurriculars that let you exercise your mental muscle (debate club, anyone?), you have a very commanding physical presence that draws people to you faster than you can say, "entourage."

love match

Your flirting style looks more like fencing than fun: It's all about attack and counterattack. An intelligent and surprisingly sensitive Aries might not understand your style of tough love, so go easy if you don't want to kill the romance before it starts.

friend match

For you, it's more like BFFTM (Best Friend for the Moment). A fire-sign friend will share your love of scathing gossip, and a Gemini will stay up and spill secrets with you all night long.

You could be a film critic, because you always have something to say—and it's not always two thumbs-up. You're extremely perceptive, so your observations are usually spot-on, but every so often your friends and family can feel like they live in a 24/7 ratings war, constantly competing for your positive opinion. One way to channel all your mental energy is to focus on learning new skills: You're never happier than when you're being challenged. But don't let your social life get lost in a jam-packed schedule.

GIVE YOURSELF
AN R RATING: RELAX!

Class president

Angelina Jolie

Boutique hotel in Chicago

June 4

· ◦ · ◦ · ◦ · ◦ · ◦ · ◦ · ◦ · ◦ · ◦ · ◦ ·

Smart, Verbal,
Intuitive

+/− You've got more influence on your friends than you know, **so be careful what you say.** A throwaway comment might be perceived by them as a scathing criticism, so think twice before declaring wedges so two minutes ago.

· ◦ · ◦ · ◦ · ◦ · ◦ · ◦ · ◦ · ◦ · ◦ · ◦ · ◦ · ◦ · ◦ · ◦ · ◦ · ◦ · ◦ · ◦ · ◦ ·

friend match

You've got a ton of acquaintances and only a few very close friends. Put a down-to-earth Capricorn on speed dial for the times when you've got a problem you can't handle on your own.

love match

Your intuition is rarely wrong, and it's leading you in the direction of a Venus-ruled artist who doesn't open up easily. Once again your gut instinct is spot-on, so put in the effort to get to know him.

June 5

You often feel like blue eye shadow: a little bit wacky and a lot underappreciated. You're ultra-creative and have strong—and unusual—ideas about what you want. (Like a pretzel covered sundae, now!) Because, you have a tendency to zone out, people assume you're spacey, but in truth you're very competitive and can get a lot accomplished once you set your mind to it. Your biggest frustration is feeling misunderstood. Just remember that everything—blue eye shadow, too— makes a comeback, so you're bound to have your time to shine.

Chamomile tea *suis desolee.*

Chef

"The Future Freaks Me Out" —Motion City Soundtrack

+/− Your biggest rival? You. **Stop psyching yourself out with doubts and fears, and you'll be unstoppable.**

YOU'RE A WORRIER BY NATURE.

love match

When you're around your crush, you speak so fast he'd have to know shorth just to decode you. Your anxieties are killing the romance quicker than garlic breath, but a patient and generous Leo might put you at ease.

friend match

The only thing keeping you from a stomach ulcer is a Taurus BFF. When you're stressing about an upcoming biology exam, she'll remind you that you always rock the essay questions.

June 6

If you were an Olympic sport, you would be archery, because you always have your eye on a target far, far away. Ruled by the idea of "vision," June 6th people never walk the easy path, preferring instead to forge their own way. (So when all your friends were cats for Halloween, you went as Cleopatra's evil twin sister—complete with a live snake pet.) You never do things halfway: It's all or nothing, black or white, no ice cream or the whole pint. Just be sure that your refusal to compromise doesn't blind you to the wisdom of what your family and friends are telling you.

friend match

A straightforward Scorpio friend can be trusted to give her honest opinion; just make sure you have your dial tuned to "Listen."

love match

The warning light should flash when a magnetic Mercury-ruled boy comes into your life, but he's so cute you're inclined to ignore the symbols. Caution: The collision of your signs means risky business.

Dinner and live jazz

Fashion photographer

Sarah Dessen

+/− Traveling the high road can be lonely, and you have a tendency to feel isolated. Remember to take pit stops and cozy up with the people you care about. You + your friends + the mall = a perfect bull's-eye every time.

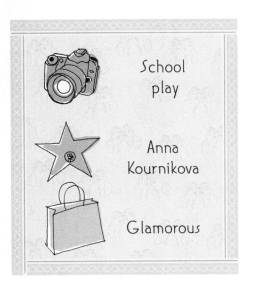

School play

Anna Kournikova

Glamorous

June 7

Entertaining, Funny, Charming

You ought to be the next American Idol, because you are all about entertaining people. Your favorite place to be is directly in the spotlight, and because you're amazing at reading people's moods, you know just how to give your fans (ahem, friends) what they want. Your favorite subject is fun, so whether you are doing some damage at the mall or lying out at your BFF's pool, you're all about letting the good times roll.

+/— When it comes to promises, you need more rehab than an out-of-control starlet. It's okay to be selfish sometimes, but be sure you're there for your friends when you say you will be or you'll find yourself in a whole new role: Social Outcast.

love match

You believe flirtation is good fun, but to a more serious and straightforward Capricorn, your flirty behavior spells L-O-V-E. Be careful about the messages you send.

friend match

A Pisces will be happy to let you have the spotlight, while she plays supporting actress. Even better? When you are being a drama queen (again!), she'll bring you back to earth.

If you were a breakfast, you would be a whole wheat toast, some orange juice, and an egg-white scramble: Totally well-rounded. You have natural skills in math, English, and art class, and you definitely have the reputation of an overachiever. (And the stress that comes with it!) Because you have very strong opinions, you tend to be judgmental just ask the last girl who tried to tell you that acid-wash jeans should make a comeback—and in your efforts to stand up for yourself can sometimes come across as rude. No worries—most of your problems can be solved by taking a daily dose of mellow.

Rose

"Manic Monday"
—The Bangles

Private
beach
in Hawaii

June 8

Dependable,
Influential,
Individualistic

+/− Super-loyal and more attached to your friends than a leash, you run the risk of holding on too tightly. Let your friends have their own opinions.

love match

When you have a crush on someone, you tend to close down every line of communication. Really this is because you're nervous, but it comes across as snobbery. An out-there Aries with a quick laugh can help put you at ease.

friend match

You and an equally intense Cancer can find yourself making like tape and sticking together 24/7. But it's important to meet new people, so beware of seeming exclusive.

June 9

You should be a superhero, because you sometimes feel like you have a split identity. Shy at school but totally outgoing at home, you've got more sides than a pair of dice and make it just as hard for your friends and family to know what your next move will be. This doesn't mean that your opinions are flexible, though; in fact, you stick to your beliefs like lint on black, and you're always trying to bring other people over to your point of view. (Chocolate ice cream is so much better than vanilla.)

Tutoring

Natalie Portman

Laid-back

love match

You tend to fall harder than the season, but a lot of hurt could be avoided if you were more selective about who—you opened up to. A water sign's fluidity and fascination with more than one side of life will make for excellent—and honest—heart-to-hearts.

+/− Keeping your emotions to yourself is not your forte, and whether you're angry, jealous, happy, or crushing, other people are bound to know it.

JUST BE CAREFUL NOT TO GAMBLE TOO FREELY WITH YOUR HEART—NOT EVERYONE IS WORTH IT.

friend match

To you, being a good friend means total honesty, and a moral Libra appreciates that she can trust your advice. Just be sure you're equally open when she gives it to you straight.

June 10

A frown is nothing but a smile turned upside down, and your life has plenty of both. June 10th people are ruled by the idea of opposites—happiness and sadness, light and dark, up-and-down—and just like a black and white cookie, you'll find greatest success by bringing different sides together as one. Passionate, sensitive, talented, and often torn in your desires (Pringles or nachos? Waffles or eggs? Prada or Gucci?), your life will have more turbulence than an airplane ride. Learn to ride out the bumps.

friend match

To most people, you seem to have the world at your fingertips, but you can rely on an earth sign when you need to share your problems. Ruled by sensitive Venus, she won't judge you or broadcast your secrets.

Change of clothes

Rock climbing

Judy Garland

love match

You're drawn to a magnetic Aries, but the fact that he's ruled by powerful and individualistic Mars means he's a rebel at heart. Don't get sucked into his orbit. Stick with a stable Leo, who won't spell serious trouble for you. Like the Sun, a reliable Leo will shine on you when you're down.

+/− Attracted to experimentation and risk, you're easily influenced by others. Make sure you keep positive people around you at all times, otherwise you may find yourself nose-diving toward trouble.

June 11

Gold

$

Rock star

Sarah Jessica Parker

Directed, Positive, Diligent

You ought to work at the post office, because you are always pushing the envelope. Your motto is "Rules are made to be broken." No matter what you do, you do it to the extreme. Having a barbecue with your BFFs? You'll stay up all night baking your own hamburger buns. Going to miss curfew by fifteen minutes? You'll go ahead and miss it by two hours. You can drive your parents and teachers crazy in your need to test limits, but you're not exactly a rebel.

+/− Competitive is your middle name, and you're always in it to win it. But sometimes the journey is more important than the finish line, so lighten up and have some fun!

FOCUSED AND DRIVEN, YOU KNOW THAT YOU'VE GOT TO BUST THROUGH A FEW GLASS CEILINGS WHEN YOU'RE REACHING FOR THE STARS.

love match

You don't have a ton of time for romance, but a driven and ambitious Aquarius just might be your A+ answer. Just remember, a little extra effort in the subject of love can lead to some major... credit from your crush!

friend match

A Scorpio who likes to walk on the wild side may seem like a blast, but the only place the two of you will be cruising together is detention. Stick with a down-to-earth and balanced Libra, who will keep your bad self in check.

You're just like a rubber ball:
No matter how hard you get clobbered, you always seem to bounce right back. The quintessential comeback kid, your natural optimism means that sooner or later things usually go your way. You love to be on the fly, zipping from school to ballet to the mall, and your friends love you for your energy, generosity, and loyalty. But just because you like to lend a helping hand, doesn't mean you let yourself get squeezed; if someone wants to take advantage of you (like a certain lab partner who's all about copying homework), you are quick to take a stand.

YOU ALWAYS LOOK ON THE BRIGHT SIDE.

Greyhound

Adriana Lima

"Unwritten"
—Natasha Bedingfield

June 12

Optimistic,
Accepting,
Loveable

+/− There's one area of your life where the glass is decidedly half empty: self-esteem. You're amazing, so own it.

love match
A Taurus troublemaker might seem like bad news, but underneath his rebellious exterior, he's got a positive attitude and a natural loyalty that matches your own.

friend match
Whenever an Aries friend starts feeling blue, your help turns her frown upside down. And she's perfect for you because she loves to be on the move just as much as you do.

June 13

You might as well be a passport, because you're all about travel and adventure. So maybe you haven't fulfilled your dreams of hiking across Europe or surfing in Mexico (cute surfer boy bonus!), but even when you are just scoping a new restaurant or sneaking into a R-rated movie, you're all about new experiences. Your friends know you for being totally courageous. (Like the time you strolled right up to that older soccer player and asked for his number!) Caution: Because you're fearless, you don't always make the best decisions.

Blue

Supermodel

Mary-Kate and Ashley Olsen

+/− Daydreaming is absolutely fine, but spending every waking moment wrapped up in a fantasy world is just like paisley on pin stripes: Not okay.

YOUR MOTTO IS "NEVER SAY NEVER."

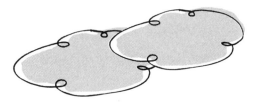

friend match

A Gemini shares your love of dreaming big and living large, and her sense of humor ensures that even if you encounter some bumps along the road, you will always be laughing.

love match

You could be a frog, from the way you jump around from guy to guy. But before you fall for the Next Best Thing, reevaluate a low-key Libra who flies under the radar as a friend.

June 14

You could be a talk-show host, because you are all about speaking your mind. Your closest friend looks to you for spot-on advice, like whether to wear those striped socks with a miniskirt (no!) or ask out the long-time boy of her dreams (yes!). But just like a talk-show host, you also let your guests have face time: You're an awesome listener—even people at the grocery store try to talk to you while you're in line buying Red Bull. But your tongue can turn scathing when you're angry, as anyone who's ever disappointed you knows. When you're feeling the urge to lecture, take a deep breath instead.

friend match

Your intuition is everything when it comes to selecting your friends, and a Virgo who balances your bluntness with a hefty dose of sensitivity scores high on the yes meter.

love match

A good-looking and hilarious Leo will be attracted to you for your listening skills. But make sure he's inclined to talk about something other than himself.

Auburn

Guidance counselor

White-water rafting in Colorado

+/− Even Michael Jordan dropped the ball once in a while, so if you make a mistake, cut yourself a break.

June 15

Turtle

Courtney Cox Arquette

Scarf? Baseball cap? Chandelier earrings?

Magnetic, Insightful, Enigmatic

If you were a cereal, you'd be Lucky Charms: You have got luck and charm to spare. It is important to you to be surrounded by people who appreciate you. Thankfully, your natural star power means admirers aren't too hard to come by. You're ultra-perceptive and understand what makes other people tick, which means that when your teachers are looking for someone to organize a bake sale, they'll look to you. (You may not know the difference between a teaspoon and a tablespoon, but you know how to make people buy whatever you're selling.)

+/− Just be sure you're not so busy watching other people watch you that you lose sight of yourself in the reflection. The most important opinion is the one you have of yourself.

love match

Boys are always making like birds and flocking to you. But you've only got eyes for a Scorpio sweetie who seems to be immune to your flirting.

friend match

A sweet-as-pie Sagittarius and a fun-loving Mercury-ruled friend will be important to you for different reasons. Fortunately, you have the ability to unify groups, and the three of you will stick together like PBB & J (Peanut Butter, Banana, and Jelly).

The best things in life are free, but when it comes to some of the most important qualities for success—like dedication, long-term vision, and patience—you have got money in the bank. Whether you're saving up cash to buy a sweet Prada bag or getting up for early a.m. jogs so you will have the fittest bikini body, you are all about getting a return for your investment. Temporary snares never get you down for long, and your positivity and natural appeal mean it definitely pays to be you. Ka-ching!

Green

Track

"Sitting, Waiting, Wishing" —Jack Johnson

June 16

Shrewd, Patient, Successful

+/− Good things come to those who wait, but life is also short. So don't sit around for too long, waiting for opportunities to come your way. Sometimes you make your own luck.

love match

When it comes to your chances with a Capricorn cutie with killer style and an adventurous streak, follow the old saying: You snooze, you lose. He's patient but not a saint, so don't think you can make him wait around forever.

friend match

Within five minutes of meeting someone, you just know if you're destined to be friends—or so you think. A fun-loving Aries might seem spacey, but she'll be a great cheerleader when you're training for that triathalon.

June 17

If you were an Olympic sport, you'd be the high jump, because you set the bar way high. No matter how much you rock the 3 Cs—acting cool, calm, and collected—in reality everything about your life is A+. Super-serious about your studies and your extracurriculars, you give new meaning to the word "perfectionist." (Your room looks like an art gallery, and you never leave the house looking less than spotless.) But everyone takes a tumble now and then, so give yourself a break.

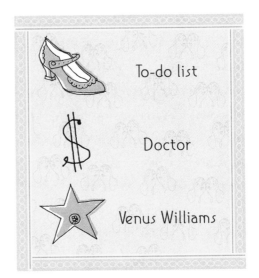

To-do list

Doctor

Venus Williams

+/− The fact that your friends won't always share your opinions is like cellulite: You can cry about it, but it's a part of life and it won't fix it to howl. So let your ladies have their own views. (And don't beat yourself up if you've got some dimples on your thighs, either.)

love match

There's only one area of your life that's less than perfect: Your love life! Your need to control is making you seem cold; loosen up and let a totally spacey (but absolutely adorable) Virgo into your life.

friend match

Patience isn't your strong suit, so you need a BFF who doesn't require constant TLC (and won't be having constant breakdowns, either). A totally together Sagittarius won't stress you out.

June 18

If you were on a reality-TV show, you'd be the contestant pulling all the strings, making pacts, and deciding alliances. You love to have fun and have charm to spare, which means you've got more pull over others than gravity. This makes you an excellent friend and a good candidate for an after-school job as a tutor or mentor, especially as many June 18th people have had to overcome a difficult hurdle early in life and know how to bounce back. A good name for that reality show starring you? *Survivor.*

friend match

You and a water sign BFF are similarly passionate but will also have a similar tendency to sweat the small stuff—and explode when things don't go your way. Learn to say sorry so you don't have to say "see ya!"

Romantic, candlelit dinner in the city

$

Talent agent

Athens

love match

Boys are like curls in humidity—no matter what you do, you can't control them. Don't force the issue, and you'll find that a Leo with a sweet streak and a hilarious sense of humor will soon be cracking you up over your math homework.

+/− You want to analyze everything, from the behavior of the new boy in your English class to the random voice mail your former best friend left you. But sometimes it's better to stop stressing and move on.

June 19

Community outreach

Paula Abdul

"All You Need Is Love"
—The Beatles

Involved, Challenging, Persistent

You are just like a book of matches, because you're all about spark. Driven, competitive, and energetic, your philosophy is love me or leave me. Some people are intimidated by your ambition—you're going to make a green homecoming float entirely out of miniature origami roses crafted by recycling all those Starbucks cups and nobody will stop you—but most people appreciate your natural abilities to lead and inspire.

+/— One thing that gets you to flare up? When people disagree with you. Let your friends have their own opinions and learn to compromise, or be prepared for your social life to implode.

DON'T LET ANYONE RAIN ON YOUR PARADE.

love match

You're right on the cusp of Cancer and Gemini, so you have a particular attraction for a sensitive fire sign, who will find your mixture of straight-up ambition and total silliness (like when you randomly bust into a dance routine at lunch) completely captivating.

friend match

Nothing gets you down more than a pessimist. (Your glass is always half full—and with a cherry on top!) Stick close to a sun-ruled gal with a natural tendency to look on the bright side.

You're just like the sun: Everything revolves around you. Charismatic, charming, and intuitive, you have an ability to make people fall for you that puts gravity to shame. You love high-energy situations and excitement, so you live for weekends, parties, summer vacations, and school dances (and can barely suffer through the day-to-day slog of classes, homework, and—gasp!—making your bed). Because you're used to laying down the law, you can be intolerant of other people's opinions and have to work hard to be more open-minded.

Jamba Juice (with an energy boost, obvs)

Nicole Kidman

Preppy

June 20

Emotional, Rousing, Charismatic

+/− You've always been emotional, but certain situations require you to have a clear head. Whether you're challenging your curfew or a C on your English paper, your best bet is to take a deep breath and stay calm.

love match

You've got people crushing on you all the time, but so far you haven't found the guy who takes your breath away. That will change when you meet a water sign with a work hard/play hard attitude that's a perfect answer to your own.

friend match

The fact that you were born near the summer solstice means that you've got an incredible influence over your friends. So make sure you use this power to build them up, not tear them down.

June 21

If you were a catchphrase, you would be carpe diem, because you're obsessed with living each day to the fullest. There's a reason you were born on one of the longest days of the year: You need time to soak up every single aspect of existence, from the taste of a frozen banana on a hot summer day to the smell of a new textbook. You have a great sense of humor and don't take yourself—or life's little snags—too seriously.

Illustrator

Rhodesian ridgeback

Florence

+/— You're all about having fun and revel in beautiful things, beautiful people, and beautiful places. Just make sure you take care of business—like homework—before you lose yourself in pleasure.

love match

You'll fall hard for a generous and artistically inclined Jupiter-ruled guy who will be more than happy to spend hours indulging in the finer things with you.

friend match

You spark attention wherever you go, and a drama-queen Aquarius might get a little jealous. But you'll share the spotlight, and her over-the-top plans (like turning your basement into a full-on spa, complete with mani and pedi stations) are more than worth it.

WHAT'S YOUR LOOK?

Best color

a. Pink   b. Green

c. Heather gray   d. Black

How do you like your coffee?

a. No-fat vanilla frappuccino   b. With soy milk

c. With a splash of skim   d. Black

If you had to describe your room in one word, it would be

a. Pink   b. Zen   c. Clean   d. Off-limits

Your fave store is

a. Victoria's Secret   b. American Apparel

c. Burberry   d. Vintage record store

You can't wait to be

a. Sixteen. Cars!   b. Eighteen. College!

c. Twenty-five. Marriage!   d. Dead. Peace!

QUIZ!

Pom Squad

Bust out the lip gloss and pink velour tracksuit: You've got more pep (and blonde highlights) than a busload of cheerleaders. But a single palette can get boring—try pretty ballet flats with a pencil skirt instead of all that glitter. Add shades of plum or teal, and fabrics like corduroy.

Eco Chick

Tree-hugger, hippie—you've been called it all. You prefer organic fabrics and socially responsible production (cottons, linens, hand-knit hats and sweaters). Green doesn't have to mean sloppy, though. So pair that funky hand-woven T with a fitted jean and cropped jacket.

Little Miss Princess

You dress like someone with a personal waitstaff (and an endless allowance for dry-cleaning). You are young and clothes are supposed to be fun, so throw a cute-colored cami on under your blazer. Or try a jewel-colored cashmere sweater instead of earth-toned.

Emo Rocker

Care to have some clothing with your angst? You love leather, skull decals, and black, black, black. Just avoid the whole Halloween-party look. A rhinestone-skull necklace paired with a vintage rocker T-shirt and straight-leg jeans hints at the dark within.

QUIZ!

Cancer Girls
are all about new beginnings

Cancer girls are deeply attuned to emotions, memories, and dreams. The first water sign of the zodiac, Cancer is all about keeping the home fires burning, which means that girls born under this sign are extremely loyal, sticking close to a small group of friends and maintaining old routines and traditions. So perceptive it can seem like a brand of ESP, they make amazingly sensitive friends and have the need to share everything with the people they let into their inner circle.

▲▲▲▲▲▲▲▲▲▲▲▲▲▲▲▲▲▲▲▲▲▲

Most likely to be: Conducting a séance at a sleepover party.

Strengths to play on: Sensitivity, intuition.

Pitfalls to avoid: Oversensitivy, unreasonableness.

Cancer

June 22–July 22

Element: Water
Ruler: The Moon

Motto:
"You're not
on the list."

June 22

Charm bracelet (it's a family heirloom)

Teacup Yorkie

Meryl Streep

Romantic, Naïve, Fanciful

If you could be a holiday, you would be Valentine's Day, because you're all about romance. Whether you're dreaming of the guy who will sweep you off your feet or fantasizing about running away to South America to become a flamenco dancer, you believe that life should be like a movie. (And you certainly win awards for being a drama queen.) 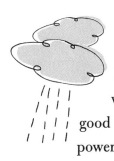 In fact, you have more highs and lows than the weather, so stick close to good friends who can help you power through the storms.

+/− April Fool's Day is not your friend, because you're always getting punked. Remember: If it seems too good to be true, it probably is!

IT'S GREAT TO HAVE IDEALS, BUT LEARN TO BE UNDERSTANDING. MAKE LIKE AN AIRLINE ATTENDANT AND DON'T FORGET: WE ALL HAVE BAGGAGE!

love match

An athletic Aries may have you getting whiplash from scoping his abs so often, but he won't satisfy your deeply sensitive side. If you want a guy who returns your love of all things romantic, look for a dark-eyed Scorpio with a penchant for guitars.

friend match

A Capricorn friend may be a little pessimistic, but you know how to cheer her up. In return, she'll make sure to keep your feet planted on the ground at least 10 percent of the time.

If you could be a candy, you would be a Hershey's kiss: You're supersweet, everyone loves you, and when you're making the rounds, there's bound to be romance in the air. Your friends make fun of you for having boyfriend after boyfriend, but you're just plain happier when you're coupling off. (You don't shy away from PDA, either. In fact, you think it's Pretty Darn Awesome.) Generous and trustworthy, you're known to both family and friends as being reliable and practical when you have to be . . . even if you'll be dreaming of first kisses while you're washing the dishes!

Ruby

Baking

Selma Blair

June 23

Magnetic,
Enchanting,
Romantic

$+/-$ Having a boyfriend is great, but needing a boyfriend is not cool. Ask yourself why you're so afraid to be on your own, and remember that you're fabulous no matter who you're with—or not with.

love match

You just love to read and sketch in your notebook, so a poetry-loving Pisces will be the sensitive and thoughtful guy you're looking for.

friend match

It's no surprise a girl whose birthday adds up to 2 will be your perfect BFF: She's ruled by the power of duos and couples, just like you. Just make sure you give yourselves time apart or you'll experience some long division.

June 24

You should have been in the Harry Potter books, because you're a straight-up wizard at whatever you choose to do. Within a month of taking up drawing, you're sweeping the state art competition for all of the prizes, but your success isn't just a result of natural skill. You are super-driven and have powers of concentration that are almost scary, **and your hobbies are almost like religion to you. As a result it's incredibly important to use your energy for good, not evil, so watch who you spend your time with.**

Your huge DVD collection

Author

Audrey Hepburn

+/− Sometimes you move forward impulsively without thinking about the effects of what you do. (Spoiler alert: It's called selfishness.) Make sure your plans don't exclude others or make them feel bad.

NO ONE WANTS TO SEE YOU GO OVER TO THE DARK SIDE!

love match

When it comes to relationships as in everything else, you can get a little carried away. Make sure the object of your affections is worth the tumble, like a Neptune-ruled music lover who is an A+ student on the sly.

friend match

You like to surround yourself with people who understand your need for alone time. An equally independent Virgo with a mind toward creative solo pursuits won't act like lint and be on you all the time.

June 25

You should be a cell phone company, because you always have good reception and can understand what other people are saying, loud and clear. Super-perceptive, you're the eyes and ears of your very own Info Operation. Whether it's the slight tic of your teacher's eyebrow that lets you know a pop quiz is on the way, or the quiver of your BFF's lips that reads, "Unhappy," you always know what's going down. Ironically, people find it hard to figure you out, because you have a private side and a tendency to keep your feelings a secret.

love match

You're excellent at hiding your emotions from other people, so even an observant Virgo does not know that he has got your head spinning. Because he is ruled by Mercury, he can't keep his feelings under wraps, so he'll be the one to make a move.

friend match

Because you're nurturing, you love to take care of people, right from helping with homework to whipping up a batch of soup when someone in your crew gets sick. A flighty—but fun—Aquarius will have you straightening out her messes 24/7.

Book club

Therapist

Linda Cardellini

+/− You have got the soul of an artist, which makes you an extremely compassionate, caring person. But you have to toughen up your skin a little bit, or else you are going to be in for a world of hurt.

Horseback riding

Summer-camp counselor

Skinny jeans and flats

June 26

Courageous, Athletic, Protective

If you were a sport, you would be cross-country, because you're in it for the long haul. Your parents depend on you for help around the house, and your friends know they can always lean on you when they're in trouble (whether they need a box of tissues, some homework help, or some serious fashion advice), since you've got your feet on the ground and your head in the right place. Naturally inclined to sports and physical activity—no couch potato slumping for you!—you're a natural team captain and leader, on or off the field.

+/− You will kick butt for your peeps anytime, but sometimes they may not welcome your in-your-face attitude.

LEARN TO PICK YOUR BATTLES.

love match

A Libra with killer tennis skills may seem a little bit standoffish, but he's just intimidated by your confident and outgoing vibe. You'll discover his sense of humor is identical to yours.

friend match

There's no doubt that you like to be the head honcho, which can lead to problems when an equally outspoken Leo wants to step up to the plate. But she'll value the same things as you—loyalty, for one—so compromise is worth it.

You ought to have lived during frontier times, because you're all about holding down the fort. You're very protective of the things that are important to you—family, friends, your grade point average, your super-killer collection of sling-back shoes—and become extremely defensive if you feel any of these things are challenged or threatened. Cautious by nature, you have the reputation of being shy because you're extremely selective about the people you open up to. But you're definitely not to be underestimated: When you want something, you go after it full speed ahead.

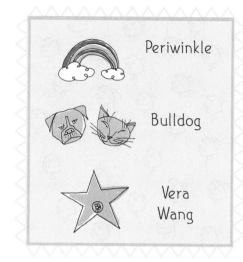

Periwinkle

Bulldog

Vera Wang

June 27

Convinced,
Determined,
Caring

+/− You'll go head-to-head with anyone, at any time, on any subject. But all that fighting is turning you into a 24/7 Lifetime drama special, so learn to let go of your anger.

friend match

You're extremely sensitive to other people's moods, so when a Pisces BFF is down, you catch a bad case of the blues. Make sure you keep some friends around who know how to cheer you up.

love match

A scorchingly hot (as well as extremely infuriating) Sun-ruled guy seems to thinks fighting is the best kind of flirtation and will love the way you give as good as you get.

June 28

Independent, Realistic, Innovative

If you could be a body part, you would be a hand, because you live your life based on how things feel. Emotion trumps reason for you every time, and if something seems right—like the new cute boy in your Spanish class or blowing $80 on a spa pedicure—you'll act first and ask questions . . . never. You love to be the center of attention and live for getting a reaction from the people around you. Positive, negative—so long as people are looking, you're happy.

Diamond studs

"Forever Young" —Youth Group

Aruba

+/− Beware of getting into trouble or acting out just to feel the glow of the spotlight; you want to be a success story, not a tragedy.

love match

In general, you listen to your heart instead of your head. A fire sign you have your eyes on means big explosions—and equally heavy damage—but you won't be stopped.

friend match

Nothing kills you more than being ignored—except being upstaged. A quieter Capricorn will let you ham it up all you want and will be your biggest fan, even when it feels like your one-woman act is tanking.

You're just like Santa Claus: You know what other people want, and you always deliver. (If they deserve it, that is!) Full of energy and big ideas, you're ruled by the idea of flight; no matter what your fantasy, you find a way to make it feasible, and you do the same thing for your friends. (When your BFF was too shy to ask out the adorable Aries she's been crushing on for years, you pulled the strings to make it happen.) You're always laughing and having a blast, which means for the people lucky enough to be your friend, every day feels like Christmas.

friend match

A serious Saturn-ruled friend won't always see the joy of trying something new, which is why you help her to experiment. And when your schemes just don't make sense, she'll give it to you straight.

love match

An earth-sign science fanatic might seem dorky, but he'll pay attention to—and care—about everything you say. Reliable and brave, he'll be the perfect sidekick to your superhero lifetstyle.

+/− You love your freedom, but ironically feel the need to control your friends. You're not a telephone, so you can't make every call.

Personal makeup artist for your BFFs

Party planner

Nicole Scherzinger

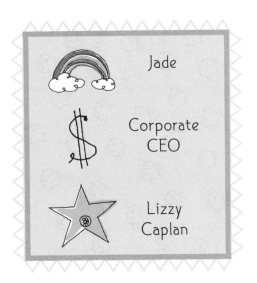

Jade

Corporate CEO

Lizzy Caplan

June 30

Technical, Motivated, Responsible

You're just like a missile, because when you want something, it's lock and load. (And when misfired, you have the tendency to explode!) Ironically, though, other people find it almost impossible to get you to conform to what they want; if it's not on your personal to-do list, it ain't gonna happen (which is why your bed has been unmade for the past three years). This makes you extremely successful at solitary pursuits and a not-so-great team member and lab partner.

+/− It is important to know what you want, but every so often it pays to play a little Simon Says. Your parents occasionally do know what's best (I know, hard to believe), so listen once in a while.

love match

You have a lot of contradictory sides, like a tendency to be shy and outgoing, serious and silly. An Aquarius dreamer who has been studying you from afar wants to get up close and personal for a better look.

friend match

Your inner circle is extremely tight and harder to get into than a VIP club, but the friends that do make it past your rigorous door policy are in for life. A totally grounded Sagittarius will be 100 percent supportive of your goals, so make sure she's on the list.

You're like a funny bone
right after it gets bumped: supersensitive and prone to hurt. You cry over Hallmark cards and digital camera commercials, and your friends value you for your ability to listen—and because you never judge. Though you have a large social circle, you spend a lot of time in your own world, blogging, drawing, or just thinking. Easily offended, you have to work hard not to take life too seriously.

$+/-$ You're definitely a glass-half empty girl and go through long periods during which you have trouble finding happiness in the day-to-day. The worst thing you can do is withdraw, so when you're feeling blue, pick up the phone and start texting.

Poetry chapbook

Head of a charity organization

Liv Tyler

July 1

Profound, Giving, Determined

love match

Your heart gets broken so often it looks like Humpty Dumpty (post-fall). That is why it is doubly important for you to risk the pain only on those people who deserve it, like an equally sensitive Pisces artist.

friend match

It's important that your BFF be someone who can help you take pleasure in the little things, and who has the patience to pull you out of your funks, like an outgoing Leo who's always looking on the bright side.

July 2

If you were a body part you would be a heart, because you're all about emotion. Strongly intuitive and very sensitive to other people's feelings, those born on July 2 fall into two categories: Those who are private, secretive, and prefer to be alone, and those who shout out their feelings to everyone and anyone. You feel things passionately and spend a lot of time daydreaming, and although you come across as confident, as a perfectionist you often feel as though you're not up to par.

Passport

Ashley Tisdale

"Nolita Fairytale" —Vanessa Carlton

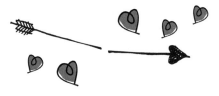

+/− If your fantasy world were a real place, you'd be a jet-setter, because all you do is go traveling. Be careful you're not using your fantasies as a way of escaping the real problems and challenges around you—like how to ask your teacher for an extension, or talk to the cute exchange student in your science class.

love match

You are ruled by the moon, which means you can be extremely moody. A dependable Taurus will know how to get you from super-stressed to completely chill and will always be there with a smile when you feel like going mental.

friend match

When it comes to friendships, you can be Intense with a capital I. A patient Libra pal deserves a plaque for putting up with all your drama, but you do your share of heroics for her, too.

You're just like a digital camera, because you're all about capturing the moment. You blog about everything from your BFF's upcoming birthday celebration to the traumatic cafeteria food, and you dream of being a journalist when you get older so you can always record what's going down. You can come across as a little standoffish, but deep down you're very sensitive and wary of getting hurt. Plus, you know that the image is clearer if you have a little distance.

+/− Nothing gets past you, because you've always got your eyes and ears open. But life's not a spectator sport, you know. So if the school's soccer team looks like fun, don't just sit on the bleachers. Get out there and play!

love match

As a water sign, you will be compelled to another aquatically oriented person, like a smoldering Scorpio with a passion for music. Your amazing observational skills will definitely complement his more intuitive approach.

Talking over coffee

Art club

Tabby cat

friend match

You tend to hang back often, **so you need a BFF who can pull you out of your shell.** A Sagittarius who loves attention will make sure you're never too far from the action.

July 4

- Social worker
- Your bright red peacoat
- Cast of *Rent*

▲▼▲▼▲▼▲▼▲▼▲▼▲▼▲▼▲▼▲▼▲▼▲

Faithful, Giving, Proud

You should be a big old tree, because you're all about your roots. Superloyal to your friends, your family, and tradition in general (your aunt had better not even think about changing her recipe for sweet potato pie on Thanksgiving Day), you feel best when you're surrounded by a group. This makes you an excellent team player and a perfect partner for a science lab, since you prefer not to work solo. In America, your birthday can be seen as an extension of the celebratory spirit of Fourth of July: All about community.

+/− It's okay to be proud of where you come from—and who you chill with—but it's not okay to look down on people who are different. If you keep your nose pointed in the air long enough, you're bound to trip up, so remember to stay level.

▼▲▼▲▼▲▼▲▼▲▼▲▼▲▼▲▼▲▼▲▼▲▼▲▼▲▼▲▼▲▼▲▼▲▼▲▼▲

friend match

You may have a ton of friends in the phone book of your Sidekick, but your Top 8 stay the same. Your best bet for Speed Dial Number One? A creative and spirited Gemini who still shares your love of ritual and habit.

love match

Just the idea of fessing up to a crush makes you need a serious dose of Pepto-Bismol. But that adorable Aquarius with the straight-A average isn't so smart when it comes to picking up on feelings, so you're going to have to speak up.

If *variety is the spice of* life, then you're a jalapeño pepper. You have more interests than a tree has leaves, and you're constantly jumping back and forth from soccer to choir to photography. Your friends change just as fast as your newest extracurriculars, and your BFFs are in and out so often you're like your own episode of *Project Runway*. Energetic, enthusiastic, and creative, you're a blast to be around but often have  trouble trying to keep promises or maintaining commitments. (Like that math homework you swore you'd work on tonight . . .)

Fuchsia

Cooking

Backpacking through Europe

July 5

Exciting,
Interesting,
Imaginative

+/− There's nothing wrong with dreaming big, but every so often you have to focus on the details. Every 100-mile race starts with a single step, so if you want to be a famous actress, try auditioning for the school play.

love match

You can be a bit wild, so look to a more stable Saturn-ruled boy to keep you in check. You're not usually the type to sit still, but lying in the park with him all day will suddenly start to appeal.

friend match

When you and your crew get together, you're the one who keeps everyone entertained. But your Number One fan has got to be a loyal Taurus friend who's seen you through all of your phases, from punk chick to Gossip Girl.

July 6

You are just like a magnet, attracting people wherever you go (and a side order of drama). You feel things passionately, and when you want something—whether it's a pair of BCBG shoes, the lead in the school play, or the hot guy you've been scoping in gym—you won't stop until it's yours. Often you feel like you're always in the middle of the conflict. Competitive and extremely social, you cannot help but involve yourself in everything—otherwise you feel left out.

School pep rally

Magazine editor

Madonna

+/− It's fine to be committed to the things and people you love, but every so often, it pays to let go. If a project isn't working out or someone's not returning your affection, you've got to loosen your grip—otherwise you're the one who will end up crushed.

love match

A Scorpio with an intense stare is one goal absolutely worth fighting for, but you're so focused on an old crush you're completely blind to his perfection. Open your eyes.

friend match

In the sandwich of friendship, your air-sign friend is the mayonnaise that holds it all together. You're the onion—some people may not like you, but there's no question that you add some serious flavor.

No one needs to tell you not to judge a book by its cover, because you're all about doing the required reading. Fascinated by how other people work, you play amateur psychologist to your group of friends, but you also spend a lot of time doing serious self-analysis. You're always honest and never shy away from expressing your ideas, even though other people don't always understand you.

AS LONG AS YOU'VE GOT A COUPLE OF GOOD FRIENDS HELPING YOU PADDLE, YOU DON'T MIND GOING AGAINST THE FLOW.

friend match

A BFF ruled by Jupiter will help you stay realistic about your expectations of yourself and others. And she won't mind playing guinea pig to your psych experiments—she's just as curious as you are.

love match

You're strongly ruled by intellect and thought, but you need to learn to pay attention to your heart: It has its own reasoning. If it beats faster every time a super-smiley January-born cutie comes around, it's time to make a move.

Living room sofa

Lavender

Punk

+/− It is great that you try to be an open book, but not everyone likes what's written between the lines. Try to be sensitive to other people's feelings; Your best friend doesn't really need to know if her butt looks fat in those jeans.

❁ ❁ ❁ ❁ ❁ ❁ ❁

July 8

BlackBerry

Babysitting

Sophia Bush

Pragmatic, Protective, Responsible

You are a firm believer in the fact that the ends justify the means. Super-practical as well as very focused, whether you're launching a new exercise routine or organizing your school's homecoming bonfire, you are all about the results. Your energy and your get-it-done attitude make you the perfect nominee for your junior class president as well as field hockey captain, and when something needs doing in your social circle—whether your BF needs to throw a fab b-day party or score a cute boy's number—you're always the go-to girl.

$+/-$ You're just like a soccer game: Always need to have a goal. But when you're hanging out with your girls, make it your Number One priority to have fun.

love match

You rock a my-way-or-the-highway attitude that can be intimidating, so you need a guy too confident to be scared off. Bonus? A sense of humor to boot. You're looking for a mischievous Aquarius.

friend match

You're a hard worker, so sometimes even your closest friends go weeks without seeing you outside of school. Everyone needs to blow off steam, so stick close to a social-butterfly Aries who won't let you go MIA.

Both you and Alice have something in common: You both spend a lot of time in Wonderland. You are deeply imaginative and curious about the world around you, and though you do spend a lot of time dreaming—of a new pesto recipe, of the world's most perfect little black dress, of ending pollution—it's not like you get lost in la-la land. You manage to keep your feet on the ground and finish the projects you scheme up for yourself.

OBSESSED WITH FINDING CONNECTIONS BETWEEN THINGS, YOU BELIEVE THERE'S A REASON FOR *EVERY*THING.

Jet skiing

Inventor

White rabbit (natch)

July 9

▲▽▲▽▲▽▲▽▲▽▲▽▲▽▲▽▲▽▲▽▲▽▲▽▲▽▲▽▲▽

Curious,
Inventive,
Open

+/− Your fave word is *"why,"* but certain mysteries are best left unsolved. People may not appreciate it if you root around in their business, so if your BFF wants to stay mum on why she dumped her boyfriend, don't push it.

▽▲▽

love match

You're a risk taker, so you'll take a chance on a Pisces with the reputation for being antisocial (really, he's just shy). This is one gamble that will pay-off: A dreamer like you, he's also sweet and loyal.

friend match

You know that it takes all kinds of cuts, colors, and fabrics to make the perfect wardrobe, and the same goes for the perfect social circle. You'll spend hours scheming up big projects together with an artistically out-there Gemini.

July 10

You are like the human version of playground games, because your personality's got a whole tug-of-war thing going on: On the one hand driven to seek recognition for your talents, you're also extremely private as a rule. A girl of few words, when you speak, you make sure it counts. And since you're always paying attention, your observations are usually spot-on. You may be inclined toward painting or sketching, both talents that make use of your extra-keen eye.

White

Architect

Laid-back

 **+/−** Often you prefer the role of spectator, but if life is a party, the place to be is not by the punch bowl. Every so often, you need to claim time in the middle of the dance floor.

love match

Although an artistic Pisces may seem like a perfect match, his social calendar (empty) will leave yours looking like a 24/7 party. You're not a clam, so it's not okay to stay in your shell; get cozy with a smoldering Scorpio who can at least convince you to leave the house on weekends.

friend match

Usually you're pretty quiet, but no one knows better than your Taurus BFF that once you pick your battle, you never say die. Luckily, she's always got your back.

You should be a sports broadcaster, because no matter what goes down (a fight in the cafeteria, a breakup, a breakdown), people turn to you for the play-by-play. Super-social, you have the reputation of a gossip, and there's nothing you like better than swapping stories with the members of your inner circle. (Your sky-high cell phone bill proves it.) You're not just about the superficial stuff, though; you have an opinion about everything and have so many random facts crammed in your brain, you're a walking about Trivial Pursuit game.

love match

Someone with quieter interests—like a poetry-loving Pisces—can help temper your go-go-go mentality and help you get in touch with what's really important.

friend match

Though you can come across as a know-it-all (admit it, it's true!), you'd actually much rather be part of a team than heading up the group. That's why you're happy to let an outspoken Aquarius friend take the reins when it comes to figuring out Friday-night plans or organizing a b-day BBQ.

+/− Adding spice to your stories is one thing, but completely making up details is different. Beware of being the girl who cried 'wolf ate my Prada bag!' If you tell too many lies, no one will take you seriously.

Teal

Yearbook
Editor

South
Beach

July 12

$ Lawyer

Pug

Blair Waldorf

Capable, Committed, Observant

+/− You have a strong personality, and you always speak your mind. Not everyone can deal with a girl who gets hers, but don't let the haters bring you down.

You're just like the pied piper, because you can always get people to follow along. Your most defining asset is your ability to be persuasive, so whether you're trying to get your parents to ease up on your curfew or are arguing your BFF out of buying purple pleather pants (ew), what you say always flies. You naturally take the lead, and the people around you find themselves unintentionally copying your style. Remember: Imitation is the sincerest form of flattery, so try not to get grieved when you see everyone rocking your fave shirt.

> YOUR TRUE FRIENDS LOVE YOUR CONFIDENCE AND HONESTY.

love match

You've got a strong personality, and there aren't many boys who can compete. A stubborn Saturn-ruled boy might seem obnoxious at first, but it's only because he's willing to give it right back to you. Admit it, you love the challenge!

friend match

An earth-sign BFF is just as studious as you are, but she also knows how to have fun. You could use a little R & R, so once in a while follow her lead and veg.

When it comes to golden opportunities—the chance to audition for the school play or ask the cute boy in your English class for his number—you make like a clock: always on time. You have an amazing ability to be in the right place at the right time, and all of your friends think of you as super-lucky. It's not chance, though; whenever opportunity's ringing, you're picking up the call, which means that no matter how rocky the road to the top, you know at some point you'll be enjoying the view.

Swatch watch

Camping in the mountains

Gymnastics

July 13

▲▼▲▼▲▼▲▼▲▼▲▼▲▼▲▼▲▼▲▼▲▼▲▼▲▼▲▼▲

Daring, Goal-Oriented, Stubborn

+/— **You've got the eye of the tiger:** When you go after something, you'll give it all you've got. **Occasionally, you'll have to wait for a long time for the perfect moment to strike, so** try to be patient and don't get discouraged.

▼▲▼

love match

It is in your nature to take risks, so a cautious Neptune-ruled boy isn't exactly your speed. Look to be swept off your feet—literally—by an athletic, outdoors-obsessed guy ruled by Mars.

friend match

You're an incredibly faithful friend, which is why you don't have patience for any fair-weather crap. Bid good-bye to an on-again, off-again Gemini and stick with a loyal Taurus.

July 14

You are just like Santa Claus, because people love to believe in you. Whether you are making a slamming first impression or spending time cultivating someone's trust, at the end of the day everyone has confidence in you. Naturally charming, you've got parents and teachers wrapped around your little finger (and more than one romantic possibility hanging off your pinkie as well). You're funny and very **persuasive**—no one wins an argument with you!

Purple

President of a university

Rio de Janeiro

+/− Though you come across as confident and in control, you're often plagued by self-doubts. Being admired 24/7 leaves you with a lot to live up to, **so** cultivate close friends who don't expect you to be on all the time.

friend match

Some people may be intimidated by a Scorpio with a tendency to hang back and observe, but you'll discover she won't judge you—or expect you to be Little Miss Sunshine all the time.

love match

Sometimes you feel like you're standing in the middle of an ocean of guys: Water, water, everywhere, and not a drop to drink! (Or a boy to trust.) You need a guy you can lean on no matter what, and a boy born under the sign of Venus is bound never to disappoint.

July 15

If life were a BMW, you'd be the steering wheel: Perfect handling and always in control. You're excellent at convincing others to do what you want them to do. (Thus the reason your two BFFs play adoring servants to your diva-ness.) Just like Madonna, you're a Material Girl, and your skills at molding and shaping the world around you extend to physical things, which is why you gravitate toward sculpture, fashion design, and interior decorating. Sharing isn't your strength, and you have to learn to work as a team member, or soon you'll be singing the blues.

friend match

You and your Leo rival are constantly at each other's throats, competing over everything from an A in English to a cute basketball player. There's a fine line between love and hate, and you'd discover you have a lot in common if you would put down the boxing gloves for a while.

love match

Love is not a compass, and it doesn't always point in the direction you expect. Don't shut yourself off to other options just because you're fixated on an autumn-born boy; the optimism and enthusiasm of an April-born Romeo might suit you better.

Bluetooth headset

English setter

Ashley Olsen

$+/-$ The ends do not always justify the means, and people are not playthings. Beware of using people just to get what you want. In this case, what goes around comes around, so watch your back.

Ice hockey

Government agent

Destiny's Child

+/− It is really great that you are so confident in your opinions, but whenever there's an argument, you make like the worst driver on the road: Always cutting people off. Learn to listen.

July 16

Faithful, Passionate, Nurturing

If you were a color, you'd be red, the color of courage, excitement, and passion. When you hit Six Flags with your friends, you book right for the biggest, baddest roller coaster, because you love to keep the thrills coming. Super romantic and easily bored, you have trouble focusing on everyday tasks like homework (and laundry—blech) and often feel torn between listening to your friends and family (bad boy who's always in detention = bad news) and following your heart (but his eyes!).

love match

Practicality? Not your thing. You're looking to be swept off your feet by someone as obsessively romantic as you are. A water-ruled Scorpio will keep things passionate, intense, and dramatic. Swoon.

friend match

You and a water-sign partner in-crime get in trouble more often than Britney Spears gets photographed. A thoughtful—and cautious—Libra might provide a welcomed balance. (Your 'rents will be so happy.)

You're just like a rocket: headed straight for the stars. It might surprise your family and friends to learn that deep down you dream of greatness—like an Emmy or a Nobel Prize—because you often come across as quiet and a little shy. Your motto? "A little less conversation, a little more action." Just because you're not running your mouth, doesn't mean you don't keep your eye on the prize, and when you're working on a project (whether it's for social studies or social survival), you're determined and persistent.

July 17

Ambitious,
Serious,
Self-Confident

Amber

Candy
striping

Environmental
scientist

+/− **They say** it takes more muscles to frown than smile, **and lately your face has been getting a workout. Lighten up and make time to be silly with your friends.**

love match

You're not immune to Cupid's arrow, but you are not looking to make yourself a bull's-eye, either. You won't have a choice when a sweet and patient Pisces takes aim.

friend match

You'll appreciate an Aquarius BFF who is just as serious about school as you are, but who also has a large network of friends and loves to have a good time. She can help you branch out, and you can help her stay grounded.

July 18

You could be a microphone, because you're all about broadcasting your opinions—and the opinions of your social circle—loud and clear. You love to debate, and you're not shy about standing up in front of the class and declaring that Snickers bars should be considered a health food. (Hello—nuts.) Very attuned to the feelings and opinions of the people around you, you're interested in making sure the voice of the common people (or, ahem, your BFFs) gets heard.

YOU'RE ABOUT MORE THAN JUST HEARING YOURSELF SPEAK.

$\$$ Political pundit

Kristen Bell

Trekking the Andes

+/− Getting rejected is like bad hair: No matter what, it's gonna happen once in a while, and the best thing you can do is get through the day and hope for a better tomorrow. If you lose out in a contest—for first violin chair or for someone's affections—move on.

love match

The moon's influence on your moods makes you swing from happy to angry pretty easily. An über-Zen Uranus-ruled guy will be a great stabilizing force. (And he makes excellent arm candy.)

friend match

You're very competitive, but you're the first person to step aside when a Virgo friend needs a leg up (or a head start). Make sure she's just as willing to be your cheerleader.

July 19

You should wrap yourself up in a ribbon, because you know just how to present yourself. You know that the proof is in the packaging, and you go out of your way to come across as confident and cool, no matter who's turning up the heat in the kitchen. A natural at dance, gymnastics, and other sports that require balance, grace, and coordination, you have an in-control attitude this unfortunately does not extend to your moods, which have a tendency to swing like you're on a playground.

YOU CAN BE EXTREMELY SENTIMENTAL.

friend match

It's inevitable that you'll butt heads with a Mercury-ruled BFF once in a while. Her philosophy is "out with the old, in with the new," but fortunately, she'll always stick by you.

love match

A quiet Capricorn boy is more wall flower than life of the party, but if you take time to get to know him, you'll see that on the dance floor of life, he makes an excellent partner.

Burberry headband

Mint green

"One Step at a Time" —Jordin Sparks

+/− Your emotional life could use some fiber, because when it comes to expressing your feelings, you're all stoppered up. Instead of being passive-aggressive when you feel a friend has let you down (removing her from your MySpace Top Friends isn't exactly subtle): Talk to her.

Gisele
Bündchen

Sporty

"(I Can't Get No) Satisfaction"
—The Rolling Stones

July 20

Adventurous, Active, Practical

You are like the human equivalent of a roller coaster: all about the ups-and-downs. One week you're teacher's pet; the next week you get a D on the pop quiz. You fall hard for the cute boy in your Math class, then dump him for his best friend. As long as you're moving, you don't care which direction you're going; you crave change (thus your ever-revolving hair color) and love to be in the middle of whatever drama is going down.

+/− It's great that you're not afraid of change, but certain things—like friendships and family members—don't have an expiration date. You need stable influences around you; otherwise you risk becoming like a doughnut: no center.

love match

Your romantic life has more drama than an episode of *Gossip Girl*, but you can't spend your whole life running through guys like toilet paper. The problem is you get bored, so stick with an outgoing, ambitious, and challenging Aquarius who will keep you on your toes.

friend match

Your BFF has her work cut out for her, since there always seems to be a crisis in your life. A patient Virgo will stay calm through the storm: Just make sure you return the favor.

If you were a game of Scrabble, you'd always be spelling the same word: *trouble.* If it seems like controversy follows you wherever you go, it's because you like to stir things up. (And face it, your pleather miniskirt doesn't help.) Bold, confident, and a 24/7 blast to be around, you love to be the center of attention and keep everyone entertained with your outrageous ideas and your spot-on sarcasm.

BEWARE OF SPENDING SO MUCH TIME PLAYING A PART THAT YOU FORGET WHO YOU REALLY ARE.

Denim

Boa constrictor

Resort in Thailand

July 21

Daring, Exciting, Active

+/− Here's another word that crops up a lot in your life: *risk.* It's great that you're so courageous, but if you keep playing with fire, sooner or later you're bound to get burned for good. It's never Okay to gamble with your health or safety.

love match

You always find yourself pursuing mischievous Aries boys. Wise up: If you meet them in after-school detention, they probably won't make the best boyfriends. A smart and sarcastic Sagittarius will keep you on your toes during regular school hours.

friend match

The last thing you need is a partner in crime—you get in enough trouble for two people as is. Turn to a level-headed Leo strong enough to talk sense into you when you want to prank the principal. (Again.)

July 22

▲▽▲▽▲▽▲▽▲▽▲▽▲▽▲▽▲▽▲▽▲▽▲▽▲▽▲▽▲▽▲▽▲▽

You believe that life is like poker: Sometimes you are up, sometimes you're down, but as long as you have the winning hand in the end, it's all good. **Your life has got more drama than a production of** *Hamlet:* **Things never stay easy for long, and you have the rocky grades (and relationship history) to prove it. Determined and persistent, you don't let the bumps get you down.**

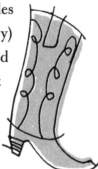

NO MATTER WHAT YOU DO OR HOW LONG IT TAKES, YOU ALWAYS END UP AT THE TOP OF YOUR GAME.

You prefer to be surprised . . .

Photography

Rock star

+/− You're a fly-by-the-seat-of-your-pants kind of girl, **but certain things—like homework and closets—require organization. Life will be a lot easier if you don't have to spend 40 minutes every morning searching for your missing Tori Burch flats. (Even the stars can't locate them in your room.)**

love match

Your attraction is straight to Aquarius: Their open attitude and take-it-as-it-comes philosophy appeals to you, and you can count on them to cheer you on when you're taking on your newest Everest. (Aquarius love your go-getter approach.)

friend match

An older earth-sign friend will have the stability you lack (and need). Plus, because she's been there and done that, she'll give you great advice when you're freaking out about your end-of-the-year evaluations.

Who's Your Ideal Guy?

1. You broke up with your last boyfriend when he

a. Named his new surfboard after his ex-girlfriend, and didn't even bother to lie about it.

b. Wrote a song about his ex-girlfriend and sang it at your school's Battle of the Bands.

c. Downloaded a picture of his ex-girlfriend for the wallpaper on his new MacBook.

2. Your idea of a perfect date is

a. Hanging out on the beach with all of your friends, body-surfing, bonfire, and s'mores.

b. Scoping out the latest French film, sharing a hot chocolate at your fave coffee shop, talking until the sun goes down.

c. His-and-hers massages, dinner on Daddy's AmEx at the best French restaurant in town. *Oh la la.*

3. What is your favorite pick-up line to hear?

a. Check out this picture of me and my boys skydiving.

b. Check out this charcoal sketch I made of you.

c. Check out my iPhone.

QUIZ!

4. What is your favorite pick-up line to *use?*

a. I know where to find the best chili dog in town.

b. I think Balzac's novels are underrated.

c. My dad owns that building/hospital/school/restaurant/hotel chain.
   (Adjust as necessary.)

5. What is your favorite room of the house?

a. The deck. *Okay, so it's not really a room, but you love the smell of fresh cut grass and watching the sun go down.*

b. Your room. *You like to be alone with a mug of tea, a good book, and your thoughts.*

c. The master bathroom. *The rainforest shower, marble tub, and fluffy towels make you feel like a princess. Plus, it's always super clean.*

6. In your fantasies, when your dream guy approaches you, what is he wearing?

a. Slouchy, shredded-up board shorts and a T-shirt that says, I only look dangerous.

b. Pencil-thin black jeans and a T-shirt that says, I only look medicated. Vintage? Preferably. Ironic? Always.

c. A Lacoste Polo shirt, Ralph Lauren pants, and boating shoes—because in your fantasies, he's sailing up to you on his father's yacht.

7. In your fantasies, when your dream guy approaches you, what are you wearing?

a. A Roxy bikini.

b. Same thing as he is.

c. A Dior bikini.

Future cast member of Jackass

Your motto is "Don't worry, be happy," and you're looking for a guy who can get down with your optimistic, adventurous attitude. Laid-back and fun-loving, you want someone who shares your love of all things outdoors and who will cover your back when you're on a mission to stink bomb the vice principal's office. A mischievous Aries—ruled by fiery Mars—is your best bet for a partner in crime. Just don't count on him to help with homework. He definitely won't be a good influence, and he won't always be there if you need a shoulder to cry on, as serious topics give him a serious case of the hives.

Future Poet Laureate (Mostly Bs)

If you were a drink, you would be a cafe mocha: deep, complex, with a little bit of an international flair. You're a die-hard romantic and looking for someone who shares your love of deep conversation and values privacy and solitude as much as you. A philosophically minded Virgo or an intense Scorpio will be ideal companions for debating the meaning of life or just lying out on a blanket and stargazing. Just beware of a tendency to completely withdraw, once you're paired up with a guy whose idea of being social involves communing with the characters in his screenplay.

Future Investment Banker

You're a typical princess, demanding the best in all things. Type-A to a tee, you're an excellent student and have a social network so large it puts Verizon to shame. You want a guy who can keep up with your frantic pace and isn't intimidated by your show-it-to-me attitude. A take-charge Capricorn, symbol of striving and ambition, will match you stride for stride. However, when you feel sad or lonely, he may not always be there to support you; when Capricorns sense weakness, they get itchier than your skin in down-market cashmere.

QUIZ!

Leo Girls

are radiant and powerful

It's no surprise Leo girls are ruled by the sun: radiant and powerful, they believe everything on earth revolves around them. Ambitious, self-confident, and in control, a Leo is bound to be the life of the party whenever she enters a room. Leos make amazingly loyal friends and fiercely frightening enemies; they can also be overly stubborn and can't always see when old habits and people need to be booted like a pair of last year's Lucite heels.

★ ★

Most likely to be: Getting the party started.

Beverage they most resemble: Orange juice—good for you in large quantities and everyone's a fan.

Strengths to play on: Leadership, refusal to lose.

Pitfalls to avoid: Dictatorship, reluctance to let go.

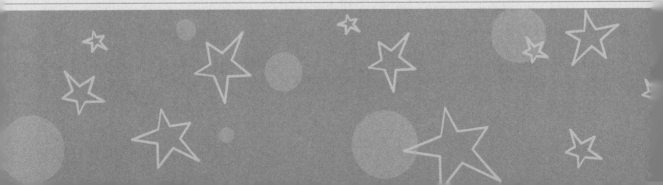

Leo

* *

July 23 – August 23

Element: Fire
Ruler: The Sun

Motto: "If you can't stand the heat, get out of the kitchen."

July 23

There's a certain expression that applies all too well to July 23rd people: You're either part of the problem or part of the solution. Ruled by themes of change and uncertainty, July 23rd people either find themselves in the role of mediator, peacemaker, or all around fixer-upper, or they get bogged down in their own insecurities and tend to withdraw. A final solution? Maintain a close network of friends (which should be no problem, since you're sweet as pie and more giving than Santa) and remind yourself how fabulous you are.

"Rock the Vote" T-Shirt

Guinea pig

"Friend Like You" —Joshua Radin

+/− You'd give the shirt off your back for a friend—or even a frenemy—in need. But remember to save some of that TLC for yourself, or you'll get left out in the cold.

love match

You may be attracted to an outgoing BMOC (Big Man on Campus) Capricorn but feel shut out when he ditches you at a party—again. Stick with a wicked-smart Scorpio who loves to stay loyal and repeat to self: "No more drama."

friend match

Your best friendship match is with other Leos, who will be sensitive to your feelings and take just as good care of you as you do of them. Even better? Joint b-day parties come summer!

July 24

When it comes to your interests, you're like a jet-setter: all over the place. Addicted to adrenaline and easily bored, you love to try new things: hang gliding lessons one week, extreme kickboxing the next. You love being the center of attention, and people gravitate to you. Your social circle is large but your inner circle is supertight; you race so much from one thing to the next, it can be almost impossible for your best friends keep up.

friend match

Your fellow fire-sign pals love your kind of fun, but things get heated with so much drama in one group. Count on a Capricorn to keep it real and remind you to chill out between adventures.

YOU'VE GOT MORE
ENERGY THAN A RED BULL.

Vintage
leather jacket

Mountain
biking

Jennifer
Lopez

love match

You might think that a Pisces photog is too quiet for you, but if you give him a chance, you will find that his easy laugh and his sensitivity to your feelings might be a welcome change from the Jackass-wannabes you usually run around with.

+/− You are a social butterfly! It's okay to enjoy a variety of interests, but your extracurricular activities (and relationship history!) has got a serious case of ADD. You have to learn how to chill out and see your commitments through.

July 25

Emerald

Apple picking

"Island in the Sun"
—Weezer

$+/-$ It's great that you reach for the stars, but if you spend all your time with your head in the clouds, you're bound to miss out on some of the here and now. Try to focus on living in the moment.

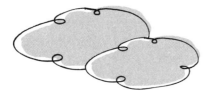

Imaginative, Idealistic, Honorable

If you were a song, you'd be Journey's "Don't Stop Believing." You dream of romantic trips to Paris and safaris in Africa, and you're convinced that no matter how many lemons life throws at you, eventually it's going to throw in some beluga caviar. Experience is everything to you, and you believe it's not whether you win or lose, it's how you play the game. Fairness and equality are very important to you.

AS AN IDEALIST YOU ALWAYS STAND UP FOR WHAT YOU BELIEVE.

love match

It's not exactly hard for you to get swept off your feet, which means you go head over heels for every Tom—and plain old Dick—who comes knocking. All that tumbling will start to hurt, so save your heart for someone who deserves it, like an adorable skater boy born in early August.

friend match

Even though you've got a strong sense of right and wrong, you're not about to tell other people how to live their lives. Good thing you won't have to with a sensible Cancer who always makes the right call.

If there is a problem—feuding friends, sibling drama, or another awful anatomy lab—you'll always be the one to step up to the plate. Life is a team sport, and you're the captain: Because you are super-practical and down-to-earth, your friends look to you to play leader. But sometimes your feet-on-the-ground philosophy can make you critical of other people's dreams, so learn to lay off the naysaying before your friends call foul. (Sure, becoming a famous actress is a long shot, but it isn't your place to remind your BFF of that every time she's dreaming of Oscars.)

$ Motivational speaker

Kate Beckinsale

Paris

July 26

★ ★ ★ ★ ★ ★ ★ ★ ★ ★ ★ ★ ★ ★ ★

Dynamic, Blunt, Influential

$+/-$ You're so focused on bringing your message—whether it's the importance of SPF or the lameness of rolled cuffs—you often don't think about delivery. Every so often, people need that spoonful of sugar, so if you think your BFF looks like a farmhand, think of a nicer way to tell her.

★ ★

love match

You like to go, go, go, and a sporty Gemini with a talent for getting in trouble will be the perfect speed racer when you're ready to tear up the town.

friend match

You called the whole pink-is-the-new-black thing way before the rest of the school caught on, but when it comes to figuring out your own feelings, you can be as dull as maroon. Count on an ultra-perceptive Pisces to help you figure it out.

July 27

You are just like a cell phone, because you always make the call. A natural-born leader and decision maker, friends turn to you for wardrobe advice, and your mom is always asking you what's for dinner. You're super-organized—you've been rocking a BlackBerry since your eighth birthday—and are skilled at solving puzzles and breaking down problems. If only you could keep your anger as tightly controlled as your schedule; you have a tendency to blow up when things don't go your way.

Medical researcher

Great Dane

Coco Chanel

+/− When it comes to telling other people what you are thinking, you are absolutely straight up. But when it comes to your own motivations you can be less than honest.

> TAKE A DOSE OF YOUR OWN MEDICINE AND FIGURE OUT WHAT YOU'RE REALLY FEELING.

love match

Not every guy gets your in-your-face attitude, but an equally dominant Leo likes you just the way you are. It works out perfectly: You like the way you are, too!

friend match

You're used to doling out advice to all of your friends, but an overachieving Capricorn BFF is the one who gives it to you straight up whenever you feel lost or confused. (Good thing she steered you away from those pleather pants.)

Your motto is simple: "Go for the gold." If life were a contest, you'd be shooting for the blue ribbon, and you believe that second place really means first loser. Whether you're playing volleyball in the gym, or vying for the attention of a cute barista at Coffee Bean, you always expect to dominate the competition. Although this makes you respected (and—face it—feared), it can be difficult for people to get close to you.

NOT EVERYONE WANTS TO HAVE A 24/7 FACE OFF.

friend match

Your people skills need work, but a completely fearless Scorpio—ruled by the dark planet Pluto—won't have any problem with your eye of the tiger approach to life. She's got her own claws out....

Kickboxing

Jacqueline Kennedy Onassis

Lavish hotel in Dubai

love match

You see relationships as almost a battle of the sexes, and you're determined to win. (Natch.) If you focus less on fighting with a certain adorable Aquarius—and more on just enjoying his company— you'd be surprised by the results.

+/− For you, it's black and white: There are winners and then there is everyone else. But to be successful you need other people on your team—not just a crowd rooting for you from the sidelines. Learn to share and work as part of a group.

July 29

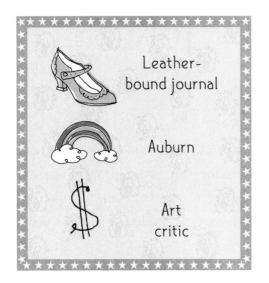

Leather-bound journal

Auburn

Art critic

Observant, Loyal, Conceptual

You are just like a tape measure, always sizing everybody up. Super-perceptive and fascinated by the people around you—from the new science teacher to the strikingly cute foreign exchange student—you're always playing amateur shrink, analyzing and evaluating everyone. For this reason, you can fit in with almost any social group; naturally understanding and sympathetic, friends (and warring social factions) look to you to resolve fights.

+/− A clique is more than the sum of its parts, and individuals are more than a part of their clique. You have a tendency to over-generalize and dismiss people before getting to know them. Try having a long talk with someone you usually only greet with a wave.

love match

You pass right over an art-loving Pisces, because you assume he's totally goth. News flash: Just because somebody wears black T-shirts and hangs out in the darkroom, doesn't make him a vampire fanatic, and a Pisces—characterized by generosity and sensitivity—might be just what you need.

friend match

You have a ton of acquaintances—from cheerleaders to drama nerds—but the girl to plug into speed dial is an easygoing and social Gemini who can slip in and out of different social scenes, just like you.

You are like a sequined black minidress in a room full of sweater sets: You get noticed. Whether you're sprinting onto the soccer field or strutting into the school dance, you make sure that your presence is felt, and anyone who's ever gone head-to-head with you in an argument (or over a free ball) knows you're a force to be reckoned with. Determined, down-to-earth, and energetic, *you keep a tight focus on the here and now* and don't spend a lot of time thinking before you act.

TRY TAKING UP A HOBBY THAT EXPANDS YOUR CREATIVE HORIZONS.

Dance team

Gwen Stefani

"What About Now" —Daughtry

July 30

★ ★ ★ ★ ★ ★ ★ ★ ★ ★ ★ ★ ★ ★ ★ ★

Strong, Charismatic, Decisive

+/− You're not big on daydreaming and think spending time with your head in the clouds will just leave you with altitude sickness. But everybody needs space to be imaginative.

★ ★

love match

If you need a good reason to add art class to your electives, how about this: A smoldering Pisces who will give you space to do your own thing and still melt your heart with a homemade photo collage for your b-day.

friend match

Independence is crucial for you, **so** you'll feel an instant connection with a Scorpio who doesn't mind marching to the beat of her own drummer (or going to the bathroom solo).

July 31

A true people-person, you play the shrink more often than jeans straight from a dryer. Your friends joke you should install a couch in your bedroom—you're always analyzing their dreams or lending an ear when they need to vent; you want to know what makes people tick. Equally interested in creative pursuits, you're drawn to painting or writing as a way to express all your ideas. Although you take great interest in social trends, you're in many ways very private.

> YOU PREFER TO HANG OUT IN YOUR ROOM RATHER THAN HIT THE MALL.

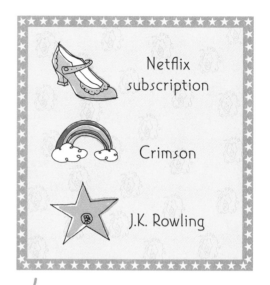

Netflix subscription

Crimson

J.K. Rowling

+/− Being a pessimist never looked good on anyone, so when you're feeling negative (this project will never work out), do your mind—and face!—a favor and turn that frown upside down.

love match

An intense Scorpio will give you plenty to analyze—and plenty of angst, too. If his hot and cold act is leaving you feeling chilly, go with a more straightforward Leo who will always listen. (Even if, bless him, he doesn't always know what you're talking about.)

friend match

A laid-back Libra is the perfect BFF for you, equally happy to hunker down in front of the last season of *Gossip Girl* or hit the mall to scope out cute guys.

August 1

You should be a contestant on Project Runway, *because* you're all about original style. But your unique point of view shows up in way more than your wardrobe selection. (Motorcycle jacket and Mary Janes, anyone?) You're a leader in everything you do, from yearbook to homecoming committee, and when you have a revelation (Earth Day party theme: Green with Envy), you're determined to get others to see the light. You like to be in charge, which can get you in trouble in situations where you're not the only one calling the shots.

love match

Opposites do attract, and the chemistry between you and a passionate Autumn-born water sign will provide explosive chemistry.

friend match

No need for a personality assessment: You know that you can be a bit difficult. That is why you need the calming influence of a Saturn-ruled BFF who will help you keep things in perspective.

Pucci sunglasses

Art gallery owner

Kate Moss

$+/-$ It's cool that you've got strong convictions, but sometimes it pays to compromise. Fighting with your little sib over the remote control will leave you with only one entertainment option: A little show called grounded.

Turquoise

Supermodel

Scuba diving in Mozambique

August 2

Versatile, Adaptable, Determined

You are just like a letter: You get around, and no matter where you go, you've always got a signature stamp on you. You change your look more often than Madonna, and you love to try out new things—field hockey, culinary club, poetry society—but no matter what you do (or how you dress), you always bring your unmistakable style, vision, and enthusiasm to it. You live for variety, but stay grounded by sticking close to loyal friends and fam. Sometimes your unique way of seeing the world makes you seem inconsistent. Be sure your pals can count on you when times are hard.

+/− Just like teachers tell you, you can do anything you put your mind to. But you know what they also say? Two heads are better than one. Do not be afraid to ask for help.

YOUR SPIRIT ANIMAL IS THE CHAMELEON: CONFIDENT AND CHANGEABLE.

love match

Your worst nightmare is a guy who wants to stick to the boring dinner and a movie routine. An outgoing and adventurous Aries will be more than happy to try out Ultimate Frisbee with you or hit the newest (spicy!) Thai restaurant.

friend match

An air-sign friend is just like snow: A little bit flaky, with a tendency to get pushed around. You can teach her something about assertiveness: Nobody tells you what to do.

If you were a song, you'd be Michael Jackson's "Thriller," because you're all about danger and excitement. First on the Viper at Six Flags and last to chicken out of mooning the rival soccer team, when the question is Truth or Dare, there's really no question what your choice will be. Interestingly, though, part of your fearlessness consists in your determination to speak the truth at all costs.

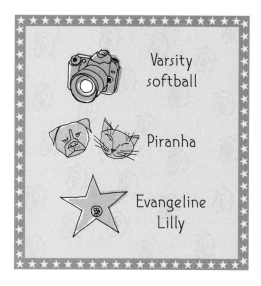

Varsity softball

Piranha

Evangeline Lilly

August 3

Courageous,
Idealistic,
Determined

WHEN YOU BELIEVE IN SOMETHING STRONGLY, YOU NEVER SAY DIE.

+/− Someone better bust out the Band-Aids, because if you keep playing Wonder Woman, sooner or later you're bound to get hurt. Some risks are not worth taking, so think twice before you act the hero.

love match

Even though you are adventurous and outgoing, what you really look for in a guy is honesty and trustworthiness. Count on a fellow Leo to make like Abe Lincoln and never tell a lie.

friend match

You can count on a Uranus-ruled BFF to be your partner in crime—and should listen to her when she wants to back out of a prank. If she smells trouble, better call it quits.

August 4

You are like the human equivalent of a campfire: Superbright, you've always got a circle of friends around you. (But if people get on your bad side, they're bound to get torched.) You are quick-witted and charming, and although your mouth often puts you in conflict with authority figures (like teachers and, ahem, parents), you try to avoid real trouble: You can peel off excuses so fast you should be a lemon zester.

Cardinal

Talk show host

You pair everything with a scarf

UNINTERESTED IN BEING A LEADER, YOU NONETHELESS FIND THAT PEOPLE COPY YOUR STYLE.

+/− You're so independent that you hate following orders. But there's no sense starting an all-out war with your mom over who loaded the dishwasher last. Ten minutes of dishes will save you an hour of headaches.

friend match

You can't stand it when people don't speak their minds, so steer clear of Pisces and Scorpio—both signs that love to keep secrets. Round out your circle with fellow Leos and truth-loving Sagittarius.

love match

You and a Libra will hit it off right away, but he'll soon tire of trying to keep you out of trouble. Look for a totally accepting Aquarius, who won't mind your mischievous side.

August 5

You're the human equivalent of a tube of deodorant: When you're around, nobody sweats the small stuff. (Plus, you always smell nice.) Totally together and cooler than an ice cube in January, you're a natural born leader, believing in the power of mind over matter and maintaining control in all situations. If some people wear their hearts on their sleeves, yours is buried in a lock box; very few people know that you're actually both passionate and extremely competitive.

friend match

You're definitely not the kind of girl who says "I love you" after meeting someone for five minutes (or five years), which is why it is important that a loyal Cancer BFF knows you care without making you say it.

love match

You keep your crushes totally under wraps, which means you often come across as an ice queen. But when it comes to a Scorpio with a wicked sense of humor, you'll have to do more than just smile if you want to make him melt.

Pearls

Comedy club

Cocker spaniel

$+/-$ On the outside, you're cool, calm, and collected. But you're often hiding both anger and disappointment. Don't wait for it to explode; talk about your feelings.

POKER FACE IS YOUR NATURAL LOOK.

August 6

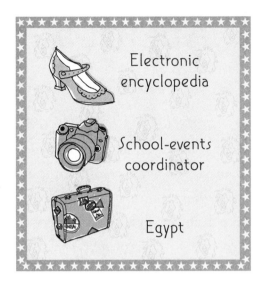

Electronic encyclopedia

School-events coordinator

Egypt

+/− It's great that you have such a unique point of view, but refusing to see things from someone else's perspective will eventually leave you rolling solo.

LEARN TO LISTEN AND COMPROMISE.

Interesting, Romantic, Original

You are just like eBay, because you're all about that one-in-a-lifetime find. Drawn to unique and unusual experiences, people, as well as things, you dream of skydiving, kicking back with a celeb, soaring to the moon, or performing with the New York City Rockettes. Even when you are stuck at home, you're always in search of the unknown; the Discovery channel is your absolute fave, and you love bouncing back and forth between social groups. Just remember that life is like Pilates: You need a strong center to get through it.

love match

You're intense about your interests, but you also have a great sense of humor, which means the Scorpio and Cancer boys are way too serious for you. A lighthearted and social Gemini will keep you ROTFL.

friend match

A Virgo friend always sees things from a different angle, just like you, and won't think it's weird when you want to scour the vintage stores for the perfect pair of cowboy boots for three weekends in a row.

If you were a number, you'd be 007: You've got so much mystery surrounding you, you might as well be a secret agent. (Repeat after me: "Bond. James Bond.") You keep your cards close to your chest and have more secrets than the deodorant aisle of a Walmart—even your best friends don't know who you're crushing on! You, however, have a nose for the truth, so whether your BFF is claiming to be over her latest boyfriend or your sister is promising she did not borrow (and lose) your new tank top, you can always smell out a lie.

Teddy bear

Charlize Theron

"Nobody Knows It But Me"
—Babyface

August 7

Clever, Funny, Investigating

+/− Some mysteries are best left unsolved; not everyone wants their dirty laundry exposed. If one of your friends doesn't want to give you the reason she stopped talking to the cutie on the basketball team, don't push it.

love match

You treat your crushes like they're Class A Confidential Material. But when an über-confident Scorpio strolls into your life (and your lunch period), you won't be able to keep your feelings under wraps.

friend match

You and a winter-born BFF will be just like Sherlock Holmes and Watson, always up in everybody's business. Just make sure you don't get the reputation of Gossip Girls. . . .

August 8

You're a one-girl theater troupe: You play all the roles. You swap outfits faster than Cher on her farewell tour (one week it's punk princess; the next it's prep) and are always exploring new interests and activities (bocci ball!). This doesn't mean you're flaky, though; you put a lot of time and effort into each new transformation and achieve success at whatever you choose to do. Realistic, responsible, and open-minded, you love to set your own path, but you'll always stop and ask for directions when you begin to wander astray.

Romantic scavenger hunt

Tropical fish

Angelina Jolie

+/− Because you shed skins more often than a snake, it's important to take time to chill out in the nest.

MAKE TIME FOR YOUR FAMILY TO HELP KEEP YOU CENTERED.

love match

One thing remains constant in your life: Tension between you and a sarcastic fire sign, who drives you crazy with his extreme arrogance. There's a fine line between love and hate. . . .

friend match

It's important for you to have a close group of solid friends who can act as your center. Make sure to stand by a loyalty-obsessed Leo and a grounded, practical Capricorn, both of whom can be good influences on you.

August 9

If you were a movie, you'd be Lean on Me: *strong,* independent, and socially perceptive. People naturally depend on you for guidance and direction. You have a lot of sway in your social circle and have your 'rents wrapped around your little finger. You have a natural ability to understand what other people are thinking and feeling, and you know how to use this to your advantage. But you never abuse your power—you're so busy providing support to your friends, you could be a bra.

BE CAREFUL ABOUT WHAT YOU SAY,
AS PEOPLE ALWAYS TAKE YOU SERIOUSLY.

love match

You are used to being in control and will be quite surprised when a scorchingly hot Scorpio manages to flip the script. Even more surprising? How good it will feel to let go.

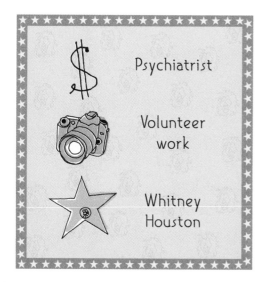

$ Psychiatrist

Volunteer work

Whitney Houston

friend match

You're usually the one dishing out the TLC, but make sure someone's filling up your plate, too. A quiet Cancer may depend on you when she's feeling down, but she'll always be there to give you a boost when you need it.

+/− Everyone knows the expression "sticks and stones may break my bones, but words can never hurt me" is untrue, and your mouth is a powerful weapon.

August 10

Pedestal

Blue

New York City
(Broadway)

+/− You feel best when you've got an audience to play to, **but confidence isn't performance art: You need to learn how to feel good about yourself, even when all the seats in the house are empty.**

Fun, Vocal, Magnetic

Anyone who would say that actions speak louder than words has obviously never heard you speak: You've got a voice that needs to be heard, and when you chime into a conversation, you are bound to shake things up. Outgoing, fun, and optimistic, you're usually in a good mood and love to be the center of attention—easy to achieve when you have a ton of admirers crowding around 24/7. You're not just a scene-stealer, though; you're a great friend, who can always be relied on to say what she means and mean what she says.

love match

You won't need to provide entertainment when a hilarious Aries is around—he'll be hogging the spotlight. You may not always want to be struggling with him for the spotlight, though; a quiet Sagittarius who loves to listen will be a 24/7 fan club of one.

friend match

You love being surrounded by a crowd, but it can be tougher to reach you on a personal level. A Libra BFF will have the patience and persistence to get to know your deepest, darkest secrets . . . and she'll still love you!

If the world had a face, you'd be its Biore Detoxifying Pore Strip: all about bringing the truth (good, bad, and really, really ugly blackheads) to the surface. A human lie detector, you see it as your mission to discover and expose the real 411 in every situation: from what's in the cafeteria's meatball mix to why your BFF is suddenly acting shady whenever she sees a certain soccer player. You need to be surrounded by people and crave attention.

WHAT'S THE POINT OF PLAYING DETECTIVE IF NO ONE'S AROUND FOR YOUR BIG REVEAL?

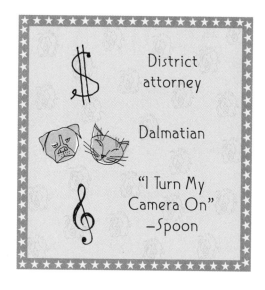

$ District attorney

Dalmatian

"I Turn My Camera On" —Spoon

August 11

Insightful, Truth-Seeking, Powerful

+/− Truth is important, but some words are best left unspoken. **Just because you found out that your friend's boyfriend used to go out with the prettiest girl in school, doesn't mean you should mouth off about it.**

love match

You have a tendency to take life super-seriously. A laid-back Libra with a love of the outdoors can help you get a more relaxed perspective.

friend match

You know what they say: "People in glass houses shouldn't throw stones." Sometimes you're so busy exposing the people around you as pretty little liars you forget to turn the microscope on yourself. Count on a no-nonsense Cancer to do it for you.

August 12

You are just like your grandmother's chicken noodle soup: traditional and nurturing, you always make everyone feel good. It's important to you to preserve old friends and habits—like pepperoni-pizza Sundays and the fact that you always wear red on Tuesdays—and you see change as a four-letter word. But your desire to maintain the status quo doesn't come from laziness or fear.

> YOU'RE INCREDIBLY ENERGETIC AND ARE OFTEN ON A MISSION TO KEEP EVERYTHING JUST THE WAY YOU LIKE IT.

Khaki

Simple

Bungee jumping in New Zealand

+/− Just like a cash register, you need to learn how to make change. You've been sitting with the same people in the caf since second grade, and your social circle is getting seriously stale. Try inviting someone new into your group, or switching up a Saturday-night routine.

friend match

The last thing you need is another BF whose idea of a super-rocking Friday night involves Chinese takeout and repeated screenings of *Sisterhood of the Traveling Pants*. Break out and get to know an outgoing (and outrageous) Aries, who can help bust you out of your rut.

love match

A cool-on-the-outside Cancer has a heart as melty as an M&M, and values close friendships and loyalty. (Just like you!)

CANDY

August 13

The number 13 gets the rep for being unlucky and people born on August 13th traditionally face many obstacles and hurdles on the road to success. Fortunately, they have the stamina and energy to overcome, and they just won't quit until they reach their goals—whether it's landing the lead in the school play, taking first in the state-wide poetry competition, or just getting the attention of the cutest guy in school. Talented and individualistic, August 13th girls have a social circle that's tighter—and harder to squeeze into—than a pair of skinny jeans straight from the wash.

friend match

A fellow Leo BFF is just like a heavyweight champion: She has to earn her title. Once you give her the green light, count on her to keep her ringer on 24/7 in case you need to talk.

love match

A preppy Saturn-ruled guy likes you, but you can't get down with someone who just wants to blend in. Be on the lookout for a sarcastic (and artistic) Scorpio who definitely marches to the beat of his own bass line.

Personal assistant

Surgeon

Sheltie

$+/-$ If you were a room, you'd have a big **KEEP OUT** sign hanging from your doorknob. You have to learn to open up about your feelings.

REMEMBER: THERE IS
STRENGTH IN
BEING VULNERABLE.

August 14

Hermès scarf

Halle Berry

"Count on Me" —Whitney Houston

Observant, Honest, Funny

In the wardrobe of life, you're the full-length mirror: reflective, brutally honest, and people can see themselves in you. A natural teacher and guide, you're a trendsetter without even trying and always have the most up-to-the-minute styles, accessories, and attitudes, which is why your friends look to you as a leader (and inspiration).

Funny, outgoing, and generous, because you can relate to almost everyone, you've *got more people sweating you than a gym class.*

+/— One of the many reasons why you make such an incredible friend is that you always pay attention. If your BFF seems quieter than usual, you're on it faster than white on rice, but remember to spend time on yourself, too.

love match

If you're looking for love, expect a Mercury-ruled guy to come your way. Just like you, he's impulsive and recovers quickly when things don't go his way. (Thankfully, since he's essentially your mirror image, that won't be a problem.)

friend match

You're always there for a creative (and flighty) Gemini friend, whether she needs homework or boy help. But when it comes time for you to get yours, turn to a fellow Leo who is just as dependable as you are.

If you were a book, you'd be *The Princess Diaries*—you've certainly already got the royal attitude. A true Leo, you're a born leader and insist on being in command. You despise getting bogged down in the details (and you can't even stand the word "chore") and instead like to focus on the big picture and the end result, which means in most groups you're the organizer, planner and, of course, the delegator. (You do not like the word "work" that much, either.) But despite the fact that you always play queen, you're not an evil dictator; you just like to see things go your way!

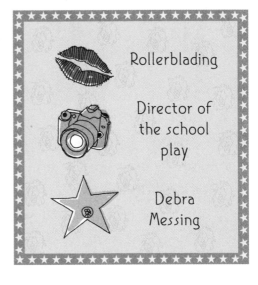

Rollerblading

Director of the school play

Debra Messing

August 15

Commanding, Decisive, Expansive

+/− You can definitely dish it, but when advice gets handed back to you, you find it difficult to swallow. Learn to take other people's suggestions.

love match

You're ruled by Venus, so you *need* to be adored. Avoid uptight water signs who are too wrapped up in themselves to give you the attention you crave.

friend match

You're definitely not afraid to boss people around, so it's important to stick close to an equally outspoken Libra who will tell you when you're out of line—before a mass rebellion develops.

August 16

You should be a blow-dryer, because you've got some serious voltage: You light up brighter than an evergreen at Christmas time and have a way of twisting people around your finger without even trying. Charming and confident, people are drawn to you like bears to honey—but you're not all sweetness. Actually, you have a very tough core that's characterized by determination and willfulness, and anyone who gets in the way of your dreams is bound to see your temper turn sour.

BMW

Fashion designer

Madonna

+/− You hold grudges so long it's a miracle your arms don't get tired. Rethink your no-forgiveness policy: You never know when you'll need to work with your arch nemesis.

YOU'D DO ANYTHING TO HELP A FRIEND.

love match

You've got guys falling for you faster than a line of dominoes, which can make it intimidating for a would-be Romeo. When you find someone you like (you + Scorpio = serious heat), make sure you let him know how you feel.

friend match

Your energy and enthusiasm are like the flu: Super-contagious. A shy Libra will break out of her shell with your help, and in return she will help you keep your cool when you're about to have a major meltdown.

August 17

If you were an amp, you'd be turned up to 11 all the time.
Energetic, motivated, and ambitious, you like to be in control and enjoy running the show—whether you're planning a group presentation or coordinating social calendars with your BFFs. Though many people think of you as extremely outgoing—what would a party be without you?—you like to maintain your privacy and sometimes come across as mysterious (which only brings the fans flocking closer).

friend match

Your argumentative attitude can turn people off ("I told you—Skittles are a thousand times better than M&M's!"), so you could use a calm and diplomatic Aquarius to help take the wind out of your sails when there's a major storm brewing.

love match

You're not a fan of following someone else's lead, so a domineering Taurus will have you looking elsewhere. I spy a confident Capricorn with a killer smile and a social calendar that is as packed as yours. Maybe your people can meet with his people to schedule something in.

Silver

Hot-air balloon ride

Cheerleading

+/− You've got energy to burn and the explosive temper to match. **Learn to take deep breaths when you're feeling angry; those extra moments might just** help you calm the winds before any major storm develops.

August 18

- Nalgene bottle
- Navy blue
- Track team

+/− Whoever said, "No pain, no gain," has obviously never been on crutches: Sometimes, the hardest way is not the best, and you have to learn to go with the flow.

Adaptable, Patient, Deep

If you were a beverage, you'd be a sports drink, because you're all about endurance. Though you'll often face difficulties—like tantrum-prone little sibs and pop quiz-obsessed teachers—you keep it cool and in control, knowing that if you want to get to the top, you have to break a sweat. A doer and not a talker, you much prefer to be out and about than reading or IMing with girlfriends.

> YOUR MOTTO IS "I WILL OVERCOME."

love match

You hate whining and complaining pretentiousness, and you'd much rather date the captain of the soccer team than the whiny emo lead singer of the local band. Go for an outdoors-obsessed Gemini who thinks a haiku is a form of martial arts.

friend match

When you're friends with someone, you're in it for the long haul. When a frazzled Virgo BFF has a mini-breakdown over final exams, you'll talk her through it, and in return she'll help put you in touch with your creative, imaginative side.

You are exactly like the ingredients in the McDonald's Special Sauce: You spice things up, and no one can figure you out. You love surprises and mysteries and it's no wonder: You've got plenty of those yourself, and even your closest friends can't always tell what is going on in your head. Extremely open at some moments, at others you withdraw completely, which means you always keep people guessing.

HONESTY IS IMPORTANT TO YOU—YOU JUST OFTEN KEEP THE TRUTH (AND YOUR OPINIONS) TO YOURSELF.

Lilac

Siamese cat

Ski lodge in Aspen

August 19

Sneaky,
Self-Confident,
Influential

+/− Life is just like a banana: better when split. **Learn to open up and share more of yourself with others.**

love match

You may keep your cards close to your chest, but you like it when other people show you their hands. A straightforward Taurus won't keep you guessing about his feelings: He's the real deal.

friend match

Your best friends may think they've got you all figured out, but you've always got surprises (and secrets) up your sleeves. If you don't want to be engaged in a constant mental tug-of-war, look for a BFF who's cool with leaving you space, like a privacy-obsessed Pisces.

August 20

If you were a book, you'd be *The Secret*. You're extremely private and tend to keep your emotions guarded from even your closest friends. Compassionate, sympathetic, as well as intuitive, you have a tendency to feel deeply and understand other people's feelings deeply, tools which make you an excellent listener and the best shoulder to cry on. This means you've got more hangers-on than a closet; just be careful to stay away from negative people, or risk getting dragged down.

Walk along the beach

Amy Adams

"Lean on Me" —Bill Withers

+/— Both you and an airport have something in common: Baggage. The biggest challenge you face is letting go of the past, but you have to learn to look forward if you don't want to trip over your feet.

love match

You're super-shy and afraid of getting hurt, but a sweet and caring Libra will never make you promises he can't keep—or make you feel stupid when you stutter over your own name in front of him.

friend match

You have a tendency to brood, so the last thing you need is a BFF who is equally as withdrawn as you. Stay away from antisocial Pisces and Cancer and reach out to a fun-loving Aries, who will make sure your main Friday-night activity isn't moping.

August 21

You're just like a fugitive, because no matter where you run to or how much you hide, the spotlight is always tracking you down. You don't try to court attention—you prefer a quiet movie with some BFs to a big blowout party with the whole school—but somehow you always seem to end up center stage. Individualistic and confident, just like a pair of strappy gold stilettos in a sea of Birkenstocks, you always stand out from the crowd. (Plus, you've got great style.)

friend match

One thing you can't stand? When people are afraid to be different. You and a radically confident Scorpio BFF will bond over the fact that you're always blazing your own trails.

love match

Guys are always trying to show off for you, but you are not looking for someone who can burp the whole alphabet. You prefer the sensitive artist type. Take heart: A Venus-ruled Romeo with a talent for guitar is headed your way.

Musical theater

Hayden Panettiere

Chic

+/− You are pretty self-sufficient, which means you never sweat the small stuff. There's no reason for you to go it alone, though. Trust other people and they'll lighten your load!

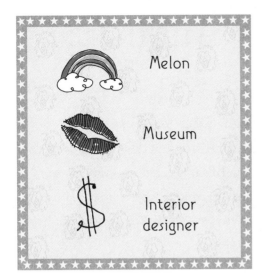

Melon

Museum

Interior designer

August 22

★ ★ ★ ★ ★ ★ ★ ★ ★ ★ ★ ★ ★ ★ ★ ★ ★

Imaginative, Patient, Seasoned

You ought to be a tree, because no matter how high you're reaching, you always stay firmly grounded. Creative and a big dreamer—you'll spend weeks designing and then sewing your own dress for Spring Fling, or redecorating your BFF's bedroom—you nevertheless stay grounded because of your practicality and ability to learn quickly. When you're on a team, you always get elected captain, and your friends are constantly asking you for homework help and fashion advice.

+/− You pride yourself on how well you learn from your mistakes, but admitting you were wrong in the first place? Not your forte. Don't be shy about leaning on someone's shoulder when you need to.

love match

A water sign will be an excellent match for you, helping bring flexibility and fun to your life while giving you the space to do your own thing. Look for a cool, laid-back Cancer with a talent for giving you butterflies.

friend match

You're superloyal to your peeps, but you don't play doormat to anybody. When a friend is acting bossy, you're the first to let her know. Just because she's ruled by the sun doesn't mean everything revolves around her.

If life were like the alphabet, you'd be the capital I: totally stand-alone. (And all about the self.) You are not exactly selfish, but you're so concerned with personal goals and ambitions (like getting first chair in the orchestra or scoring the cutest date for your friend's b-day bash) that you sometimes seem oblivious to other people's needs. Your motto is live and let live, and just so long as no one gets in your way, it's all smooth sailing. But anyone who blocks you from getting what you want is going to see the stormy (and scary!) side of your personality.

MacBook

Pitbull

"I Want it That Way" —Backstreet Boys

August 23

Intense,
Poised,
Logical

+/− To say you're ambitious would be a massive understatement. **True, all's fair in love and war, but you should still play by the rules of engagement.**

love match

When you find a Capricorn with a take-no-prisoners attitude, nothing will stop you from winning his attention. Be prepared for a roller-coaster relationship: The fights will be epic. (And the making up is even better!)

friend match

Your schedule's so packed, it could be a suitcase, and sometimes you need to straight-up chill. Count on a Cancer to be there when you need quality down-time at home or in front of the TV.

Virgo Girls

are serious and selective

If life were a house, Virgo girls would be its founda-tion: down-to-earth and all about structure. Virgos are choosy about everything from footwear to friends. (Hardly anyone makes it past the velvet rope.) With a tendency for controlling behavior, they often find themselves in the role of organizer. Their very private nature can be frustrating for the people who are trying to get close.

◆ ◆ ◆ ◆ ◆ ◆ ◆ ◆ ◆ ◆ ◆ ◆ ◆ ◆ ◆ ◆ ◆ ◆ ◆ ◆

Most likely to be: Color-coding their closets.

Freezer item they most resemble: Vanilla ice cream. Pure but surprisingly complex; also a tendency to freeze.

Strengths to play on: Logical, respected by many.

Pitfalls to avoid: Heartless, feared by more.

Virgo

August 24 – September 22

Element: **Earth**
Ruler: **Mercury**

Theme song: "I Feel Pretty"
(Pretty Good About
Blowing You Off. . .)

August 24

You should be a comb, because you are forever untangling knots and problems. Naturally gifted in math and science, you can knock out a Sudoku puzzle in under five minutes and don't read mysteries because you always predict the ending. But your skills extend far beyond school: You're thoughtful and perceptive.

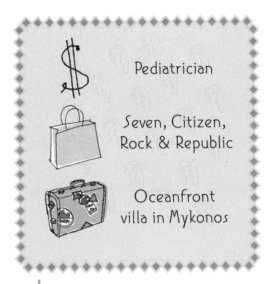

Pediatrician

Seven, Citizen, Rock & Republic

Oceanfront villa in Mykonos

+/− You like sniffing out the truth but leave your own thoughts and feelings totally hidden—**and since not everyone's as good at playing Sherlock as you, your friends and family often feel like you're one giant mystery. Clue them in.**

YOU'RE TOTALLY CLUED IN TO HOW YOUR FRIENDS ARE FEELING AND CAN ALWAYS HELP THEM FIND SOLUTIONS TO THEIR PROBLEMS.

love match

You're harder to decode than a Rubik's Cube, so you need a guy with the patience to take it slow (and keep at it when the going gets tough), like a steadfast and determined Taurus.

friend match

You're picky about everything, from fabric (cashmere and cotton only) to food (nothing spicy!). But nothing compares to how selective you can be when it comes to picking a BFF. A creative and sweet-tempered Gemini is just as curious as you are, but with a slightly more social side to keep you from going hermit.

August 25

Your motto is "If you've got it, flaunt it," and you strut your stuff so hard you make Naomi Campbell look like a slouch. Blessed with brains and beauty, and determined to be appreciated for both, you're the life of the party and are always seeking the spotlight. Though naturally gifted at school, you actually have one true passion in one subject and one subject alone: fun! You love to blast music and dance around with your BFFs or scope out cute boys at the mall, and being around you is like having the ultimate VIP pass to a 24-hour party.

friend match

Your biggest secret? Though you seem to have it all (and have more MySpace friends than a Claire's boutique has rhinestones), you're prone to moments of feeling alone and misunderstood. An intuitive Pisces will always make you feel appreciated, even when the rest of the world seems to have turned its back.

love match

If flirting was an Olympic sport, you'd take home the gold. But do not be surprised if an adorable, quirky Gemini suddenly gets you tongue-tied. He's too confident—and clever—to fall for your usual tricks. (And you love it.)

$+/-$ You are one of those girls who makes popularity look totally effortless—people just like you. But do you like yourself? Don't feel like every spare second has to become a social hour. Find things that you enjoy doing on your own, and take time to smell the flowers.

Stylist

Club opening

Blake Lively

August 26

Hazel

Stage crew

Hamster

+/− You're used to playing a supporting role while your best friends hog the spotlight. Don't let them upstage you; you're a superstar, too.

> SOMETIMES YOU'VE GOT TO TAKE THE LEAD AND SHOW EVERYONE WHAT YOU CAN DO.

Self-Contained, Accepting, Cooperative

You're just like ballroom dancing: All about partnering. When you play basketball in gym (blech), you'd much rather set your pal up for the winning basket than lead the team in scoring, and even off the court, you prefer to keep a low profile. Private and independent, you occasionally get the reputation of being standoffish, when in reality you just like to work your magic behind the scenes. Just make sure you don't get stepped on in the process— your efforts need to be appreciated.

love match

Anyone who knows you will say you're a total sweetheart, but because you're shy, you can come off as kind of aloof. Thankfully, a Taurus will set his eyes on you—and be unstoppable on his mission to get to know you better.

friend match

Friendship is definitely the most important thing in your life, and you don't like to roll anywhere without a solid crew of friends. Not everyone can get down with your stick-to-me-like-peanut-butter style, but a totally devoted Leo BFF will be into playing jelly.

If life were like a wiener, you would be the bun: all about the underdog. When your school's soccer team is kicking serious butt on the field, you can't help but root for the losing team, and in general you tend to stay away from competition because you do not like anyone to go home upset. Whether you're raising money for the local soup kitchen or protesting the use of animal fur in clothing, your strong ideals and sense of fairness mean you're always trying to do the right thing.

Children's book author

Baking

Sarah Chalke

August 27

☆ • ☆ • ☆ • ☆

Caring, Idealistic, Passionate

+/− It's great that you hold such strong beliefs about right and wrong, but keep in mind that opinions are just like first-draft essays: Most of the time, they're meant to be revised. Listen to what other people are saying and keep an open mind.

love match

A fellow Virgo is perfect: He's cool, smart, sensitive, and never steps on the little people. Basically, he's you in boy form. (Without the fabulous clothes and hair, natch, but you'll have to forgive his ratty baseball hat.)

friend match

Whenever your friends get depressed or discouraged, you're ready to play cheerleader so fast you should keep emergency pom-poms in your locker. You and a Libra have that in common, which makes you perfect cocaptains of your own private squad.

184

August 28

If you were a subject in school, you'd definitely be language arts. You've got a way with words, and you know just what to say to get people to see things from your point of view. ("Pushing back my curfew to eleven thirty will only encourage responsibility.") But you are not just about argumentation; you love dishing out advice, too.

YOU PLAY THE ADVICE COLUMN FOR ALL OF YOUR FRIENDS AND FAMILY, WHO CAN ALWAYS COUNT ON YOUR WISE WORDS AND SYMPATHETIC EAR.

This month's issue of the *New Yorker*

Film critic

LeAnn Rimes

$+/-$ Your mind is just like a pie chart, all about facts and figures. But you're often so focused on the details that you miss out on the big picture. Work on your "zoom out" function.

friend match

When a Gemini friend needs advice, she comes to you. And when you need to shut off your brain (which runs a mile a minute) and laugh your butt off, you can count on her to throw an impromptu Rihanna dance party in her bedroom.

love match

Sometimes a picture really is worth a thousand words. For example: Picture yourself with that gorgeous, brooding, sensitive Scorpio. Then shut up and kiss him already! (One word: Amazing.)

You must love to go to restaurants, because you're all about ordering. You hate chaos more than anything, and you're always bringing structure and organization to whatever you do—from cleaning up your room (natch) to dividing up the homecoming dance committee into different functions. (One group does decorations; one does refreshments; one does nominations.) You're happy to lose control when it comes to having fun, though, and are the first to shake it on the dance floor when the music starts blaring.

friend match

You and a type A Sagittarius will just compete over who can throw the best b-day bash. (And bake the best brownies, as well as do the best downward-facing dog...) What you need is a social, laid-back Gemini who just wants to have fun.

love match

Ironically, although you are used to doing the steering, you'll be happy to take the backseat when an outspoken Taurus comes along. Trust and believe: Wherever he's taking you, it's going to be a blast.

Morning hike

Feng shui

Owner of a boutique hotel

+/− You hold yourself to such a high standard it's like *Mission: Impossible,* and then you beat yourself up for failing. Everyone makes mistakes, so ease up on yourself and spend time with people who can help you laugh about the slipups.

☆ • ☆ • ☆ • ☆

August 30

Flat iron

Cameron Diaz

Spa resort in Japan

+/− If you were nylons, you would definitely be the control top. You can't manage everything, so learn to ease up and let things unfold naturally.

Organized, Reliable, Determined

You should be a diamond engagement ring: rock solid and always shining. Super-dependable and very ambitious, whether you're strength-training before a big soccer game or spearheading a car wash to raise money for the student council, you're all about getting results. Hugely confident, you have a ton of friends and are always playing social coordinator for your inner circle—and your shoulder is cried on so often it's permanently soggy. Just be careful that lifting up your friends all the time doesn't leave your arms—and spirit—exhausted.

love match

Though you're a straight-A student, you often need help when it comes to a different letter: R & R. Let a fun-loving Aquarius with a low-key outlook help you take the mess out of your stress.

friend match

You love your independence, so sometimes you just need to do your own thing. Steer clear of a Cancer who will stay on you like a dog on a fire hydrant, and surround yourself with freedom-craving signs, like Capricorn and Sagittarius.

Just like a reality-TV star, your motto is "No press is bad press." Very concerned with being at the center of attention, you're a social butterfly and a blast to be around. (No one needs to tell you to get the party started.) But although you crave recognition, you are not just about surface. You are extremely perceptive and sensitive to other people's feelings, and the reason you like to be looked at is simple: Just like any great leader, you want to be an example.

Gold

Politician

Grace Kelly

August 31

Dynamic, Influential, Fun

+/— If a cell phone rings on a Friday night and there's no one around to answer, is it really ringing? You'd never know, since you've got the thing surgically attached to your ear. Don't let alone time freak you out; turn off your phone (yes, and computer) once in a while and practice some privacy.

love match

You take rejection superhard, which can make you afraid to reach out. You won't have to take a chance on a Taurus: He'll make it clear how he feels from day one. (And he's totally here to stay.)

friend match

You and a Scorpio friend are like fireworks: beautiful, fun to watch, and absolutely not to be played with. Once you guys pair up, the rest of the school had better watch out.

September 1

You are just like a human vacuum cleaner, all about cleaning up other people's messes. Strictly no-nonsense, your can-do attitude means you're always picking up the slack and taking care of business. A natural leader, your ambition and desire to reach the top make you a stellar student and a stand-out member of any team. Just as long as no one gets in your way. You have a temper that makes Cruella De Vil look warm and fuzzy!

Burgundy

Advertising executive

Little black dress

+/− In certain situations, quitting is actually the right thing to do; it's okay to give up on an extracurricular or avoid taking the field when you have a sprained ankle. (And you know you have to toss that deadbeat dude to the curb when he starts acting shady.)

YOUR MOTTO IS "NEVER SAY DIE."

love match

You know what they say about all work and no play? Boring. Look for a dreamy and imaginative Pisces to sweep you off your feet and make you forget all about your homework.

friend match

You believe that honesty is the best policy, so you'll love how a down-to-earth Taurus always gives it to you straight. (Even when she criticizes your fave purple platforms.)

You are like the perfect pair of black boot-cut pants:
You may not be about frills and flourishes, but you're hugely practical and infinitely popular. You hate fakes and phonies (in everything from bags to people), and you're a big believer in letting your actions speak for themselves. You may not gush over how much you love your BFF, but you'll throw her the best b-day party ever and be there with a box of tissues the day her dog is put to sleep.

friend match

You are just like Head & Shoulders shampoo: You hate flakes. **You'll find greatest compatibility with fellow earth signs, who are just as reliable as you.**

love match

You're too disciplined to let yourself get carried away by whims and spur-of-the-moment ideas. **But one of the great things about love is that you can't control it, so don't be surprised if an ultra-romantic Scorpio has you acting crazy.**

Kipling messenger bag

Professional football game

Salma Hayek

$+/-$ **You've got drive that would put a car to shame:** Ultra-determined and very disciplined, **you're always turning in assignments early and asking for extra credit. Make sure you're not just going through the motions, though. Let some passion and inspiration into your life.**

Lime green

Playwright

Bora Bora

September 3

You'd make one bad cookie, because you're always breaking out of the mold. Innovative and original, you aren't afraid to have different opinions, interests, hobbies, and shoes than everybody else. For you, "conform" is a four-letter world, and you find it just as difficult to follow rules as you do to follow trends. Way ahead of your time, the outfit you're rocking this year may take another two to reach the masses—and by then you'll be on to something else.

+/− You have a lot of trouble opening up to others and don't like to explain yourself. But if you want to bring people around to your point of view, you have to show them that there's a method to the madness.

love match

You pick guys the way you pick shoes: You want to be the very first to appreciate their charm. A quirky nonconformist Pisces with a talent for photography will appreciate your unique point of view.

friend match

Although you crave closeness and have the ability to feel deeply, **it's hard for you to open up. Count on a loyal (and extremely talkative) Gemini to bring you out of your shell.**

If you could be a toy, you would be legos: all about building, putting things together, and watching things stack up. Superorganized and detail-oriented, you're always helping your friends redecorate their rooms or clean out their closets. Naturally inclined toward science and art, you like to work with your hands—and have got such a talent for getting the project done, you could host your own show on HGTV.

> REMEMBER THAT YOU DESERVE A LITTLE TLC, TOO!

Habitat for Humanity volunteer

Cockatoo

Beyoncé Knowles

September 4

Methodical, Capable, Constructive

+/− You love helping out, and your 'rents can always count on you to babysit your younger sibs or rake and bag leaves—just as your friends count on you to give fashion advice and find lost homework in their lockers. Don't be afraid to ask them for help, too!

love match

Crazy in love? Not so much. You keep your head firmly on your shoulders at all times. But a certain Sagittarius sweetie with a killer smile—and the ability to make you laugh when you're feeling stressed—may change your perspective.

friend match

You'll always go the extra mile for your friends, so you deserve a BFF who will always go the distance for you. An ultra-loyal Taurus will always be there for you.

September 5

They say if wishes were horses, beggars would ride—and you'd be sitting pretty with a whole stable for yourself. Prone to daydreaming, you're excellent at visualizing what you want (homecoming queen!) and then making it happen. (Even if you have to launch a smear campaign against the rest of the court.) Extremely ambitious, you believe you're fated for greatness—just make sure your head doesn't get too big, or that crown you're after will start to feel a bit tight.

Peach

"Daydream"
—Lovin'
Spoonful

Funky

+/− You walk a fine line between fun and foolish. Rules like "always wear your seat belt" exist for a reason, so don't try to innovate.

YOU BELIEVE RULES WERE MADE TO BE BROKEN.

love match

It's great that you dream big, but you could use a solid and reliable honey to keep you grounded. A trustworthy and dependable Taurus will make sure that you don't lose sight of what really matters.

friend match

You love pranking people and pushing boundaries, which is why you need a practical Capricorn BFF to set you straight if you're heading for trouble.

September 6

If you were a game, you'd be poker: All about chance.
Those born on September 6 are extremely subject to coincidence and luck. It seems like life is always throwing you curveballs, and no matter how hard you swing, you just can't seem to knock it out of the park. Spontaneous and very focused on the present, you often get accused of not planning sufficiently.

BE PATIENT AND KEEP YOUR EYE ON THE PRIZE, AND YOU'RE BOUND TO GET A HOME RUN.

friend match

Your life goes up and down more often than a roller coaster, so it's important that your friends stay constant. Buddy up to a Leo who will never disappoint you, even when the going gets tough.

love match

Romance is super-important to you so look for a Scorpio who loves candlelit picnics and walks on the beach as much as you.

Magic 8-Ball

Stand-up comedian

"Accidentally in Love" —Counting Crows

+/− Just because something doesn't go your way, doesn't mean it wasn't "meant to be." Often, people make their own luck: Trust yourself and don't give up so easily when you hit a bump in the road.

Mock trial

Rihanna

Road trip

September 7

Determined, Competitive, Diligent

If you were a book, you'd definitely be in the self-help section, because you're all about achieving a personal best. You've got your eye on the prize—whether it's an A+, MVP, or the cute boy from science class—and there's nothing you like better than the feeling of struggling to get your way. In fact, you're more about the means than the ends. You don't trust anything that comes too easily. If it's worth anything, it must be worth fighting for.

+/− It is great that you set high standards, but every so often you need to make like an elastic waistband and loosen up.

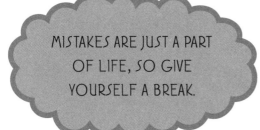

MISTAKES ARE JUST A PART OF LIFE, SO GIVE YOURSELF A BREAK.

love match

It's great that you always want more, more, more, but all that chasing after what's bigger and better just leaves you winded. You need a laid-back Aquarius who takes pleasure in the little things.

friend match

You and an ambitious Capricorn are both super-opinionated and intent on getting what you want. Your butt heads over everything from the last bagel to the front seat in the car, but you also encourage each other to do your best.

You could be a preacher, because you're all about keeping the faith. You stick up for your beliefs religiously, and you're just as loyal to your friends and family. You're not about walking the straight and narrow, though; original and inventive, you often forge your own path and have a tendency to keep secrets. Your heart is like the final frontier: Even your BFF has no clue what makes it beat faster.

Newspaper editor

Golden retriever

Pink

September 8

Serious, Stubborn, Dynamic

+/− There's another way that you're like a preacher: You're always telling people what to do! Understand and try to accept that other people have different beliefs and attitudes than you do. Variety is the spice of life.

love match

When it comes to matters of the heart, you're more mysterious than the contents of your school's hot dogs. A patient Gemini will take on the challenge of winning you over—and he'll have enough surprises of his own to keep you interested.

friend match

You love to have the last word, which means that fighting with you is about as fun as a three-hour extended calculus exam. But it pays to listen up, so count on a Libra BFF who will always give it to you straight.

September 9

You are under so much pressure you could be a barometer. It feels like no matter what you do you're always facing down difficult situations—from psycho phys ed teachers to ultra-demanding 'rents—but the truth is that most of the pressure you feel comes from within. Driven, confident, and influential, you've got a ton of power over your peeps and don't take that responsibility lightly.

Leather recliner

Pilates

Michelle Williams

YOU'RE ALWAYS PLAYING SOCIAL CO-ORDINATOR AND DOLING OUT SPOT-ON ADVICE.

+/− You might as well be on a treadmill, always running, running, running. Sometimes it takes the most confidence to be still and reflect, so don't be afraid of what will happen if you pause to look in the mirror. You're fabulous, so own it.

love match

You're super-independent, so you can't stand needy guys who want to check up on you all the time. A confident Taurus will let you do your own thing.

friend match

The last thing you need is a high-drama BFF who will stress you out with her 24/7 crises, so stick with a fun-loving Aries or totally chilled-out Gemini who will keep things mellow.

If your heart wore a sign, it would read, "No Trespassing."
Ultra-guarded, you keep your deepest thoughts, feelings, and wishes to yourself, and your desire for privacy extends to school and your social life: You won't try out for the school musical, but you'll be the crucial go-to girl behind the scenes. Secretly, though, you might long for the chance to break out of your shell.

WHETHER YOUR DEEPEST DESIRE IS TO JOIN THE TRACK
TEAM OR TO POST A SHORT FILM ON YOUTUBE,
SEIZE THE DAY AND GO FOR IT.

friend match

You can be very intense, **which is why you need the goofy influence of an Aries BFF. Whether she's cracking a sarcastic joke or just pulling a funny face, she'll always lighten the mood.**

Brown

College professor

B&B in Notting Hill

love match

It's true that opposites attract: You're attracted to creative and outgoing people with a wild streak. **Just be careful of falling for an artistic Aquarius who is flightier than an airplane; you need someone who will encourage your dreams, like a sweet and supportive Gemini.**

+/− Your teachers never have to tell you to pay attention: You're always taking notes. But try turning some of that attention on yourself.

September 11

Amusement park

Bohemian

"Crazy"
—Gnarls Barkley

Free-Spirited, Nurturing, Dramatic

If you were an awards show, you would definitely be the Oscars: all about dramatic choice. You always find yourself hitting a fork in the road and having to make big decisions on behalf of your friends and family. (Should you take a vacay to Disney World or the Bahamas?) Daring and fearless, you always follow the road less traveled (major highways are such a snooze!) and have a tendency to plunge headfirst into a new opportunity without giving much thought to the consequences.

+/− Other people may strike you as just like a Rubik's Cube: Impossible to crack, and probably not worth the effort. If you spent more time listening—and less time lecturing—you'd figure out what you're missing.

love match

You seem to be attracted to a carefree Aries whose motto is carpe diem. It's great that he lives for the moment, like you, but be careful that the two of you don't find yourself sharing a love seat in detention!

friend match

Your life is more high drama than the latest Hollywood blockbuster, and you could use the steadying (and practical) influence of a clear-headed, no-nonsense Virgo.

If you were a late 1990s catchphrase, you'd be, "word," because you're all about language and logic. Thoughtful and dedicated to truth, you mean what you say and you say what you mean. (And you'd make a killer journalist.) You're always checking up on your fave blogs (and updating your own), and even though you're not super-outgoing, you're naturally drawn to debate and argumentation.

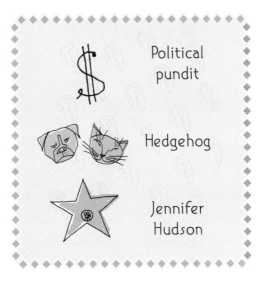

Political pundit

Hedgehog

Jennifer Hudson

September 12

Honorable, Witty, Fearless

+/− You should be careful of making promises to your friends and family that you just can't keep. (Like helping your mom spring clean and tutoring your BFF in the same weekend.) You're not a doctor, so there's no reason you always have to be on call.

love match

A super-logical Libra is always arguing with you on issues from the ethics of euthanasia to the best brand of cereal. He would be perfect for you, so turn the convo in another direction . . . like the best time for the two of you to catch a flick.

friend match

You have trouble setting boundaries, so an ultra-demanding BFF will just stress you out. An imaginative and independent Pisces, on the other hand, will give you space to do your own thing and inspire you to channel different energies.

September 13

You'd make a fierce boxer, because you're always ready to knock 'em out. Competitive and driven, you face down (and throw down!) any obstacle that gets in your way, whether it's your brownnosing rival for first chair in orchestra or a gigundo math final exam. Sometimes it seems like you were born under a lucky star: You're so good at getting your own way that to others it looks like magic.

> YOU KNOW THE REAL TRUTH: YOU MAKE YOUR OWN LUCK WITH DETERMINATION AND PERSEVERANCE.

Scarlet

ER doctor

Stella McCartney

+/− Your single-minded focus is admirable, but just like a pair of fitted jeans, sometimes the best way to be is relaxed. The weekends were invented for a reason, so don't spend the whole time studying or trying to perfect your soccer punt.

love match

When you like a guy, you're on it like a missile. Stand back, put down the big guns, and see what comes to you. An adorable and chilled-out Aquarius—the perfect antidote to your on, on, and on outlook—might be waiting for a break in the ammunition before approaching.

friend match

When you're on a mission, you can be pretty ruthless. You need a BFF who will remind you that not everything has to be do-or-die, like a silly, prank-loving Aries.

You should rename yourself Siskel or Ebert, because you're a natural-born critic. Ultra- perceptive, you feel the need to change and better the world around you, always suggesting different ways your school could improve homecoming (smoke machines! A Deejay instead of a band!) and dishing out advice to your friends and family.

 YOU'RE A TAKE-CHARGE KIND OF GIRL AND GET IMPATIENT WHEN OTHERS AREN'T EQUALLY ON THE BALL.

friend match

You're just like the Viper roller coaster: Not for the faint of heart. Surround yourself with confident Gemini and Leos, who aren't oversensitive and can give as good as they get.

Your blog

Amethyst

Environmental lobbyist

love match

Face it: You're not going to get excited about a guy who lays down and lets you walk all over him. You're not at Crate&Barrel, so why shop for a doormat? You need a guy who will stand up for himself, like a smart and opinionated Taurus.

$+/-$ You're used to being the commander in chief, but it can be fun to work as part of a crew now and then. When your pals decide they want to make a short film, volunteer to do the camera work.

❀ ❀ ❀ ❀ ❀

Concert in the park

Ballet

Polo shirts and cardigan sweaters

September 15

Expansive, Motivated, Ambitious

If you're a golf tournament, you will surely be the masters. Once you strike on a passion, you're determined to become the best at it. (Thus the gorgeous cashmere sweater you made during your knitting phase.) You're super-patient and can come across as shy, but people who mistake you for being happy to stay in the shadows had better  watch out—you're just waiting for your moment to claim your place in the sun.

+/− You dream of having a house so big it could feature on *MTV Cribs*, seven Bentleys, and a private plane to boot. But money won't make you laugh or give you a hug when you're feeling sad.

FOCUS YOUR AMBITIONS ON BEING A GOOD FRIEND, AND YOU'LL GET WAY MORE PAYBACK.

love match

You need a guy to show you the beauty in the simple things, like a sporty Sagittarius who loves hiking, biking, and just playing around outside—no credit card necessary, no drama allowed.

friend match

You can be super-closed off when somebody has hurt or disappointed you, but an ultra-perceptive Pisces will be able to tell when something's up.

You should be a cheerleader, because you're all about spirit. Energetic and dedicated, you never let life's bumps get you down for long, and your positive attitude means everyone wants to bask in your glow. You're always looking to do more, better, and you have the patience and determination to see the payoff. Your parents and teachers can have trouble controlling you, since you never back down when you feel your beliefs have been compromised. (Like your belief in a midnight curfew!)

Toy poodle

Prom committee

Alexis Bledel

September 16

Courageous,
Honest,
Sweet

YOU'RE USED TO GETTING WHAT YOU WANT.

+/− It's great that you're so fearless, but there's a fine line between spunk and stupidity. Make sure your energy doesn't pull you in a dangerous direction; keep both feet on the ground.

love match

Up until now you've always crushed on out-there Aries and ultra-outspoken Taurus, but a super-supportive Sagittarius will be a good mellowing influence.

friend match

When you want something, you'll go after it no matter what the risks. A diplomatic and practical Libra will let you know whether your endgame is worth all the trouble.

September 17

If slow and steady wins the race, somebody better be preparing your blue ribbon. Those born on September 17th are characterized by great perseverance. You are totally unstoppable when you have a goal, and though you may not take the fastest route to the finish line, in the end your sheer determination and force of will mean you'll come from behind to take the prize. (Even if "the prize" is the cute private school boy you've been scoping out in the park.) You seem serious to others, but you're more complex—and funny—than you sometimes let on.

DON'T LET YOUR INTENSE FOCUS TURN INTO TUNNEL VISION!

Maroon

Veterinarian

Rome

+/− You have high standards and can be quick to judge. But friends aren't teaspoons, so don't be so quick to say they don't measure up. Try seeing things from their perspective for once, and you just might learn something new about yourself.

love match

You're pretty independent, but that doesn't mean it wouldn't feel nice to be appreciated by a special someone. You like a guy who listens, so a patient, relationship-oriented Cancer is your best bet.

friend match

Spontaneous you are not, but when you're not playing Serious Student, you've got an offbeat sense of humor that craves expression. Look for a quirky Aries BFF to crack up with.

September 18

You're just like an iPhone: super-popular, you always create a public stir. (And it's a total mystery how you actually work.) Though people gravitate to you and you often find yourself at the center of attention, you're extremely secretive and closed off to all but the inner circle. And a position on your VIP list is never guaranteed: When you feel hurt, betrayed, or threatened, you can shut the door on even your closest friends. But when you're at your best, you really do light up a room.

love match

In a lot of ways an extremely private person, you're drawn to people with a similar penchant for secrecy: Like an artistic Pisces who knows the value of unspoken communication.

friend match

You and a temper-prone Scorpio are like a match held over a tin of explosives: The smallest spark, and everything blows up. Look for a more even-tempered Libra, who won't turn every disagreement into a major meltdown.

+/− You do not like conflict, **so** you'd rather withdraw than fight. But you're not a Crock-Pot, so why sit around stewing? When something upsets you, talk about it.

Ivory

School play

"Lucky"
—Britney Spears

$\$$ Wedding planner

French poodle

Jackie O

September 19

Tasteful, Elegant, Organized

You could easily be a beauty salon, because you're all about keeping up appearances. It's not just looks you care about (though you always look fab): Your room is always super-neat, and you'd never dream of turning in homework that wasn't triple-checked for accuracy. Some people accuse you of superficiality—but they're just jealous of your perfect hair. You know all about the importance of inner beauty, and have plenty of it to go around.

$+/-$ You are always looking for bigger and better things, but don't forget about the little people.

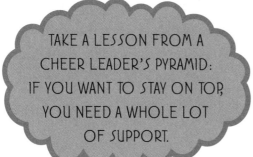

TAKE A LESSON FROM A CHEER LEADER'S PYRAMID: IF YOU WANT TO STAY ON TOP, YOU NEED A WHOLE LOT OF SUPPORT.

love match

Whenever a new cute boy walks through the doors, you catch a bad case of the Love Bug. Don't ignore the importance of loyalty and constancy—a Leo who has stood by as your friend all these years may be the real Prince Charming.

friend match

You need friends who will help you keep things in perspective (a bad hair day is not an excuse to skip school), like a totally together and infinitely practical Capricorn.

If you and your friends were in *Entourage,* you'd play the manager. You're always serving as social coordinator for your crew and mediating disputes between your two BFFs when they're squabbling. Super-social, diplomatic, and responsible, you're a great team player and an awesome friend. Although you're usually responsible and practical, when it comes to matters of the heart, you're always getting swept off your feet.

Christian Louboutin pumps

Candlelit dinner

Student council

September 20

Organized,
Shrewd,
Observant

FOR SOMEONE SO IN-THE-KNOW, YOU'RE CLUELESS WHEN IT COMES TO YOUR OWN FEELINGS.

+/− Everybody makes mistakes. (even you!) Rather than beating yourself up when you hit a snag, try to figure out what you can do differently next time.

love match

You fall head over heels so often they should have a private place for you in the ER. Make sure the trip is worth it: Look for a guy who's as caring and responsible as you, like a Taurus.

friend match

An Aquarius BFF can trust you to be 100 percent honest when she's in danger of going off the rails (a miniskirt and Puma sneakers is so not homecoming formal wear!), and you can count on her to help you laugh off your funks—she's always in a good mood.

September 21

If you were a body part, you'd be the tongue: All about good taste. You've got an eye for style and are always scoping out the newest trends, but you've got your finger on the pulse of more than just fashion. Perceptive and intuitive, you can always read how other people are feeling and know how to move—and motivate—a crowd.

> A TRUE TRENDSETTER, EVEN YOUR OPINIONS ARE ALWAYS *AU COURANT.*

The latest issue of *Vanity Fair*

Faith Hill

"Uptown Girl" —Billy Joel

+/− Appearance may be everything, but it's also true that the most attractive thing a girl can have is a whopping dose of self-confidence. It doesn't matter what your classmates think of you, so stop looking over your shoulder to see who's watching.

friend match

You've caught a bad case of the frenemies: Haters who try and make you feel insecure because they're jealous of your rocking style. Quick fix? Pick up a loyal (and honest) Cancer who won't undermine you.

love match

You change love interests more often than you change shoes. But certain people never go out of style, like the charming class-clown Aries who always makes you crack up.

September 22

You have got a bad case of restless legs syndrome: You always have to be moving. Driven, outgoing, and easily bored, you like to be challenged by new places, people, and things. You'll never hit the same restaurant twice, and the list of extracurriculars you've tried (and dumped) reads like an advertisement for attention deficit disorder. But no matter what you're doing, your strong personality and strength of character mean you always make your mark.

friend match

There's only one constant in your life: your friends. You're very picky about who you let get close, and a Sagittarius who likes to go, go, go is your perfect partner in crime.

love match

When you like someone, you act like you're gearing up for a military attack: Your motto is "Ready, set, charge." Give the cavalry a rest and let a laid-back Libra—who might just make you want to settle down (gasp!)—find his way to you.

Indigo

Travel writer

Las Vegas

+/− Good things come to those who wait, and sometimes the most important thing you can do is sit still. Take a break in your 24/7 marathon of activities to relax at home or spend some time daydreaming.

Libra Girls
love harmony and equality

Libra is represented by the scales because Libra ladies are all about balance. One of the most socially attuned signs of the zodiac, Librans feel the need to be in harmony with the people around them. They weigh their options carefully and can be seen as fickle because it's hard for them to commit. Ruled by Venus, they love beauty, fun, and the finer things in life. They can also be superficial and a little self-involved.

Most likely to be: Asked to homecoming by four different people.

Candy they most resemble: Sour Patch Kids— the perfect blend of tart and sweet.

Strengths to play on: Popularity, sense of fairness.

Pitfalls to avoid: Procrastination, inability to make choices.

Libra

September 23– October 22

Element: Air
Ruler: Venus

Motto: "Why do today
what you can
put off until tomorrow?"

September 23

In the MTV Movie Awards of life, you'd always take home the prize for Best Breakthrough Performance: Breaking all the barriers, surmounting difficulties, and crossing limits is your whole raison d'être. You are an ambitious dreamer: You want to be the best student/friend/teacher/clarinet player/soccer goalie ever but often seem to face major obstacles on your road to success.

> A TRUE WARRIOR, YOU NEVER GIVE UP AND YOUR PERSEVERANCE ALWAYS PAYS OFF.

Tangerine

Professional athlete

"Taking Chances" —Celine Dion

+/− You're just like a witch on a broomstick: Always flying off the handle. If you're going to do battle for something you want, do the prep work beforehand. Figure out your talking points and anticipate objections.

love match

You can be super-serious, so you need a guy who will lighten things up and inspire you to laugh off the tough times. An Aries with a cool here-for-the-party attitude will help you shake off the blues.

friend match

Maybe it's because of all the hard times you've seen, but people need a nutcracker just to break through your shell. Try letting the optimistic attitude of a happy-go-lucky Aquarius rub off on you.

You might as well be a passport, because you're always traveling around. You can't stand to sit still and love to dream up all the places you're going to visit (Costa Rica, Paris, Barcelona). Your philosophy is if you're not moving forward, you might as well be going in reverse. But it's not just your feet that peddle around: Mentally and spiritually, you were born to wander, to experiment with different interests and hobbies and to switch social groups faster than your old BFF can say, "Call me."

friend match

You treat friends like fish fillets: Good for three days at most. **The problem?** You haven't found your BFF soul mate, like a quirky Aquarius who loves to dream up new vacation destinations.

love match

You're ruled by the love-dominated number 6 and the planet Venus, so romance is important to you. An intense and passionate Scorpio will sweep you right off your feet.

Ice skating

Goldfish

Victoria Beckham

$+/-$ You can't help that you're bored easily. But you're flightier than an airplane, and sometimes when the going gets tough, it's important to rough it out.

INSTEAD OF RUNNING FROM CHALLENGES, EMBRACE THEM.

September 25

$ Gossip columnist

★ Catherine Zeta-Jones

Retro

Hard-Working, Witty, Determined

You'd be the perfect judge on *American Idol*: You love to be in the spotlight, and your greatest talent lies in critiquing and exposing flaws. Naturally inclined to journalism and photography, you're always blogging about ways your school could improve. (Starbucks in the cafeteria, anyone?) You can be extremely sarcastic and anyone who's ever been on the wrong side of one of your scathing jokes knows that when it comes to you, the tongue is mightier than the sword.

+/− Your sarcastic sense of humor leaves all your friends ROTFL. But be careful about tossing out caustic commentary super-casually, since you never know who could be the next casualty. (And your teacher will not be amused by your impression of her.)

love match

They **say** you catch more flies with honey than vinegar. **Obviously you don't want insects buzzing around, but every so often give your tongue-lashings a rest and let the Aquarius you're crushing on see the sweet side.**

friend match

You work your butt off, **so on weekends take a break to hang out with a Capricorn BFF. She's got a good sense of the big picture, so she'll keep you from feeling overwhelmed.**

If practice makes perfect, then you're a perfect 10. A complete perfectionist and highly critical of yourself and others, you believe if you're going to do something, you should do it right. Your clothes, report card—even your sock drawer!—are all totally flawless, and you serve as an example and inspiration to your friends.

YOUR MOTTO IS "TRY, TRY AGAIN," AND WHETHER OR NOT YOU FIRST SUCCEED, IN THE END YOU ALWAYS GET WHAT YOU WANT.

Lemon

Choir

Serena Williams

September 26

Persistent, Secretive, Satirical

+/− You've got a lot of wisdom to share and enjoy playing teacher to your friends. But they're already in school seven hours a day: They don't need extra classes. Loosen up and let them instruct you once in a while—in the subject of fun, for example.

love match

You clam up around guys because you're worried about coming across as stupid. But there is no Flirtation Script, so you can't miss a line. Look for a Leo who will make you feel comfortable.

friend match

You are so responsible, sometimes it feels like you should skip straight to your eighteenth birthday. But everyone deserves the chance to play five-year-old, so cozy up to a hilarious Gemini who will teach you the values of finger painting and food fighting.

216

September 27

You're just like Spider-Man, always trying to play the hero. You're extremely driven and set the bar so high you might as well be a pole-vaulter, and any little slipup leaves you feeling blue. Although from the outside you look like you have it totally together, because you're unable to cut yourself a break, you're often troubled by feelings of insecurity.

SENSITIVE AND INDEPENDENT, YOU STICK CLOSE TO A SMALL GROUP OF TRUSTED FRIENDS.

$$+/-$$ **Remember not to sweat the small stuff.** Everyone makes mistakes: Don't dwell on yours. Nobody expects you to be perfect, so try relaxing your own standards and you'll be much better off.

love match

You're A+ at everything except loosening up and having fun. Aquarians are known for their open and joyful attitudes, so a boy born around Valentine's Day just might give you much-needed tutoring.

friend match

You need a BFF who is just like a calculator: You can always count on her. A Taurus who is fiercely loyal is the obvious choice. Even better, she'll give you a lift when you're feeling down on yourself.

You should be arrested for vandalism, because you're always breaking hearts. You rock what you got, and people want what you rock: Your undeniable charm and over-the-top confidence mean that you've got people swooning for you all over town. Ironically, though you look for strength in other people, you're always making (not-so-grown) men—and former BFFs—cry. Of course it's not on purpose! But admit it: you savor the attention.

A DIE-HARD ROMANTIC, YOU'RE A BIG
FAN OF ALL THE FINER THINGS IN LIFE.

friend match

You have a lot of star power, so you need a BFF who can hold her own when it's time to shine. Look for an ambitious and high-octane Leo who will serve as more than your wingman.

$ TV star

Naomi Watts

Couture

love match

You treat guys like sidewalks: Made to be walked on. For someone to stand out he'd better not act like a doormat. You need the strength and toughness of a supermasculine Taurus.

+/− You tend to have a tremendous influence on other people, but with great power comes great responsibility. Keep in mind that when you make a cutting comment about your friend's new hairdo, she'll be totally devastated, so think before you speak.

September 29

Jade

Photography

Chow Chow

Technical, Intense, Capable

If you were a piece of exercise equipment, you'd be the stability ball: always trying to find balance. Your mood has more swings than a typical playground, and you often go from feeling like you're on top of the world to feeling like the world's sitting on top of you. Although you're supersmart and extremely accomplished, you're plagued by doubts about your self-worth.

+/− Part of the reason why your emotions are so all over the map is that you don't really know what you want. Pretend you're an algebra problem, and dedicate time to figuring yourself out.

IT'S EXTREMELY IMPORTANT TO STAY CLOSE TO FAMILY AND FRIENDS WHO MAKE YOU FEEL VALUED.

love match

A sensitive and perceptive Pisces will understand and accept you intuitively— no embarrassing confessions necessary!

friend match

Nothing's more important for you than having loyal friends close by who can serve as a stabilizing influence. Pick an Aries who will always make you smile, and a Taurus to be your rock during hard times.

219

You should be a detective, because you're all about uncovering the truth. A perfectionist, you always do your homework before expressing your opinion. (And you have a lot of opinions.) Whether you're holding court about melting polar ice caps or the importance of flax seed oil, you're an idealist who likes to get behind a cause.

A NATURAL LEADER, YOU HAVE A FORCEFUL PRESENCE AND KNOW HOW TO COMMAND PEOPLE'S ATTENTION.

September 30

Curious, Knowledgeable, Impressive

+/− You're just like an encyclopedia: You've got all your facts together. But some issues aren't a matter of right or wrong, so don't freak out when others don't agree with what you say. They're entitled to their own opinions.

love match

You like a guy with smarts—and he needs to be confident, too, if he's going to keep up with you. Sparks will fly when you start arguing with a brainy Aquarius—good thing you can always kiss and make up!

friend match

You tend to be super-defensive—and you're not shy about going on the attack, either. Take a lesson from a chilled-out Libra, who can teach you how to play nice with others.

October 1

You should compete for

Best in Show, because you're all about being top dog. It's not that you're aggressive or overly ambitious, but your clear head and ability to see the whole picture make you stand out from your peers. You're naturally social and like to be surrounded by a small group of fans (um, friends) all the time. Your

philosophy? There's no point in being leader unless you're leader of a pack.

RELAX AND HAVE FAITH IN YOURSELF.

Dolce and Gabbana eyeglasses

Head of a cosmetics company

Power suit

+/− Generally, you've got a ton of confidence. But because you're a perfectionist, you're also plagued by fears that you'll never be good enough. All your stressing is a recipe for failure.

love match

You've got your own ambitions (like being elected class prez), so you don't have time for a me, me, me Taurus. A super-supportive Aquarius, on the other hand? Vote yes.

friend match

You value the way an earth-sign friend sticks by you and she values your uniqueness and fearlessness. You help her strut her stuff, and she helps keep you grounded.

October 2

You're just like Z100: When you're on, everyone tunes in to listen. Charming, persuasive, and allergic to sugarcoating, you always say exactly what you feel—even if the truth hurts. (Your BFF had to know that her lime-green coat was puke-worthy.) But it's not like you're always running your mouth; you say only what you need to say to get your point across, making you the top choice for Debate Club president, and a fierce enemy.

YOU'VE GOT A
SERIOUSLY SARCASTIC SIDE.

friend match

You can't stand girls who play dumb, so look out for a smart and sassy Scorpio who can more than match you in a game of verbal sparring.

Crimson

Comedy club

"Honestly" —Cartel

love match

You appreciate an up-front attitude and despise game playing, so a mischievous Aquarius who keeps his feelings hidden will leave you feeling cold. A straight-up, cards-on-the-table Taurus is the perfect remedy.

+/− Be careful that people do not mistake your bark for a bite. It's great that you have got such a strong sense of humor, but you have to make sure everybody is laughing with you.

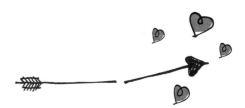

October 3

Latest issue of *Nylon*

Maltese

Yoga

+/− You're so focused on what other people think of you, you lose sight of the only opinion that really counts: your own. Self-confidence will always be fashionable, so take time to work on yours.

Intense, Hip, Influential

You should be the host of Project Runway: You always know what's in and what's out. Über-trendy and super-fashionable, you're also a social butterfly constantly IMing and texting. You need to stay up-to-date on the latest gossip just as badly as you need the latest dress from fashion week. In fact, staying *aucourant* is a major driving force in your life, but that doesn't mean it's always out with the old.

YOU VALUE OLD TRADITIONS, GOOD FRIENDS, AND FAMILY TIME

love match

You may like the way a fire-sign hottie looks in his soccer jersey, but you need a relationship that's based on more than a mutual love of the mirror. Try a laid-back Aquarius who actually listens.

friend match

Your b-day-party invite list reads like a who's who of all the big names at school, but watch out for frenemies masquerading as friends. You know when push comes to shove, a loyal Libra has got your back.

You're just like the girl with the little curl: When you're good, you're very, very good, and when you're bad, you're horrid. You always do exactly what you want, which can bring you into conflict with the people around you (especially the 'rents). But you're so charming that you usually get your way. You're super-social and your friends admire you for your unique point of view and your ability to lead by example. But you could use a yoga session or three to learn something about flexibility.

+/− It's great that you're confident and always giving yourself a pat on the back, but sometimes what you really need is a kick in the butt.

Dance captain

"Trouble" —Pink

Sailing in Tahiti

October 4

Funny, Stubborn, Social

DON'T BE SATISFIED WITH THE BARE MINIMUM; PUSH YOURSELF TO ACHIEVE MORE.

love match

Sparks will fly between you and an equally hot-tempered Scorpio, but all those explosions will just lead to a blowout. You need a fun-loving and social Aries who will let you take the lead.

friend match

You definitely don't need a BFF who's going to bring out your bad side, so stay away from a prank-pulling Aquarius who's always parked in detention. Instead, stick close to a sweet-tempered Leo.

October 5

You're like a one-woman court of law: You're determined that there'll be justice for all. Your deep sense of honesty means you're determined to bring the truth to light, whether you're exposing your little bro as a cookie-stealing culprit or staging a rally to warn people about the dangers of global warming. You  have a tendency to put the causes you support ahead of your personal happiness, but you're not all work and no play.

$ Lawyer for the ACLU

Rescued dog

Kate Winslet

YOU LOVE TO HAVE FUN.

+/− Life isn't fair, and it's great that you want to change that. But don't waste your energy on losing battles. (Like whether you can sleep over at your BFF's house when her parents are out of town.)

LIKE A GARDENER, LEARN TO PICK AND CHOOSE!

love match

You have a tendency to lecture, so if it seems like your crushes are always tuning you out, maybe it's time to try listening . . . and go for a sweet Sagittarius who admires your strong opinions.

friend match

You consider yourself independent, but the truth is you like a solid crew to back up your cause du jour. Look for a Libra who shares your sense of fairness.

If you were a bumper sticker, you'd say, "Seize the Day": You're all about living life to the fullest, and no matter what snags you hit (like massive amounts of homework or nagging younger sibs), you're determined that nothing's going to get in the way of your good time. You're fatally allergic to boredom, so you seek out adventure and excitement. Deeply romantic, you fall head over heels so often it's amazing you don't have a permanent concussion.

friend match

You want a BFF who knows how to keep the good times rolling. A unique and confident Gemini will keep things lively, but will also be a perfect movie buddy on the (rare) occasions you want to veg.

love match

You fall hard and fast, so you better make sure the tumble is worth it. A lively and intelligent Aquarius makes the perfect plus one to a party, and will also provide a mellowing influence when your life is getting too crazy.

Fuchsia

Rock climbing

Harajuku

+/− You are definitely a glass-half-full kind of girl, but it's okay to give in to the blues every now and then. If you try to be Miss Suzy Sunshine 24/7, you are bound to burn out.

"Go Green" tank top

Debate team

Rachel McAdams

October 7

Committed, Idealistic, Charming

If you were a movie, you'd be *Rebel with a Cause.* You're always fighting for something—whether it's cruelty-free lip gloss or longer lunch periods—and even though you're often in trouble with 'rents and teachers, people can't help but admire your fire. You're a strong believer in honesty and have a reputation for bluntness, but you're so charming (and well-intentioned) that people usually forgive even your most outrageous observations.

+/− You might as well be deaf, 'cuz you never listen. You can't stand when people tell you what to do, but keep in mind that your teachers and parents may be piping up with opinions that will actually help you.

☆ • ☆ • ☆ • ☆

love match

You and an equally rebellious Scorpio will go together like a marshmallow in a microwave: hot and unexpected, with a tendency to explode. If you both keep a wrap on your temper, you can avoid the blowups.

friend match

You're constantly getting into scrapes, and you need a BFF who's going to stick by your side when your parents (or the cops!) crack down on your latest protest, like an ultra-loyal Leo.

If you were a date, you'd be a hot-air balloon ride: romantic, unusual, and all about reaching new heights. It seems you fall head over heels for a new crush every week, but it's not just a killer smile and a set of dimples that make your insides shivery. You see the beauty in the world around you, and get just as excited about a gorgeous sunset or the mystery of the tides as you do about basketball-playing cuties.

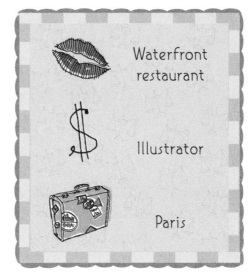

Waterfront restaurant

$

Illustrator

Paris

October 8

YOU'RE PASSIONATE AND FREE-SPIRITED.

Imaginative, Romantic, Capable

+/− People need a passport just to get in touch with you, because you're often off in your own world. Daydreaming is fine, but learn to touch down in the real world every so often. Your friends and fam miss you!

love match

You've got a poet's soul, and no one's a better match for you than an ulra-artistic, sensitive, and perceptive Pisces, who will share your love of deep conversation and traditional romance.

friend match

A sarcastic Scorpio may rub some people the wrong way, but you love her off-beat sense of humor and passion for trouble. Nice is all well and good, but you like to keep things spicy.

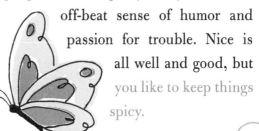

October 9

Multi-talented, Observant, Inspirational

If you had a superpower, it would be X-ray vision: You can see straight through people. Incredibly perceptive, you have intuition about what other people are thinking and feeling that comes from the heart, not the head; you really care. People send the love right back your way; you have a ton of friends and not-so-secret admirers. Although artistically inclined, you've got a superphysical side and often need to shake it on the dance floor.

Pink

Teen help line

Quiet ranch in Montana

TAKE TIME TO SORT YOUR FEELINGS OUT.

+/− As spot-on as you are when it comes to figuring out what's going on with your friends and family, you're way off when it comes time to turn the eye inward. Your feelings are like your closet: A big old mess.

❋ ❋ ❋ ❋ ❋

love match

A lot of guys are intimidated by you, but don't dismiss a sensitive Cancer who likes to hang back as one of them—he may be quiet, but he's got the inner strength to more than match your own.

friend match

In your group of friends you naturally take the lead, so the most important thing to watch out for is backstabbing, which is why you have your loyal Leo BFF to keep your followers in line.

If you were a bag, you'd be a woven tote made from recycled plastic bottle caps: You're all about doing more with less. Inventive and practical, you're excellent at multitasking and managing your time and have been saving up your allowance since you were three. (Guess who'll be rocking a Beamer by her sweet sixteenth!) A natural born problem solver, whether your BFF has a curling-iron crisis or a homework meltdown, you're the one she calls.

YOUR FACE MIGHT AS WELL BE LISTED
NEXT TO "RESPONSIBLE" IN THE DICTIONARY.

friend match

There's no harm in letting someone help you loosen up. Look for a fun-obsessed Aries with a huge social network.

love match

When it comes to relationships, you'll pass on the drama. Instead go for a practical and ambitious Sagittarius who admires how you're always playing Ms. Fix-It with real-life problems.

Krazy Glue

Persian
cat

Coco
Chanel

$+/-$ It's great that you're cautious with your time, energy, and cash. (Let's face it—none of it grows on trees.) But there's no harm in having a blowout once in a while, so don't be afraid to give a little.

October 11

iPhone

Cocktail party

Michelle Trachtenberg

+/− Like a musician, you like to keep things harmonious. You avoid problems like the plague—but that also means that you don't take chances.

YOU'LL NEVER DISCOVER YOUR LOVE OF THAI FOOD— OR A NATURAL TALENT FOR FIELD HOCKEY—IF YOU'RE AFRAID TO TRY NEW THINGS.

Charming, Accepting, Secure

If you were a snack cake company, you'd be Hostess. You see it as your role to bring people together and make them feel comfortable, and you're never happier than when you're socializing at a friend's pool party or organizing an impromptu mall trip for your girlfriends. Supersweet and easygoing, you can't stand to be alone and are always seeking out fun, but that doesn't mean you're a risk taker. In fact, you're not a fan of changing it up.

love match

You dream of finding True Love Forever. You might think a mischievous Scorpio with a talent for trouble is too rebellious for you, but deep down he's as sweet and loyal as they come—and just as romantic as you!

friend match

You're all about giving people second chances, but if you're always getting stepped on by a self-centered Leo, then it's time to give her the boot. Friendship is like traffic: It flows best when it goes both ways.

You should be a musical, because you're all about the show stopping performance. Extroverted, talkative, generous, and fun, you're always looking to do things Bigger and Better: You throw the best parties, you give the best gifts, you have the juiciest secrets. But you're not just a social butterfly. You're extremely smart and can't stand airheads and flakes.

YOU LIKE TO BE SURROUNDED BY *LA CRÈME DE LA CRÈME.*

Periwinkle

Screenwriter

Glamorous

October 12

Social, Generous, Dependable

+/− The whole world is your stage, and you are definitely making the most of your time in the spotlight. Remember to keep other people's feelings in mind, and be careful not to treat your friends like your fan club—or else you're bound to get booed!

love match

You're smart without feeling the need to flaunt it, and people who are always bragging (like a pretentious Sagittarius) make you feel queasy. A breezily intelligent Aquarius is a much better bet.

friend match

You may come across as superficial, but actually you despise people who are all about surface. A supersweet Cancer might not share your love of socializing, but your connection will run deep.

October 13

You're like an Oreo that's been left out too long: one tough cookie. You always go for the gold—no ifs, ands or buts—and you can't stand whiners and, quitters. You're a super-serious student and fierce competitor (whether you're vying for the title of MVP on your summer soccer league or trying to land a date with the cutest boy in school); nobody wants to get in your way. You make a frightening enemy: The words "forgive" and "forget" aren't in your vocab.

> GIVE YOURSELF A VACATION AND RELAX ONCE IN A WHILE.

Any black-tie event

Class president

Bulldog

+/− It pays off that you treat school like a job (all those As!), but you're a briefcase away from acting like a straight-up fifty-year-old. Loosen up and have some fun!

love match

You never give second chances, but you'll have to take it easy on a serious and sincere Cancer who's doing his best. He's not a mind reader, so give him time to get close to you before you write him off.

friend match

You don't win any warm and fuzzy awards for first impressions—the truth is, you're shy deep down so can often come across as standoffish. A perceptive Pisces will know how to break through your barriers.

October 14

If you were weather, you'd be an even 75 degrees: Moderate and comfortable, you leave the highs and lows to other people. It's important for you to avoid extremes. You keep disappointments from turning into major meltdowns, and you know that just because your crush shoots a smile your way, it's no excuse to start planning your wedding (unlike some of your friends). Practical and reserved, you often seem older than your years.

friend match

You're so together, you make Martha Stewart look like a hot mess. But every so often you should let a giggly, fun-addict Aries help you tap into your inner child.

love match

You're not the most outgoing person in the world, which is why a romance between you and an equally reserved Virgo never gets off the ground. Love is about risk, so take a chance on a passionate and expressive Scorpio.

Northface backpack

Tan

Summer house in the Hamptons

+/− Moderation in all things is a good philosophy in theory, but there are some things—like laughter and dark chocolate—it's Okay to OD on once in a while.

LET YOURSELF INDULGE MORE OFTEN.

October 15

Music critic

Beagle

If it doesn't have sparkles, you're not interested!

Magnetic, Knowledgeable, Challenging

You're just like a dog, always laying claim to your territory. Surprise! Your fave place to stake out is usually right in the middle of the spotlight, though you're not just about upstaging your peeps. You've got more personal attraction than a magnet, so when you speak, people listen up. You may not get voted Miss Congeniality any time soon, but you're a lock-in for Miss Honesty.

YOU GET PROPS FOR BEING A GREAT LEADER AND TEAM MEMBER.

+/− Like the eye of a tornado, you're always in the middle of a storm. It's great that you do your own thing no matter what, but a little bit of compromise can go a long way when it comes time to smooth over a rough patch with a disappointed friend or a scandalized teacher.

love match

You've got plenty of admirers, but for a guy to move up on your Most Wanted list he's got to be laid-back and smart, an overachiever and a social dynamo. Luckily, a January-born boy meets all the requirements.

friend match

You're always on the go, and sometimes things get so crazy you have trouble keeping your feet on the ground. Count on a down-to-earth, balanced Libra to do it for you.

If you had your own TV show, it would be just like *Judge Judy*. You've got a million opinions, and you're always making the call—about whether a new hairstyle is fabulous or frightening, or whether a boy is the real deal or counterfeit. But that doesn't mean you're inclined to judge a book by its cover. You're open to other people and different opinions; it's just that you've got a talent for sizing up the situation in a snap.

Hybrid car

Walk in the park

After-school job at a clothing store

October 16

Discriminating, Practical, Fair

+/− You like to practice what you preach, but you could use a little sermon on pushing yourself. Don't be afraid to test your own limits and try something—like advanced trig or basketball—that you haven't done before.

love match

Since you're ruled by Venus, you know how to turn on the charm, but you're also down-to-earth and looking for someone with more than a cute smile. Let your instincts lead you to a laid-back Libra with his priorities in order. (In other words, you first!)

friend match

A super-indecisive Gemini will count on you to give her guidance, and her crazy inventive ideas (like a coed finger-painting party) will help you break out of the same old, same old.

October 17

If life were a circus, you'd be the tightrope walker: all about balance. You try to walk the straight and narrow, but at heart you're a daredevil, which means you're always doing the seesaw between keeping your feet on the ground and flying off to find adventure. You love to take chances (and aren't afraid of a few slipups), and because of your self-confidence, you make like a cat and always manage to land on your feet.

Violet

Field hockey captain

London

+/− They say that pride comes before a fall, and unless you change your self-satisfied attitude, you're bound to take a major tumble soon. Don't be afraid to admit when you're wrong. Mistakes are like back pimples: Everyone's had a few, even if no one admits it.

love match

You love the thrill of the chase, but if a secretive Scorpio is giving you the runaround, bid him *hasta la vista*. An Aries is quirky and spontaneous enough to keep things interesting, but he won't lead you on a wild-goose chase.

friend match

You want a BFF, not a parole officer, so stay away from uptight Virgo and conservative Cancer. But you also need someone who gives it to you straight, like a loyal and straight-shooting Leo.

You're just like a telescope, always looking ahead.

A natural leader due to your supercharged energy and over-the-top ambition, you'd also make a great motivational speaker: You've got the imagination to dream big, but you know how to keep it real. You're not just about being on the top of your game, though.

YOU HAVE A DEEP PASSION FOR YOUR PRIVATE INTERESTS, AND WHETHER YOUR HOBBY IS BAKING OR BADMINTON, YOU ALWAYS TAKE SOLO TIME TO ENJOY IT.

friend match

You can be a little shy around new people. That's why you need to stick with a fire-sign socialite who can help you navigate your way around any party.

love match

Even though you come across as confident, when it comes to guys you often go Jell-O. Let an Aquarius who starts off as a friend appreciate your sweetness, and the romance will follow.

Friendship bracelet

Documentary filmmaker

Casual

+/− *Non. Nyet. Nein.* No. It's an important word, so get familiar with it in as many languages as possible, and then don't be afraid to bust it out when your BFF is nagging you for homework help or your shady ex "just wants to catch up."

October 19

Yellow

Columnist for your school newspaper

"So What" —Pink

Open, Independent, Lively

You better like the taste of sock, because you are always putting your foot in your mouth. Totally outspoken and opinionated, you have a tendency to blurt out whatever you're thinking. Your policy of brutal honesty may get you into a lot of trouble, but people have to respect you for always saying what you mean and meaning what you say.

YOU CAN'T STAND LIARS AND FAKES, AND YOUR IDEA OF SERIOUS TORTURE IS GETTING (OR GIVING!) THE SILENT TREATMENT.

+/− You blow up faster than a volcano. But you cool off just as quickly, and when you fight with your BFFs. the damage is never long-lasting. Life's too short to hold grudges.

love match

Admit it: You love attention. There's no harm in a little bit of flirtation, but make sure you don't spread yourself too thin—and miss out on an adorable Aquarius who's looking to be your one and only.

friend match

You can't stand when people keep secrets from you, so stay away from Pisces and Scorpio, who tend to be some of the most private signs. Stick with a tell-it-like-it-is Taurus or an honesty-only Virgo.

If you were a classic Madonna song, you'd be "Vogue." You always know what's in and what's out, but you're more interested in setting the trends than in following them, which means you're often slightly out of step with your peers. Your style, beliefs, and opinions place you firmly in the avant-garde. You would rather be admired than accepted, and your desire to be influential is so strong that you take criticism like a two-year-old takes a calc test: badly. Take out those ear phones and listen to the feedback once in a while.

October 20

Enthusiastic, Logical, Influential

+/− Your spirit animal might be the mule, because you are super-stubborn. Once you get an idea in your head, you can become obsessive about it, but knowing when to let go will save you lots of headaches in the end.

love match

When you fall for a guy who's strongly influenced by Mercury, you'll be in and out of fashion so often it will make your head spin. Time to vote him off and stick with a more stable and forward-thinking Capricorn.

friend match

Sometimes you feel like no one understands you. Thank God for an artistic and original Pisces who completely appreciates the methods behind the madness.

October 21

If you were a word, you'd be "supercalifragilisticexpialidocious": imaginative, unique, and totally original. You march to the beat of a different drummer, and though you're extremely smart and quick-thinking, you have a deeply emotional side that often gets you into trouble. (You're just like a soccer goalie, always on offense). But on the surface you can be ultra-charming and agreeable.

Saffron

"That's Just the Way We Roll" —Jonas Brothers

Trekking through the Amazon

+/− Here's a more basic word you need to get familiar with: "acceptance." You have a tendency to be supercritical of your friends and family, especially when you feel they've let you down. Remember, nobody's perfect!

YOU CAN'T STAND BEING TOLD WHAT TO DO AND ARE ALWAYS LOOKING TO SET YOUR OWN RULES.

friend match

There are a ton of people who wish they were in your inner circle, but that place is reserved for a trustworthy Leo, who has the two qualities you value most in a friend: honesty and loyalty.

love match

You can be extremely stubborn, so stay away from a Taurus who will just want to butt heads. At the same time, you hate pushovers. Find balance with a self-assured Libra who knows how to compromise.

If you were a magazine, you'd be Allure: *You're naturally* magnetic and appealing. The theme of attraction is dominant in your life. You've got people falling over themselves for you just like a set of dominoes, and you have a similar tendency to get swept off your feet. But for the most part you leave the loving to your admirers and keep your emotions under wraps. You often find yourself controlling other people—and situations—by keeping your cool.

friend match

You can be a little crazy, so you need your super-steady Capricorn to bring you back to earth once in a while. It's a fair trade: You bring the spice to her life.

love match

When it comes to love, you like to think you know just how close you can get to fire without getting burned. But a magnetic Scorpio who's as skilled in the art of charming as you will crank up the heat.

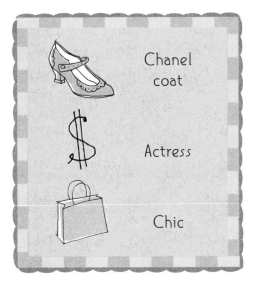

Chanel coat

$ Actress

Chic

+/− Life is not a power struggle, so it shouldn't be all about control. A constant game of tug-of-war is going to land you nowhere but flat on your butt.

LOOSEN UP AND LET PEOPLE SEE THE REAL YOU.

Scorpio Girls

are passionate, dynamic, and explosive

Ruled by the dark body Pluto, Scorpio girls are a coloring book's worst nightmare: They never stay inside the lines. Passionate, dynamic, and explosive. They crave the best things in life but they also veer toward the creative, different, and bizarre. Deep thinkers, they are secretive, serious, and can be overcome by pessimism. They make intense friends and tempestuous enemies—"forgive and forget" is not in their vocabulary.

* *

Most likely to be: Breaking curfew.

Theme Song: "Gimme More." (And more and more and more . . .)

Strengths to play on: Creativity, passion.

Pitfalls to avoid: Recklessness, anger.

Scorpio

* * * * * * * * * * * * * * * *

October 23–
November 21

Element: Water

Ruler: Pluto

Dessert item they
most resemble:
Dark chocolate.
Irresistible, decadent,
and sinful.

October 23

You should be part of an improv troupe, because you're all about thinking on the fly. Spontaneous and energetic, you get bored easily and are always looking for excitement. You can't stand planning in advance and are always ready to see where the week takes you. No matter how hard you try to find balance, you often feel like you're playing on a seesaw: If one part of your life is going well, another part is bottoming out.

Lime green

Travel writer

Tarantula

+/− You're just like the cream filling of an Oreo cookie: always in the middle of something. Your friends don't need you to get involved with their fights, so learn to look away when a conflict doesn't involve you.

> YOU HAVE A LOT OF GREAT QUALITIES, BUT STABILITY IS NOT ONE OF THEM.

love match

Nothing bores you more than the same old dinner-and-a-movie routine, so be on the lookout for an artistic Pisces whose idea of "date night" involves breaking into the aquarium with a picnic basket.

friend match

You need a rational and quick-thinking Capricorn BFF who can talk you down when you're on the verge of a blowup.

October 24

You should be a magnifying glass, since the two major themes of your life are discovery and detail. Deeply curious about the world around you, you're an excellent and serious student and a deeply attentive friend. But you're not happy unless you can share your "Eureka!" moments with a wide social circle. The last thing you want is to be shut up in a room with your nose in a book.

friend match

Your mouth is like a broken door: It just won't stay shut. **A fellow water sign ruled by the mellowing influence of Neptune, like a Pisces girl, can help you learn to go with the flow.**

> YOU LIKE TO SHARE YOUR THOUGHTS AND OPINIONS WITH OTHERS.

love match

The one thing you keep to yourself? Your crushes. You are terrified of rejection, so you prefer to keep your feelings under wraps, but a patient Leo with a talent for listening might be the guy to spill your secrets, (and give your heart) to.

Bronze

Museum

Archeologist

$+/-$ In the Radio Shack of life, you play the remote control. You're always trying to dictate what your friends and fam are up to and love to have power over your peeps. Remember, your loved ones aren't playthings, so hit the off button on that attitude.

October 25

Prom
committee

Katy
Perry

San
Francisco

* * * * * * * * * * * * * * * *

Physical, Substantial, Dependable

You should be set in the middle of an engagement ring, because you're just like a rock. Solid and dependable, you're always there when your friends need a shoulder to cry on, and no matter what crisis comes your way, you'll be sure to have your feet on the ground. You're ruled by the themes of form and structure.

+/− You have a tendency to get stuck like superglue in your habits and routines. It's fine to have a comfort zone, but it's not fine to give up on expanding it. Try to do things that frighten and challenge you.

YOU'RE AN EXCELLENT PLANNER AND ORGANIZER AND DESPISE FLAKES AND SPACE CADETS.

love match

Some people thrive on roller-coaster romances, but you're looking for more of a smooth ride. There's no question that you should cozy up with a Leo or a Taurus, two of the zodiac's most grounded signs.

friend match

A Gemini, ruled by the changeable Mercury, is as flaky as you are reliable and drives you crazy with broken plans and missed engagements. Virgo, an earth sign, shares a Gemini's traits of fun and independence without all the drama.

If life were a marathon, you'd be the Nike Air Pegasus shoe: You make things run more smoothly. You'd make an amazing event planner, because you're excellent at organizing and bringing people together. Good thing you're already getting practice: A natural leader, you're always hosting the best b-day bashes and organizing food drives for the local soup kitchen. You're independent but feel the happiest when you're working for the greater good.

Cream

Class social chair

Blair Waldorf

October 26

Organized, Astute, Active

+/− It's great that you work so hard, but don't forget to make time for your friends. That A+ on your bio test looks good hanging from a fridge but won't giggle with you for hours or give you a hug when you need one.

love match

You have an ambitious side and you need a guy who's content to let you step into the spotlight, like a super-supportive Sagittarius who doesn't mind playing arm candy to your A-list star power.

friend match

Though she couldn't organize her way out of a paper bag, your Gemini BFF is your fave party-planning assistant. She's a social butterfly, like you, and plus, while you are stressing out about color coordinating plates and napkins, she reminds you that it's supposed to be fun!

October 27

Ready and Aim got nothing on you: You're all about Fire. Dynamic and impulsive, your moods swing from scorching temper to sunny optimism to fiery passion, which means it's almost impossible for your friends to predict what you're going to do next. Spontaneous as well as creative, you're always trying to give the impression of dependability when in fact you often feel totally off balance.

Kleenex

Gymnastics

Secluded spa with your BFFs

THE SUPPORT OF CLOSE FRIENDS AND FAM IS CRUCIAL TO YOU.

+/− When it comes to your emotions, you're just like dark chocolate—superintense. It's crucial that you learn to express yourself. If you try to keep your feelings on lockdown, it will end with a breakdown.

love match

You come across as strong and independent, but you're very sensitive to rejection and are deeply afraid of opening up to someone else. Avoid the influences of Venus and quick-changing Mercury, and look for a generous, talkative Leo.

friend match

You need a friend who can weather your mood swings and keep you calm when you're about to blow. An even-keeled Aquarius or a diplomatic Libra can help you keep things mellow.

You should have been a Boy Scout, because your motto is "Always be prepared." Cautious, serious, and smart, you like to know how things work, and you never try anything—whether it's a new exercise regime or a different kind of frozen yogurt—without doing all your research. Your parents never have to nag you to do your homework, and you're a classic overachiever, but one kind of activity is missing from your miles-long to-do list: Fun.

friend match

Opposites attract, and your life is definitely in need of some dramatic reversals. Buddy up with an explosive, spontaneous, and always-on-the-go Aries and unearth your inner troublemaker.

love match

An overachieving Aquarius with a ton of social clout may seem uninterested in you, but the truth is you don't exactly come across as warm and fuzzy. Dig your nose out of the books and try giving him a smile.

$$+/-$$ You've got everything planned, from your college of choice to your honeymoon destination (Bali!). Often the best part of an exciting road trip is the unexpected detours.

ALLOW YOURSELF TO
WANDER OFF THE PATH.

October 29

Cherry
Blossom

Foreign-film
festival

Talent
agent

+/− You are a master at keeping your lips sealed, **which means your peeps can trust you not to spill their deepest secrets. Keeping confidences is one thing—keeping your feelings on lockdown is another. If you're upset, learn to speak up.**

Convincing, Secretive, Intellectual

If you had a catchphrase, it would be "Eureka!" because you're all about discovery. Innovative and supersmart, you're full of new, bright ideas about the best way to do things: from what to do with leftover baked potatoes (hash browns, anyone?) to how to solve that killer algebra equation. Your talent for thinking clearly and creatively makes you a leader at home and at school.

YOU'RE OFTEN HAPPIEST
WHEN YOU'RE PUTTING
YOUR SKILLS TO WORK
FOR A GROUP.

love match

You have a tendency to overthink. Make sure you are not so focused on the intelligentsia that you tend to neglect your emotional needs. If your heart starts beating faster every time a Pisces musician walks by, it's not a chemical reaction caused by his cologne.

friend match

You're an excellent friend and can always be counted on to keep your promises. Make sure you choose peeps who will throw the love back at you, like ultra-dependable Leo and sweet-tempered, giving Libra.

You are like a scenic lookout point on a winding mountain road: You're all about overseeing everything. When it comes to taking charge, you've got no problem directing others, but you also have the rare ability to really listen. You always lead by example, and your peers respect you for it. October 30th people will face several major periods of challenge in their lives, but their courage and persistence will see them through.

Red Bull

TV network executive

"What About Now"
—Daughtry

October 30

Organized, Confident, Attentive

> YOU ALWAYS LEAD BY EXAMPLE, AND YOUR PEERS RESPECT YOU FOR IT.

+/− You've got a supersharp vision of how things should be, but be sure not to focus too much on the little things. Part of your talent is being able to see the big picture, so stand back and let it happen.

love match

When you see something you want, you have to have it, and your friends totally dig your take-no-prisoners approach to love. Just make sure the spoils of war are worth the effort. Focus on a cool, perceptive Capricorn whose fresh perspective and witty comments will have you cracking up.

friend match

You love having a big social circle, but you're ruled by the super-independent number 3, which means you also need your space. An introspective Virgo is more than happy to roll in a group, but she's also down for private time.

October 31

There is no doubt what your Halloween costume should be: With your superhuman ability to laser right in on the truth of any situation, you should be one of the X-Men. You pride yourself on your attentiveness and your dedication to detail, and the fact that nothing gets by you undetected means you make a great friend and an even scarier enemy. Second choice of costume? A warrior princess.

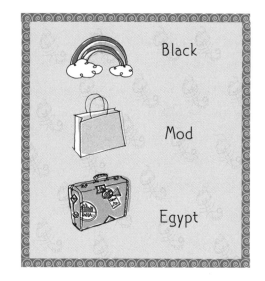

Black

Mod

Egypt

YOU'RE OFTEN RUNNING INTO MAJOR CONFLICT.

+/− You're distrustful of anyone and everyone, which makes it difficult for people to get close. Channel Gwen Stefani and make your new motto "No Doubt."

love match

You are amazing at reading people, so if you think the shy Pisces with the mysterious smile has hidden depths, trust your instincts and pursue him. A Pisces guy will love your independence and fearlessness, while you're attracted to his creative and offbeat take on the world.

friend match

You'd make a terrible tree, because you're super-afraid to branch out. A Libra will be sensitive to your allergy to all things new—and she has the loyalty you crave—but she'll encourage you to let more people into the inner circle.

Your friends need matching hard hats, because you're a walking Danger Zone. Forceful, determined, and completely fearless, you pursue your goals with relentless determination and can't be bothered with rules or warnings. You believe the ends justify the means and have no problem being sneaky when it comes to getting yours.

friend match

A Virgo pal is also all about honesty, which is why you go together like PB & J. You'll let her know when she's being uptight, and she'll tell you when your schemes are headed for disaster.

YOUR IMMENSE SELF-CONFIDENCE MEANS YOU'RE A "GET WHAT YOU SEE" KINDA GIRL.

love match

Much as this might surprise you, you could use a guy with a more conservative outlook. Not that you want a weenie, but a grounded Capricorn might just be the stabilizing influence you need.

Oversize sunglasses

Intern at the local TV station

"My Way"
—Frank Sinatra

+/− You're whips mart in most ways, but you've got all the common sense of a cucumber. And though it's great you don't second-guess yourself, you'll never learn from your mistakes if you don't take the time to reexamine them.

Forest green

House party with mutual friends

Stylist

November 2

Influential, Powerful, Adaptable

You're like a chameleon in reverse: You'd rather make the world adjust its colors than try to blend in with the world. A social powerhouse, you're a trendsetter and a dynamo at making over everything from your BFF's wardrobe to your math teacher's attitude. (Who knew he could smile?) You have a tremendous impact on the people around you, giving you the power to transform situations according to your will.

+/− Change freaks some people out, but not you. When opportunity knocks, you roll out the welcome mat. But it's important to stick with your commitments, so remember you don't always have to open the door.

YOUR ATTENTION SPAN BARELY CARRIES YOU THROUGH A MOVIE.

love match

There's no chance of committing to just one guy. But watch out for a taste of your own medicine (de flakiness) in a gorgeous Mercury-ruled Gemini who will have you wishing for a little one-on-one time.

friend match

You've got the energy of Times Square on New Year's Eve, but sometimes you just need to chill. That's when you should seek out a laid-back Libra, who'll keep you from stressing out too much.

If you were a game, you would be chess, because you're all about thinking three moves ahead. Persistent and focused, you keep calm under pressure and know how to wait. But you're not a procrastinator. When the time is right, you work passionately and energetically. Everyone knows not to argue with you; nothing gets under your skin, and even when your temper's burning, you stay as cool as ice.

Lilac

Yoga

Haute couture

November 3

Persistent, Concentrated, Triumphant

YOU DO NOT LIKE TO LOSE.

+/− You're so concentrated you're just like orange juice from a can, but when it comes to your feelings, you've got a serious block. Give your heart a de-freeze and learn how to express yourself emotionally.

love match

You're not the type to give your affection away freely, but let an expressive and artistic Pisces show you how to open up.

friend match

Sometimes your sarcasm can get out of hand. A straightforward, sensitive Cancer will always tell you when to lay off the abuse—and she'll help you figure out what's really got you mad.

November 4

You should be a wooden spoon, because you're always stirring things up. You have a knack for causing controversy and are always provoking people with your up-front attitude and unusual beliefs. Luckily, your wicked sense of humor and charm means (for the most part) you're more of a lover than fighter.

> YOU KNOW JUST HOW TO PUSH OTHER PEOPLE'S BUTTONS, WHICH MEANS YOU MAKE A FIERCE ENEMY.

Unlimited-minutes cell-phone plan

Talk-show host

Siamese cat

+/− You take everything—from the fact that your math teacher springs a pop quiz on the class to the fact that your BFF snags the last walnut brownie—superpersonally. Not everyone is out to ruin your life, so ease up on the defenses and learn to let the small things slide.

friend match

You're not just about causing problems. Your fun and outgoing approach to life means you're always ready to get the party started, so surround yourself with upbeat, sun-ruled friends who are always ready to shake their groove thang. (And who will have a mellowing influence on your temper.)

love match

You're as stubborn as, well, an ox, so the last thing you need is to pair up with an equally bull-headed Taurus. Look for a water-sign Cancer who knows how to go with the flow.

November 5

If you were a TV show, you'd be the Discovery Channel's Mythbusters: An ultra-realist, you're obsessed with uncovering the truth and can't stand liars, braggers, or flakes. You've got a sharp eye for scams (and slimeball guys), and your friends depend on you to make the right choice in every situation.

COURAGEOUS AND UNAFRAID OF CONFRONTATION, YOU ALWAYS DEFEND YOUR BELIEFS AND OPINIONS.

friend match

Your Cancer BFF can be super-shy, which is why you're always sticking up for her. The trade-off? Her sweetness and loyalty mean that you always have someone to share your stories with.

love match

A diligent Sagittarius will share your love of truth and learning, so if you're looking for hours and hours of deep conversation—and someone who won't break his promises—look no further.

Library card

Salmon

District attorney

+/− You mess around in everyone else's private business so much, you should be a private investigator. Focus on your own issues and leave the snooping to the professionals; otherwise your fed-up friends are going to put you out of business.

Amusement park

What don't you do?

Rebecca Romijn

November 6

* * * * * * * * * * * * * *

Energetic, Stimulating, Optimistic

You should be a stair climber, because you're all about stepping it up. You've got energy that's more infectious than the flu, and people can't help but be charmed and motivated when you're around. More bubbly than champagne and super-self-confident, you can't stand the word "no," and are driven to succeed.

+/− You're a whirlwind of activity, always blasting from one obligation to another. But unless you learn how to press pause once in a while, you're bound to do damage to both yourself and your close relationships.

YOU'RE THE GO-TO GIRL FOR CHAIRING UP THE SOCIAL COMMITTEE OR ORGANIZING AN EARTH DAY EVENT.

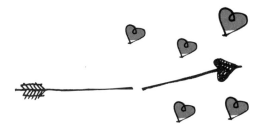

love match

It's great that you're so ambitious, but maybe one of your goals should be to let yourself really fall for someone. An über-romantic Scorpio will help you forget about deadlines and school drama for a while.

friend match

When it comes to your friends, your philosophy is the more the merrier. But for someone to lean on when you're not feeling like the life of the party, stick with a quiet, loyal Virgo.

If you were a type of Ford, you'd be the Explorer. Always down to try something new, you're adventurous, brave, and deeply curious about the world around you. A teacher's dream student, you keep your straight-A average not because you're a suck-up but because you actually love to learn. But you're not a bookworm.

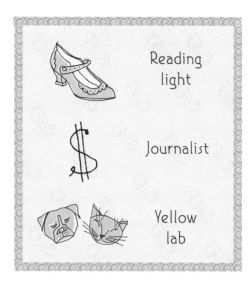

Reading light

Journalist

Yellow lab

YOU LOVE HAVING FUN AND NEED CONSTANT STIMULATION TO KEEP YOU HAPPY.

November 7

* * * * * * * * * * * * * * *

Curious, Adventurous, Entertaining

+/− You like to stay on the move 24/7, and your cell phone is practically glued to your ear. Part of the reason you like to surround yourself with people and noise is that you're not supercomfortable when you're on your lonesome, so take time to cultivate a better sense of self.

love match

You've got a ton of not-so-secret admirers, but don't let anyone get too close; deep down, you're worried that the real you isn't so lovable. Allow yourself to open up to an intuitive and trustworthy Aquarius who likes you, Nutella-and-popcorn obsession and all.

friend match

Watch out, 'cuz some of your friends are just like beachgoers: ready to pack up and go at the first sign of bad weather. You need a friend who will stick it out through thick and thin, like a loyal Leo.

November 8

If you were a TV show, you'd be *Crossing Over*: all about pushing every single limit of human experience and breaking boundaries. You're drawn to experiences that others might find frightening. (No wonder you're obsessed with watching *Law and Order: SVU!*) And trouble has a way of riding your coattails.

PERCEPTIVE AND INTELLIGENT, YOU'RE PASSIONATELY DEVOTED TO PURSUING YOUR INTERESTS AND ARE CAPABLE OF GREAT SUCCESS.

Bungee jumping

"Danger Zone" —Kenny Loggins

Safari in South Africa

+/− The people and things that attract your attention are just like trees: super-shady. There's beauty in the everyday, too, so take time to figure out that *fun* and *danger* are spelled differently for a reason.

love match

The last thing you need is a danger-prone Aries to encourage you to step over your limits, so try a more conservative Capricorn who will keep his (and your) feet on the ground.

friend match

You're just like King Midas: Whatever you touch turns to gold. But the thing that really needs a glowing makeover is your attitude, so stick close to a sunny, upbeat Leo who will help you smile.

You're just like a triple-fudge sundae with whipped cream and hot fudge sauce: all about indulgence. Temptation is a major theme in the lives of those born on November 9th, and you're always giving in to the here and now pleasures with very little thought for tomorrow's consequences.

SPONTANEOUS AND FUN-LOVING, YOU WELCOME
CHALLENGES AND NEW EXPERIENCES.

friend match

A Virgo BFF has a good sense of when to pull the plug on your big ideas (like when they're going to get you grounded), while a Gemini helps encourage your giggly, silly side.

love match

Don't let a sun-ruled guy with an outsize ego pull you into his orbit. You deserve to be the queen of your own universe, so choose a confident and devoted Taurus who will treat you like one.

Cheerleading

Nikki Blonsky

Boho chic

+/− You're always out to have a good time, but because your danger meter is slightly off-kilter, you don't always realize that what you're doing is risky. Learn to tune in to your inner voice when you're having second thoughts about swimming in the mall fountain.

November 10

Sewing kit

Interior designer

Brittany Murphy

Creative, Self-Assured, Magnetic

The ruling symbol of November 10th is the butterfly, because those born on this day are all about metamorphosis. Your change is not just personal, however: Creative and productive, you are able to transform the materials around you into something fabulous and new. (Like when you turned an old pair of jeans into a handbag). A social butterfly (what else?), you attract people to your offbeat sensibility and your confidence.

+/− Although friends flock to you, you have a tendency to view them as audience members in the One Woman Theater of You.

CULTIVATE YOUR LISTENING SKILLS AND LEARN TO BE MORE SENSITIVE TO OTHERS' NEEDS.

love match

You can't stand people who always stick to the same old routine, so a Sagittarius—ruled by themes of movement, travel, and change—will share your love of exploration and help to keep things fresh.

friend match

You definitely march to the beat of your own drummer, but a Cancer friend is totally feeling your rhythm. And because she's superloyal, she won't blab to all your other peeps about your lucky stuffed bear or tendency to put ketchup on everything.

If you were a vegetable, you'd be a carrot: Most of what you've got going on is happening underground. Although you come across as cheerful and together, you've got hidden depths of feeling and thought that rarely get displayed. Powerful and driven, you like to control not just the way you appear to others but the people and things that are close to you.

YOU HAVE A NEED TO BE AT THE CENTER OF YOUR GROUP AND TEND TO TAKE CHARGE.

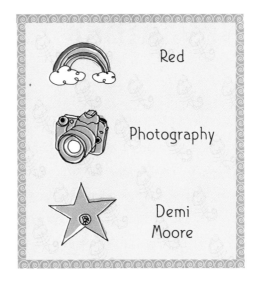

Red

Photography

Demi Moore

November 11

Persuasive, Colorful, Energetic

+/− Remember that what doesn't bend breaks. It's okay to ask for what you want, but if life throws you a curveball, learn to take a swing instead of stalking out of the game.

love match

You like to be admired from afar, but the second a guy gets too close, you push him away. News flash: Losing control is the best part, so go all in for the smoldering Scorpio who catches your eye.

friend match

Don't feel you have to act 100 percent together just to keep the admiration and loyalty of your peeps. True friends should want you to open up no matter what you're feeling, so don't be afraid to open up to a sensitive Pisces when things aren't going your way.

November 12

You should be a Sephora store, because you're all about beauty. You love to create and be surrounded by the finer things, which is why you're always redecorating your room or obsessing about what to wear. Magnetic and persuasive, you attract people more easily than a picnic does ants. Just be careful not to get carried away on the waves of admiration: What matters most is how you feel about yourself.

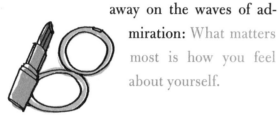

Swarovski necklace

Poodle

Anne Hathaway

+/− Like a black-and-white cookie, you need both the light and the dark, so if you're not comfortable discussing your fears or troubles with your friends, at least write them down in a journal.

> THE WORLD KNOWS YOU AS CHARMING, OPTIMISTIC, AND RADIANTLY SUNNY.

love match

The boys flock to you like you've got the latest Halo cheats for Xbox. Make sure you choose one who's digging more than just your smile, like a Pisces who doesn't care about the surface stuff.

friend match

It's great that you have a ton of friends to go out with, but make sure you have at least one to stay in with when you're feeling down, like a sweet-tempered Cancer who's all ears when you need her.

November 13

You should be a newspaper, because you've always got something to say about what's going on in the world. Curious and inquisitive, you've got the gossip on everything that goes down at school, from the politics of popularity to the most recent makeups and breakups, and you're never afraid to voice your opinion. But when it comes to self-knowlegde, you can be surprisingly thin, which means you've been accused of being superficial.

friend match

Your girlfriends had better share a love of drama; there's nothing you like better than a gossip session. Be sure to include a bluntly honest Sagittarius who will tell you when it is time to hush up.

ZIP YOUR LIPS
ONCE IN A WHILE AND LET
YOUR FRIENDS SPEAK.

love match

If it seems like you're always attracting guys for the wrong reasons, maybe it's because you've been playing dumb. You cannot truly open up until you know yourself better. (Not even to a smart fellow Scorpio who is your perfect match.)

Baby blue

Eurotrash

"Dirty Little Secret"
—All American Rejects

+/− There may be an "*i*" in listening, but if you keep bogarting the conversation every time your BFF wants to vent, you'll discover that the only "*i*" that will apply to you is the one in the word ditched.

Kindle

Apricot

Anthropologist

November 14

Self-Assured, Thorough, Observant

You're just like the zoom lens on a camera, because you're all about seeing closer, clearer, and deeper. Detail-oriented and curious, though you're always asking questions about the world in general, you've got clearly defined interests, a strong point of view, and the ability to focus.

YOUR NATURAL CONFIDENCE AND INDEPENDENCE MEAN YOU DO YOUR OWN THING WITHOUT WORRYING.

+/− Whether you're trying to figure out why your BFF is acting strange or who has been slipping love notes in your older sib's locker, you're always ready to bust out your detective skills. Be sensitive to the fact that your friends and fam may not always want to be the subject of your very own mystery show.

love match

You and an individualistic Pisces are the perfect match: Both of you are always trying to see beneath the surface, and both value deep connection but still appreciate space to do your own thing.

friend match

You love how an Aquarius shares your curiosity about the world. Even better? Her up-front attitude means she'll remind you when your snooping is about to get you in trouble.

If you were a sci-fi flick, you'd be *Close Encounters of the Third Kind.* The lives of those born on November 15th are ruled by themes of random meetings, chance occurrences, and unlikely events—and when opportunity comes knocking, you always answer the door. Independent and courageous, you're not the kind of girl whom people mess with.

Student disciplinary committee

Python

Sarah Jessica Parker

November 15

Measured, Just, Courageous

> YOU HAVE STRONG VALUES AND BELIEFS, BUT YOU ARE CAREFUL TO PICK YOUR BATTLES.

+/− You're just like a Boy Scout: Always prepared. But you're so busy expecting the worst you miss out on all the good things going on around you. Try to look on the bright side once in a while.

love match

You're usually calm, but when it comes to relationships, you can be a little volatile. Try to stay away from guys with an equally explosive emotional spectrum and stick with a sweet, chilled-out Libra.

friend match

Honesty is super important to you, but because you're super-protective of your friends, you'll conveniently forget to tell your emotional Pisces friend about the smack talk you heard behind her back. In return, you expect 100 percent loyalty and support whenever life throws you a curveball.

November 16

If you were a reality-TV show, you would be *Top Chef*: A natural leader, your commanding presence means you always bring the heat. (And if other people don't like it, they can get out of the kitchen.) You have tendencies to rebel against your parents and teachers largely because you like to be the one in control, but you're definitely no dictator.

PART OF WHAT MAKES YOU SUCH A GREAT LEADER IS YOUR ABILITY TO LISTEN.

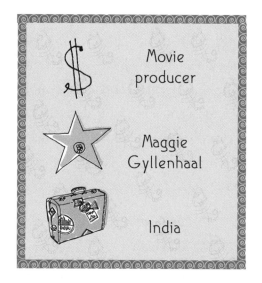

$ — Movie producer

Maggie Gyllenhaal

India

+/— Don't forget the little people on your quest for success. Give credit— and accept help—when it's due. You may have come up with the Spanish bullfighting theme for homecoming, but make sure to shout out to all the peeps who helped transform the gym into an arena.

love match

When it comes to relationships, you wear the pants—until a Leo ruled by the number 1 throws you for a loop. A little competition will keep things interesting, but both of you must learn to compromise.

friend match

You do know for certain that a super-supportive Cancer friend is always there for you—but how about putting her to use? You have a tendency to deny it when you're feeling down. Instead, try opening up.

If you were a song, you'd be "Bridge Over Troubled Water" —you're always helping to smooth things over, join two sides, and establish a connection between opposite positions. You can't stand disagreements or drama, and you often act as the glue that holds your social network together, negotiating compromise between your two squabbling sibs or playing matchmaker for your BFF.

YOU'RE SO USED TO TALKING AND THINKING ABOUT
OTHER PEOPLE, IT CAN BE HARD FOR YOU
TO DISH ABOUT YOURSELF.

friend match

You can help resolve disputes between a type A Virgo preplanner and a play-it-by-ear Gemini. Just be sure that in return you get the support you need.

love match

A perceptive and thoughtful Pisces wants to know more about you, not your fifty best friends, so try focusing the conversation on the things that get you pumped.

Tan

Poetry slam

Model UN

+/− You pride yourself on your ability to stay supercalm under pressure, but sometimes the fact that you always keep your cool makes you seem like a straight-up ice queen. Learn to be more emotionally open.

November 18

Fashion photographer

"Tied Together With a Smile"
—Taylor Swift

Swiss Alps

+/— You have spot-on intuition, so learn to listen and trust your gut instincts. If you get the feeling that the new cutie in class has some kind of shady secret, you're probably right, so make Mystery Man history.

Intuitive, Emotional, Social

You should be an aerobics instructor, because you've got energy to burn. Though you may come across as totally together, your thoughts and emotions race faster than an Olympic sprinter, and you're always looking for new ways to stay stimulated. Highly social, you love to be the center of attention. You definitely play hard, but work hard? Not so much.

YOUR CREATIVITY AND VISION ALLOW YOU TO SUCCEED EVERY TIME.

love match

You have too many different sides to you—right from social butterfly to dirt-bike enthusiast to tree hugger—and a get-what-you-see Taurus might be too boring for you. But do not underestimate the power of a dude you can depend on. Bonus? His excellent hugs.

friend match

You've got a ton of people vying for a spot in your inner circle. You love all the admiration, but you also know what really matters is the kind of old-school loyalty you get from a Leo BFF.

If you had a motto, it would be "*Vive la revolution!*" You're all about change and improvement, but you're not just a girl with big ideas; your take-charge attitude and practical outlook mean you  find a way to make your dreams a reality. Even if your friends aren't sure about taking a stand, you'll persuade them to play a part. Playful, trendy, and fun-loving, you take a break from changing the world to let the good times roll.

Megaphone

Staying in and watching a movie

Jodie Foster

November 19

Convincing, Strong, Confident

+/− If you've got something to say, you're not the type to keep it under wraps. But sometimes it really is best to be seen but not heard—like during your history final exam, for example.

love match

You're a family-oriented girl, so you hate it when guys talk smack about their sibs. Look for a quiet and honest Cancer who values the nest as much as you, without being a momma's boy.

friend match

A BFF ruled by the erratic planet Mercury changes her mind practically every second and is always turning to you for advice. Despite her flakiness, her energy and enthusiasm make her a perfect partner when it's time to fight the good fight. (Uh, curfew.)

November 20

You should have been a boxing champion, because you're a natural born fighter. You act out sometimes against your 'rents (do they really think nine o'clock is an acceptable curfew?), but the truth is you're extremely loyal to your fam and always willing to do battle for the people close to you.

Jack Russell terrier

Op-ed columnist

"Underdog" —Jonas Brothers

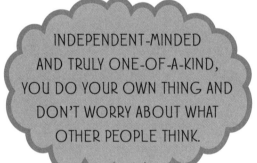

INDEPENDENT-MINDED AND TRULY ONE-OF-A-KIND, YOU DO YOUR OWN THING AND DON'T WORRY ABOUT WHAT OTHER PEOPLE THINK.

+/− You've got a biting sense of humor that keeps your friends rolling in the aisles. But not everyone is happy to be the punch line of one of your jokes, so be sensitive to other people's feelings when you're about to break out the scathing stand-up routine.

love match

You're often attracted to bad boy Aries and flaky-as-pie-crust Gemini, but do you really want a guy who will always keep you guessing? An individualistic and confident Scorpio will keep things interesting without playing games.

friend match

You're ruled by the number 2, so you can be a little oversensitive sometimes. An earth-sign friend will keep you grounded and remind you to pick your battles.

If you were a piece of jewelry, you'd be a single strand of pearls: Classic, classy, and elegant. But just because you're not interested in passing trends doesn't mean you're old-fashioned. You make your own trends and are often pioneering a new way of thinking about an old problem or a fabulous spin on a traditional idea (like whipped-cream-topped pumpkin muffins on Thanksgiving).

friend match

You need friends, not fans, **so don't be afraid to get really close to someone who will tell it to you like it is, like an honesty-loving Libra or even a bluntly realistic Capricorn.**

love match

Any guy who wants you to change for him isn't worth your time. You'll find plenty of acceptance in a down-to-earth Aquarius who thinks your unusual outlook is totally inspiring.

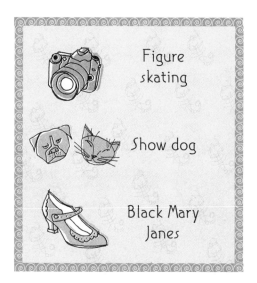

Figure skating

Show dog

Black Mary Janes

+/− You're so cool you could give an ice Popsicle a run for its money, **and you always do and say the right thing. But don't be afraid to act silly or reveal one of your embarrassing secrets— revealing the truth of who you are is always the coolest thing to do.**

Sagittarius Girls

are practical, optimistic, and honest

Those born under the influence of Sagittarius are like the 90-inch flat screen in the Best Buy of life: The only thing that really matters to them is the big picture. They make the best students, as they are constantly seeking to know and understand more about the world and the people in it. That desire for clear sight and change means they love travel. They have a tendency to set standards too high for anyone to reach.

* * * * * * * * * * * * * * * * * * * *

Most likely to be: Skipping off to
Cabo for spring break.

Exercise they most resemble: Yoga—concerned
with emotional enlightenment; difficult to follow.

Strengths to play on: Eagerness to learn, ability
to take the broad view.

Pitfalls to avoid: Refusal to hear different
opinions, inability to focus.

Sagittarius * * * * * * * * * * * * *

November 22– December 22

Element: Fire

Ruler: Jupiter

Theme Song:
"Climb Every Mountain"
(Get Every A)

* * * * * * * * * * * * * * * * * * * *

November 22

* * * * * * * * * * * * * *

If you were a national monument, you would be Philadelphia's Liberty Bell: All about freedom. Strong-willed and extremely independent, you demand the right to make your own choices and feel frustrated when people (like, ahem, your parents) try to impose limits on what you can do.

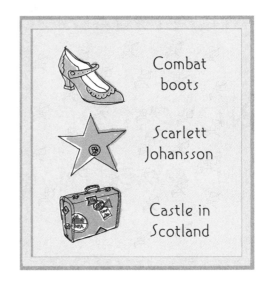

Combat boots

Scarlett Johansson

Castle in Scotland

YOUR FRIENDS RESPECT YOUR TAKE-ME-AS-I-AM ATTITUDE: YOU'RE NEVER AFRAID TO BE 100 PERCENT YOURSELF.

+/− It's fantastic that you've got such a fighting spirit and great that you're such a protective friend, but don't be so quick to jump into the frontlines. Pick your battles, and don't necessarily think that your pals can't—or won't—stand up for themselves. Friends are not fragile butterflies.

love match

If there's one thing you can't stand it's when a guy feels like he has the right to tell you what to do, so definitely stay away from bossy Taurus and look for a more easygoing Aries.

friend match

You and a supersweet Virgo are just like freshly baked bread: You're the hard exterior; she's the mushy soft inside. Together, a perfect pairing.

November 23

If you were a catchphrase, you'd be "Prove it to me."

You never follow rules just because someone says you should; from an early age, you gave your parents grief because you refused to accept their because-I-said-so arguments. In general you don't care what other people think but can ironically be supersensitive about certain lingering insecurities (and quick to take offense).

> YOU ARE SHARP-WITTED AND INDEPENDENT.

friend match

You admire a Pisces for her inventive fashion sense and I-don't-care attitude, and she admires you for always saying what you mean. Don't be afraid to let her help you tap into your creative side.

love match

You've got a great sense of humor, so you should be looking for a guy who can laugh at himself. A fun-loving Aries isn't afraid to make a fool out of himself and can help you loosen up when you're feeling uptight.

Jet Skiing

Miley Cyrus

Grunge

+/− You're just like the filling in an Oreo cookie: always in the middle of something. Try to cultivate a thicker skin when it comes to the issues that get you really riled up.

November 24

Aqua

Katherine Heigl

New York City

Spirited, Loyal, Involved

If you were a sports car, you'd be a foreign Ferrari: Unusual, a little flashy, and bound to be admired wherever you go. Deeply social, you're a fan of long conversations and need to be surrounded by people who understand and support you. You're an excellent friend; on the flip side, you have a tendency to hold grudges when people have betrayed your trust and make a scary—and outspoken—enemy.

+/— You often wish you were more like foundation: blessed with the ability to blend. You often feel different from the people around you and wish to be more "normal." Understand that, really, there's no such thing and embrace all of the qualities that make you you (and fabulous!).

* * * * * * * * * * * * * * * * * * * *

love match

You love to debate, and you need a guy who won't be intimidated when you defeat him point by point in an argument, like an über-confident fellow Sagittarius who's a big fan of long convos.

friend match

You and a BFF are both ruled by the dynamic number 2, which means you like to be on the go 24/7. Remember to make quiet time with a low-key Cancer when it's time for R & R.

If life is a highway, you're a cross-country truck driver: All about the long haul. You've got the patience and persistence to pursue your goals no matter what the obstacles and look for friends who share your desire to succeed. Though you have a ton of energy, you come across as cool, quiet, and reserved. You enjoy being alone but also have the capacity for deep and unwavering attachment.

Life list

Novelist

Christina Applegate

November 25

* * * * * * * * * * * *

Constant, Thorough, Accomplished

MAKE SURE THE PERSON'S WORTH IT BEFORE OFFERING A LIFT.

+/− You're a true perfectionist and are always painstakingly careful about what you do and say. Reality check: Unlike *The Hills,* life is unscripted, so let loose and allow your unregulated side to shine.

* *

love match

When you like someone, you refuse to see the negatives in him. But if an Aries is keeping you jumping through hoops, it's time to call off the circus. A loyalty-minded Leo will be the perfect remedy for the drama.

friend match

A Gemini is always going through ups and downs, and you'll be there no matter what the weather. In return, she can help you loosen up and laugh at yourself when things take a downturn in your life.

November 26

Interesting,
Free-Spirited, Unique

You're just like the smell of gasoline: Love you or hate you, you're 100 percent unique. Deeply creative, you do things in your own way and at your own speed, but there's no doubt that you make things happen. You are curious and inventive but you are also blessed with a practical side that helps keep your ideas grounded in real life, and you are always working to find a balance between your imaginative and down-to-earth sides.

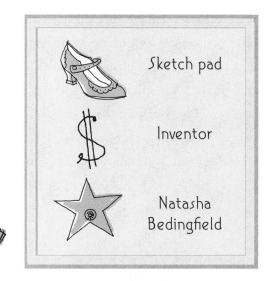

Sketch pad

Inventor

Natasha
Bedingfield

+/− It's cool that you don't care what other people think. But you may play better with others than you know.

YOU'LL NEVER KNOW WHETHER PEOPLE UNDERSTAND YOU UNLESS YOU'RE WILLING TO SHARE YOUR THOUGHTS WITH THEM!

love match

It's hard for you to be in a relationship because you're so independent. Look for a guy who will give you space to do your own thing, like a Cancer who values privacy or a Sagittarius who's always on the move.

friend match

You're drawn to a Pisces BFF because of the unusual, intuitive, and individualistic way that you both see the world. And who else will spend an entire afternoon finger painting your walls?

* *

If you were a line dance, you'd be the Electric Slide. If you're not the one creating the drama, you'll be in the middle of it faster than you can say, "Oh, no, she didn't." Spontaneous, fun-loving, and full of more energy than a twelve-pack of Red Bull, you're so busy bouncing off the walls you often don't notice you're getting battered.

YOU NEED TO TAKE SOME TIME FOR R & R TO AVOID PERIODS OF ANGER AND FRUSTRATION.

friend match

Pair up with a Leo. She has just as much energy as you do, but her steadiness and optimism mean she never goes through periods of boom and bust and can help you find stability.

love match

In your case laughter really is the best medicine, so you'll know it's love when a class clown Aries keeps you in stitches. (Even when you are doing—blech—dissections in science class.)

Magenta

Club in Ibiza

Mary-Kate Olsen

+/− Your whirlwind energy—and the tantrums that accompany it—can cause more damage than hurricane season in Florida. You need the stabilizing influence of close friends and family, so lean on them for help. (And learn to say, "I'm sorry.")

November 28

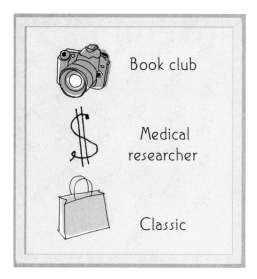

Book club

Medical researcher

Classic

* * * * * * * * * * *

Profound, Natural, Sensitive

If you were an old TV show character, you'd be the Lone Ranger. You're supersmart, but school still feels like a seven-hour-a-day prison sentence to you. You'd much rather be learning on your own terms, and your desire for independence extends to every area of your life.

ALTHOUGH YOU HAVE A SHARP AND SPOT-ON SENSE OF HUMOR, YOU OFTEN COME ACROSS TO OTHERS AS SERIOUS AND EVEN INTIMIDATING.

+/− You have a naturally logical mind and are quick to pick an argument to shreds when it isn't up to par. But you don't always hold yourself to the same standards, so before you start throwing stones, make sure you're not sitting in the middle of a house of glass.

* *

love match

You come across as snobby when in fact you're just private. You've got a lot in common with a Cancer in your class—he's just as introspective as you are—but somebody has to make the first move, so try breaking out of your let-him-come-to-me routine.

friend match

You find a natural counterpart in the logically minded, diplomatic, and sweet-tempered Libra. But stay close to the silly influence of a goofball Aries, who will help keep things light.

You should be an elevator operator, because you're always pushing buttons. Energetic, smart, and opinionated, you're always provoking others with your unusual ideas, unflinching honesty, and in-your-face attitude. Nothing infuriates you more than liars and fakes, and though some people may find you intimidating, everyone has to respect you for always telling the truth and speaking your mind.

Emerald

Day at the beach

Lit mag

November 29

* * * * * * * * * * *

Challenging, Dynamic, Influential

+/− It's great that you're not afraid to express yourself. But there are times when you should reserve judgment, like when your BFF tells you she's thinking of joining the cheerleading squad. Your job as a friend is to be supportive, not critical.

* *

love match

You should come with a big "Fragile" sign, because people better handle you with care. Your tendency to explode means you need a guy who's not going to press the detonator, like an Aquarius who doesn't mind admitting when he's wrong.

friend match

A Libra BFF is super-patient, but even she'll get fed up if you don't stop picking fights. Take a lesson from her cool-as-a-cucumber demeanor and chill.

November 30

* * * * * * * * * * * * *

Your spirit animal should be a tiger, because when it comes to getting what you want, you always know just when to pounce. Patient and hardworking, you also possess an intuitive side that means you can sense when to act. Whether you're whipping up a new outfit from an old tank top or turning a pair of jeans into a pillow covering, you're always making the most of what's given to you.

YOU KNOW HOW TO DO A LOT WITH A LITTLE.

Silver

Kaley Cuoco

Cancun

+/− You like to be in control of everything from your social calendar (planned a month in advance) to your burger toppings (extra ketchup, absolutely no onions). Take a lesson from cotton and loosen up.

love match

A mischievous Aries tries to seduce you with charm, but you respond better to openness and honesty. Look for a Sagittarius who'll be willing to spill—and share—his soul.

friend match

You and a Virgo share a love of matching stationery sets as well as spotlessly clean bedrooms, but for sheer giggly fun and a mellowing influence, go ahead and send a Gemini a friend request.

December 1

If you were a type of candy, you'd be Skittles: Fun, colorful, vibrant, with a totally unique flavor. Outspoken and upbeat, you follow a policy of strict honesty that borders on brutal bluntness. But your charm and sense of humor mean your friends always forgive you for your most outrageous comments, and in general your desire to spill comes from a desire to share.

YOU'RE GENEROUS WITH EVERYTHING FROM YOUR ADVICE TO YOUR TIME TO YOUR SHOES.

friend match

 You need a BFF with lots of energy and the desire to try new things, so a homebody Cancer will just have you yawning. Pair up with an outgoing Aries who's a social butterfly, like you.

Nighttime picnic

Dalmatian

Sarah Silverman

love match

You love to be admired and have the rep of being an outrageous flirt. But make sure you're not courting all the wrong kinds of attention. The kind of love you really need goes far beneath the surface, so try cultivating a deeper relationship with a quiet and sincere Aquarius.

+/− You're just like McDonald's: always open. But in certain cases, it's better to keep your opinions to yourself, like if you think your friend's jeans look like a sausage casing.

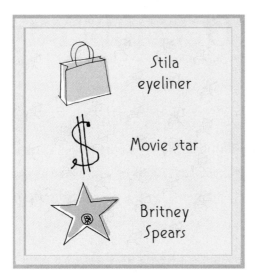

Stila eyeliner

Movie star

Britney Spears

December 2

* * * * * * * * * * * *

Dynamic, Spirited, Active

You should be on the silver screen, because you're all about being larger-than-life. You have a tremendous presence; when you walk into the room, people bow down or step out of the way. You believe that life is a boxing match, and you're looking for an all-out knock-out victory. Your tendency to see things in terms of struggle means you often hold grudges, and you're prone to furious and frightening temper tantrums when people disappoint you.

+/— It is great that you are so ambitious and strong, but winning really isn't everything. No trophy or award in the world will comfort you when you're feeling down or make you crack up when you need to giggle, so work on strengthening your ties to your real winnings: your friends.

* *

love match

You've got superhigh standards and are always saying that none of the guys you know can measure up. Make sure you're not just pushing people away before they can reject you—a patient, devoted, and supersweet Cancer comes pretty close to perfection.

friend match

You expect honesty and integrity from your BFFs, and anyone who gets close to you had better know how to calm you down when you're about to blow. A level-headed Libra has all these qualities.

CANDY

You and sliced bread have something in common: You're both totally ingenious. Creative, innovative, as well as extremely independent, no matter what your passion—from writing to knitting to the boy in your science class— you dedicate yourself to it with attentiveness and skill that borders on the truly genius. You do your own thing and never seek out attention or flattery; in fact, you crave privacy.

Oversize headphones

Art club

Adopted cat

December 3

* * * * * * * * * * *

Concentrated, Secretive, Innovative

+/− It's great that you're self-sufficient, but you graduated from kindergarten, so you should know how to play with others. Let your friends take you out on Saturday night and try to maintain closer contact with the people you love.

* *

love match

A handsome Cancer who appreciates your need to be alone but understands the importance of having a small group of close friends will make sure that you don't put the "her" back in hermit.

friend match

You need a BFF who values privacy and independence above all else and won't be offended that you have a tendency to keep secrets, like an equally mysterious and private Pisces.

December 4

* * * * * * * * * * * * *

You should be a Nike ad, because you always "Just Do It." When you want something, you pursue it relentlessly and you don't let anybody or anything stand in your way. You jump so many hurdles you should compete on the Olympic team, and you're no stranger to struggle. Sometimes you're so focused on your goals you neglect the needs of family and friends, and your desire to dominate means you can be kind of bossy.

Dinner and dancing

Professional athlete

Tyra Banks

+/− You're amazingly strong, **but** even you have limits, so learn them. You can't be a star soccer player and social VP and the editor in chief of the yearbook, so take a shot at saying once in a while.

love match

You're all about power, but you haven't yet given in to the greatest power of all: L-O-V-E. You'll never truly fall unless you're willing to let go, so try letting someone else—like a super-popular Leo with a powerful presence—take the lead for once.

friend match

You and a stubborn Taurus are bound to butt heads 24/7, but you do need a BFF who is strong enough to tell you when you are out of line, like a grounded and confident Capricorn.

December 5

Being you is like sporting a tube top to a formal garden party: Both require a ton of confidence. You're blessed with a strong belief in your ability to pull things off, whether you're assembling your social studies project at the last second or rocking leather pants to homecoming. In general, your confidence is justified—things have a way of turning out right for you—but you have to learn when to admit it on the rare occasions you need help.

love match

You're just like a pizza: Made to share. You cannot stand secrets and need a guy who is willing to spill his hopes and dreams, like an open-hearted and expressive Aries.

$ Personal shopper

Funky

"Lose Control" —Missy Elliot

friend match

You sure know how to rock what you've got, but you could use some help knowing when to rein it in a little—for example, busting out into a karaoke rendition of "I Will Survive" at your parents' X-mas party might not be the best idea. Trust a down-to-earth and laid-back Libra to let you know when to lay off the theatrics.

$+/-$ It is really great that you are so positive, but you need to stop dismissing people as haters just because they are not all roses and sunshine. You might benefit from constructive criticism, so open up your ears.

Vintage Polaroid camera

Orchid

School-events coordinator

December 6

* * * * * * * * * * *

Pragmatic, Perceptive, Capable

You ought to be a jeweler, because you've got an eye for that diamond in the rough. You can make the best out of any situation, and you're always able to spot things—like antique bedside tables and grungy-looking guys—that with just a little bit of polish will sparkle like new. Extremely practical, you're a born organizer and manager.

+/− It's great that you're always looking ahead, but if you don't pause for breath, you're going to miss out on a chance to stop and smell the roses. Life's too short already, so make time to appreciate it.

YOUR COMPETITIVE NATURE MEANS THAT YOU'RE ALWAYS OUT TO WIN.

* *

love match

You need to respect the object of your affections, and that means no whiners, moaners, or self-pitiers for you. Ideally, you need a guy who's as strong-willed and competitive as you, like a take-charge Taurus.

friend match

When someone disappoints you, you have a tendency to drop the friendship faster than a socialite drops names. Buddy up with someone who will teach you the value of perseverance and communication, like an extra-patient Cancer.

You're just like an original
Picasso painting: one of a kind, with a totally unique perspective. Those born on December 7th never blend in with the crowd, and though some people might consider you weird, the fact that you always do your own thing regardless of what other people think is an admirable and enviable trait. Unsurprisingly, you're attracted to people who are also brave enough to march to the beat of their own drummer.

Turtle

No one rocks pink tights like you.

"Imagine"
—The Beatles

December 7

* * * * * * * * * * *

Imaginative, Sensitive,
Individualistic

+/− You're deeply creative, so it's normal that you spend a lot of time with your head in the clouds. Just make sure you don't forget to touch down in the real world every so often. A girl can't live on dreams alone.

* *

love match

Even though you just love to express yourself, when it comes to romance, you do your best impression of a clam. It's crucial that you find someone you can be yourself with, like an even-tempered and non-judgmental Aquarius.

friend match

You need a BFF who's not afraid to take the road less traveled, like a creative and visionary Pisces. But for a more social influence who will keep you from perma-hibernation, look also to an independent and fun-loving Gemini.

December 8

* * * * * * * * * * * * *

Both you and an Olympic high-diver have something in common: You're all about diving in headfirst. No matter what you're working on— from an English project to a difficult friendship—you throw yourself into it 100 percent. Generous and energetic, when it comes to your emotions, you lay everything out on the table, and you feel deeply responsible for the well-being of everything and everyone around you.

DYNAMIC AND FULL OF LIFE, YOU WILL ACHIEVE GREATNESS AS LONG AS YOU DON'T GET IN YOUR OWN WAY.

love match

Because you love unusual and mischievous people, you're often drawn to guys who aren't prepared to return your affection, like a shady Scorpio with a wandering eye. Down-to-earth doesn't have to mean boring; once you try out a dependable Leo, don't be surprised if you never go back.

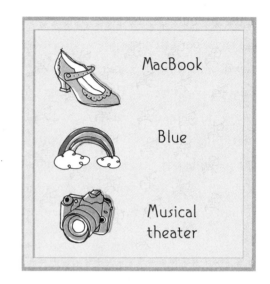

MacBook

Blue

Musical theater

+/− You'll tackle any project, no matter how difficult. But ask yourself if the rewards are worth the effort. It might be easier to write an essay than build a scaled-down version of a Native American village; similarly, if you have to put in months of energy to a relationship that's not getting better, it's time to pull the plug.

friend match

A Virgo with both creative and pragmatic tendencies is a moderate version of you: All the talent, half the angst. Occassionally, let her do some of the venting.

December 9

You deserve an award for Best Performance, because you're always the star of the show. You love to be the center of attention, and you've got a knack for sniffing out (or starting!) drama. Imaginative and prone to flights of fancy, you're always playing casting director, and putting yourself in the role of heroine, leader, or diva.

THOUGH A LITTLE SHY NOW, YOU WILL GROW TO BE
A TRUE EXTROVERT WITH A BIG PERSONALITY.

friend match

You're super-protective when it comes to your posse, so a Capricorn who shies away from confrontation can rely on you to have her back. In return, she can help mellow out your outrageous energies and keep you grounded.

$ Entertainment reporter

Bollywood

Puerto Rico

love match

People who only see your outgoing side would be surprised to find out that you're shy when it comes to boys. You need a dependable guy with a relaxed attitude to balance out the more fiery side of your personality, so you can trust a Libra to make you feel comfortable.

+/− You can definitely command attention, but you don't always have to steal the stage. Sometimes it's nice to play a supporting part and let someone else have the chance to shine for once.

Morning hike

Raven-Symoné

"I Shall Believe"
—Sheryl Crow

December 10

Appreciative, Introspective, Calm

If you were a subject in school, you'd be philosophy—super-deep. Extremely private, you often come across as shy when in fact you're just busy reflecting on the Big Questions—like why are we here? Idealistic in the extreme, you have a logical mind but faith and belief (in everything from friendship to religion to the beauty of nature) are very important to you. Modest and sweet-tempered, you don't seek out attention. But because you can seem so mysterious, there are actually more people paying close attention to you than you ever realize.

+/— You love being alone, but other people deserve to see you shine, so do not always hide your glow. Just make sure you maintain connections with friends who will help you break out of your comfort zone.

* *

love match

You're way more comfortable flirting over AIM than in person. But wouldn't it be nice to LOL face-to-face? A sweet-tempered Cancer who has homebody tendencies might actually be your perfect match—if one of you can be convinced to stop hiding behind the keyboard and make the first move.

friend match

Your BFF had better love lengthy and serious chat sessions. Fortunately, a profound Pisces would much rather debate morality with you than catch up on the latest episode of *The Hills*.

You're just like the flavors in a cafe mocha: intense and super-deep. Serious and dedicated, you apply yourself vigorously to your goals and are difficult to stop. A thoughtful person by nature, you also have a commanding physical presence: When you walk into the room, everyone looks. It's hard for you to hide your emotions, and your moods, opinions, and, yes, occasional tantrums have a huge effect on the people around you.

Burgundy

Town carnival

Museum hopping in Italy

December 11

* * * * * * * * * *
Purposeful, Powerful, Influential

YOU'RE SURROUNDED
BY GREATNESS, SO STOP
FOCUSING ONLY ON THE BAD!

+/− It's nice that you're willing to fight for what you want, but swimming upstream is bound to leave you exhausted. Follow the current once in a while.

* *

love match

You're a quick study in almost everything you do, but a big failure when it comes to the subject of fun. You could use a little laughter in your life, so depend on a class-clown and prank-prone Aries to keep you ROTFL.

friend match

The fact that you have extremely high standards means you have a tendency to be judgmental. Lean on a Libra who will remind you to keep a balanced and fair perspective.

December 12

Expressive, Poised, Persuasive

Ballet

Puggle

Jennifer Connelly

You should be a one-woman theater company, because you're all about putting on a show. Expressive, open, and persuasive, those born on December 12th are ruled by the themes of motion and body language. You definitely know how to play a part—from dutiful daughter to victim of a homework-eating dog—but in general you're graceful and comfortable in your own skin. You know that appearance counts, and you make yours work for you.

+/− You're a genius at reading nonverbal signs, but not all of your friends are so lucky. So quit it with the silent film.

WHEN YOU'VE GOT AN IMPORTANT POINT TO MAKE, SAY IT.

love match

You make it your business to get noticed, but just make sure all of that strutting and blustering isn't keeping guys from getting to know the real you. Stick with a sensitive—as well as ultra-perceptive—Scorpio, who will see past the facade.

friend match

You have a tendency to be drawn to the superficial aspects of life and could use a friend who will remind you that beauty is more than skin deep and all that glitters is not gold, like a profound Pisces.

December 13

You're just like HDTV: You've got the big picture, sure, but it's your ability to see the details that really makes you special. Careful, precise, and patient, you never shy away from projects that other people consider impossible—like creating a wall-size fresco in your bedroom or landing a date with the star basketball player—but you can get tripped up by your desire to make everything perfect. (Do you really need to flat iron your hair for two hours?)

friend match

A competitive Capricorn will just bring out the worst of your type A tendencies. You need a BFF to remind you that a straight-A average isn't all there is to life, like an outdoorsy and open-minded Aquarius.

love match

Sometimes you feel like if you don't do or say the Exact Right Thing, your crush will write you off for good. News flash: The best relationships are the ones you can be goofy in, so look for a hilarious Aries who makes you laugh—and won't care when you snort soda out of your nose.

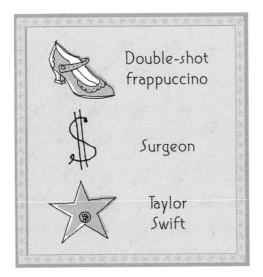

Double-shot frappuccino

$ Surgeon

Taylor Swift

+/− It is true that practice makes perfect, but past a certain point, practice also means that you're avoiding getting out there in the game. You don't want to get stuck in a rut trying to make everything just so, so learn how to move.

December 14

Your diary
(with a lock,
of course)

Vanessa
Hudgens

Emo

* * * * * * * * * * * * *

Original, Provocative, Daring

You and a jar of spaghetti sauce have something in common: It is hard to get you to open up! Although you may often come across as outgoing and very social, in reality you have an intensely private side that you rarely reveal to anyone. You have got a ton of acquaintances and admirers but only a few very close friends, and though you may let people in on where you're headed for a Friday night, you hardly ever share your true feelings and thoughts. If you assume others just wouldn't understand, try giving them the benefit of the doubt— they may surprise you.

+/— It's no wonder your friends get frustrated trying to figure you out: You seem to be harder to unravel than a knee-high lace-up boot. But keeping all of your complexity to yourself will just leave you feeling alienated and frustrated.

LEARN TO SPEAK UP ABOUT YOUR TRUE OPINIONS AND FEELINGS.

* *

love match

You have a forceful will and you're very persuasive, but when a smoldering Scorpio with a secretive nature starts getting close to you, you'll step back and let him take the lead.

friend match

You and a Cancer can totally relate: She, too, values privacy and a small circle of close friends. She won't force you to talk about what you're going through, but her sensitivity and trustworthiness mean you'll be inclined to share more.

If you had a motto, yours would be "Go big, or go home." Confident, open-minded, and supersocial, you like to live large and in charge. People gravitate to you because of your natural positivity and optimism, and you don't mind rolling with a big entourage. On the flip side, your refusal to see the dark side means that you can become attached to people who don't deserve it.

YOUR PHILOSOPHY IS, THE MORE THE MERRIER!

Your friends

Pink

"Here's to the Night" —Eve 6

December 15

* * * * * * * * * * * *

Cheerful, Social, Popular

+/− It's great that you're so naturally sunny, but if the clouds are rolling in on the horizon, it might not be the best time for a parade. You must learn to accept hardships and disappointments realistically, and face problems head-on.

* * * * * * * * * * * * * * * * * * * *

love match

The Gemini you've been crushing on is popular, cute, and charming, so you refuse to acknowledge that he may not be worth your feelings of hopeless devotion. Dig deeper when you meet a quiet and rock-solid Taurus, and you may find the diamond in the rough.

friend match

You're a blast to be around and are always making your friends feel good. Just make sure you have your own cheerleader, like a supportive Leo or a Cancer who admires your social skills.

December 16

* * * * * * * * * * * * *

If you were a book genre, you would be fantasy. People born on December 16th are some of the most imaginative of the entire astrological year. Creative and artistic, you see things differently from your peers, and whether you're assembling a mural out of discarded plastic bottle caps or penning a short story entirely in rhyme, you're always testing limits and pushing boundaries.

YOU CRAVE PRIVACY AND FREEDOM.

$ Film director

"Hot N Cold" —Katy Perry

Vineyard in California

+/− Your emotional life has so many ups-and-downs it should be its own roller coaster at Six Flags. Your friends have problems, too, so lay off the venting sometimes and learn to listen.

❋ ❋ ❋ ❋ ❋ ❋ ❋ ❋ ❋

love match

You're deeply romantic, and you fall in love faster—and harder—than you can say, "ouch!" Make sure you get to know a guy before declaring him your One and Only and pay special attention to an artistic Pisces with the same values as you.

friend match

You often disappear into your own world, so it's good to have a grounded earth-sign Virgo to bring you back from the clouds and remind you of the day-to-day pleasures (and obligations) of this planet.

December 17

* *

You and a gym teacher have something in common: You're all about physical education. Down-to-earth, practical, and grounded, you limit your beliefs to the things you can see, touch, taste, and smell. Ruled by themes of body and earth, you're not interested in flights of fancy or superficiality. You gravitate toward dependability and solidity in other people.

SERIOUS AND FOCUSED, ONCE YOU SET YOUR MIND TO SOMETHING, IT'S IMPOSSIBLE TO STEER YOU FROM YOUR PATH.

friend match

You take things super-seriously and could use some friends around you to help you lighten up, like a laid-back, social Libra and an energetic, fun-loving Gemini.

love match

Nothing seems to irritates you more than broken promises, so very adorable Aries with a habit of telling little white lies will just drive you crazy. Stick with a solid-as-they-come Taurus or an affectionate Cancer.

+/− You're definitely not a fan of team sports; you prefer to always roll solo. Like a kindergartener, you need to learn to share. Don't be afraid to open up to others and show off your inner shine—make time to hit the movies or have a makeover night with good friends.

Camping
candy

Cooking

Outdoorsy

December 18

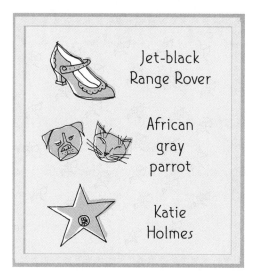

Jet-black
Range Rover

African
gray
parrot

Katie
Holmes

You and a whale share something in common: You're all about living large. When you commit to something—like heading up the decorator's committee for homecoming—you see it through no matter what, and you see it through in a big way (2,000 handmade paper vines to go along with the jungle theme, anyone?). But just because you see the big picture doesn't mean you ignore the details. You can be quite crafty and precise when it comes to using your hands and your head. But try some spontaneity when it comes to your heart.

+/− You have unstoppable quantities of energy, but just like when you're driving, it sometimes pays to REDUCE SPEED AHEAD. Going full throttle will just lead to burn out, so try to appreciate the journey and not just the destination.

ATTENTIVE AND FOCUSED,
YOU MAKE SURE
EVERYTHING IS JUST SO.

* *

love match

Having a boyfriend is awesome, but having a boy friend is even better. Make sure your guy gets you and can serve as your support system, like a loyal Taurus whose steadfastness will help you achieve your goals.

friend match

Sometimes you crave absolute privacy; at other times you spill all your secrets faster than you can say, "Dish." You might run hot and cold sometimes, but a Libra who is laid-back like lukewarm water will be able to go with the flow.

You have your own version of black magic, because you were born to raise hell. Dominating and brave with a wild streak, you're just like the taste of cilantro: People might love you or hate you, but they always have an opinion. It doesn't bother you when people don't feel your vibe, though. You always do your own thing, and your philosophy is to either take it or leave it.

Sapphire

Hockey game

Government agent

December 19

* * * * * * * * * * * *

Deep, Daring, Indomitable

THE HATERS ARE PROBABLY JUST JEALOUS THAT THEY'RE NOT AS GUTSY AS YOU!

+/− You hate to confess that something's getting you down. **But life can be pretty lonely without someone to talk to, so share your problems with your close friends—that's what they're there for.**

* * * * * * * * * * * * * * * * * * * *

love match

You are totally comfortable in your own skin but have a very honest time expressing yourself verbally to other people—especially guys. Look for a Libra who is all about long convos. He'll help unravel your tongue when it's twisted into knots.

friend match

You've got an ironic sense of humor, **so you have no time for people who don't get you or who are easily offended. Luckily, an Aquarius shares your sharp wit and can also smooth things over if other people's feathers get ruffled.**

December 20

* * * * * * * * * * * * * *

You should have your picture in the dictionary next to the word "because": you're always causing things to be. Ruled by themes of production and efficiency, you have a lightning-quick speed and brilliance that means you launch—and complete—projects with an ease that makes other people gawk. No wonder you find yourself in positions of leadership; you are always looking at the broader view as well as the big picture.

Jimmy Choo sling backs

Magazine editor

Victoria Beckham

+/− You like to get things done, and you want them done ASAP. **But** sometimes mastery requires patience and time, so focus on one thing and don't be so quick to jump from project to project.

love match

You're quick to do everything, including form opinions about other people. Be careful that you're not judging books by their covers. A quiet Scorpio may be much smarter—and more attentive—than you give him credit for, and his poker face may be concealing a brilliant sense of humor.

friend match

You can be pretty bossy and have a tendency to push your own point of view. A fellow Sagittarius with strong opinions of her own will remind you that variety is the spice of life. (And to chill with the lecturing!)

* *

You're just like a ninja: silent but deadly. You don't need to run your mouth to command a room, and whether or not you've got your lips on lockdown, you make sure people know how you feel—and do what you want. Intimidating and powerful, you use all of your energy and focus to achieve your goals, and whether or not you use verbal skills or just body language to communicate, you're always making your point clear.

love match

You need a guy who won't keep his feelings on lockdown, or you're both bound to suffer in silence. A Libra values honesty and communication above all else and can help you open up.

friend match

You and a Cancer may have been best buds since you were in diapers, but don't let that stop you from expanding your horizons. An expressive, take-charge fellow Sag makes a great partner in crime.

YOU LIKE TO KEEP YOUR POSSE SMALL, AND YOU LIKE TO KEEP THEM CLOSE.

Black

Judge

Morocco

+/− You're supersensitive when it comes to understanding other people's moods. When it's your friends' turn to read you, however, they'll find you're a closed book. If you're struggling with a problem, don't stew on it—open up!

WHAT'S YOUR STRESS STYLE?

When things don't go your way, you

a. Scream.   b. Take a deep breath.   c. Cry.

d. Treat yourself to a Frappuccino.

You're most often called

a. Drama Queen.   b. Reliable.   c. Princess.   d. Pessimist.

The last thing that stressed you out was

a. When the barista screwed up your order. *How hard is a latte?*

b. Performing a choir solo in front of the whole school.

c. When a drama geek beat you out for the lead in the student play.

d. When you flew to Europe. *You were convinced the plane would crash.*

When you don't get something you want, you usually blame

a. Other people.

b. Poor planning.

c. Your parents, for giving birth to you.

d. A cruel, unfeeling world.

What's your favorite word?

a. Now.   b. Please.

c. But.   d. Figures.

A LASHER

Anger Management much? Your temper's as hot as Miami in August. Before you blow, take a walk with a chill Pisces or philosophical Aquarius to put things in perspective.

A PROBLEM SOLVER

You're great in a crisis—you know a major meltdown never solves anything. Just don't keep your own emotions on lockdown. Try venting to a strong Taurus.

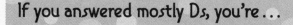

A WHINER

Your BFFs have a 24/7 invite to the biggest pity party in town—yours. And it's never your fault—you have more excuses than a dog has fleas. But taking blame is the first step to making change. Ask advice from a practical Sagittarius or calm Cancer.

A FATALIST

Little bugs you since you expect the worst, anyway. Your why-bother attitude is a way of avoiding disappointment. But a little hope could get you what you want. Take a leap with the help of a brave Leo or optimistic Libra.

QUIZ!

Capricorn Girls

are confident, persuasive, and determined

Astrologers agree that Capricorn is the hardest sign to categorize, as there are many different kinds of people born under its influence. But they all share one thing in common: Just like the bubbles in champagne, their single goal is to get to the top. Ruled by fateful Saturn, they share a driving ambition and a desire for power.

- -

Most likely to be: Campaigning for social vice president.

Vegetable they most resemble: Artichoke. Prickly exterior. Hard to get to the heart, but totally worth it.

Strengths to play on: Drive to succeed, ability to take things in stride.

Pitfalls to avoid: Tendency to step on the little people, refusal to compromise.

Capricorn

December 22 – January 20

Element: Earth
Ruler: Saturn

Motto:
"Because I said so."

December 22

Your philosophy is "Slow and steady wins the race." A queen of to-do lists and a natural planner, you've got everything in your life mapped out in advance, from the outfit you're going to wear to school in a week to the location of your wedding in fifteen years (Aruba). It's not that you're stubborn when it comes to walking a certain path, it's just that you always have a clear idea of where you want to end up.

National Honor Society

Tropical fish

Jordin Sparks

+/− You've got a ton of rules, like no side ponytails after 1995 and no speaking in class without raising your hand. But rules are meant to be broken, so try tossing out the list of dos and don'ts.

love match

You're definitely not the kind of girl who skips from crush to crush, so you need a guy who, like you, is happy to stay out of the game. A super-supportive Taurus will have eyes only for you.

friend match

Your tongue is so sharp it could be a pair of scissors, so you need to find a BFF who can roll with your scathing sense of humor, like a good-natured and mischievous Aries. Bonus: Her constant pranking and laissez-faire attitude will keep you cracking up.

December 23

You're just like a jackhammer: always breaking new ground. Whether petitioning your school to get a Taco Bell in the caf or being the first girl to win the state math competition, you're always looking for ways to do things bigger and better. But although you're definitely a dreamer, you're no radical or rebel: In fact, you tend to be very cautious when it comes to pursuing your plans, and you consider problems carefully before you try to tackle them.

friend match

Face it: You can be bossy. At first you may not appreciate it that an equally strong-willed fire sign gives as good as she gets, but after a while you'll love her for keeping you in check. (And being your Number One ally)

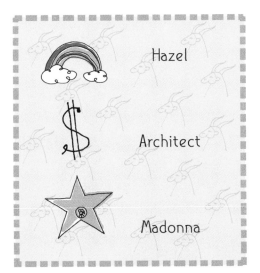

Hazel

Architect

Madonna

love match

You love the thrill of the chase, so a Mercury-ruled Virgo who's not giving you the time of day will set your heart beating faster. Keep your eye on the prize and remember that his private side makes it difficult for him to open up— but once you bring the heat, he's bound to melt.

+/− You should be a crotchety old grandmother, because you can't stand it when people talk back to you. Lose the old-woman attitude and listen when people have other points of view; it's the only way to learn.

Seeing a play

Stephenie Meyer

"Breathe"
—Anna Nalick

December 24

Visionary, Dramatic, Emotional

You are just like a dog swimming in the ocean: No matter how rough the waves get, you always keep your head above water. Those born on December 24th can typically expect lives filled with emotional challenges—and rewards—more intense than other people's. Intuitive as well as passionate, you're quick to react (both positively and negatively) to other people.

THOUGH YOU OFTEN SWEAT THE SMALL STUFF, YOU TAKE EQUAL AMOUNTS OF JOY IN LIFE'S LITTLE PLEASURES.

+/− You may be supersmart, **but** when it comes to learning from your mistakes, your report card would blush. When something goes wrong, do not pretend it didn't happen. You'll never be able to avoid tripping up if you don't look back down the path to see what made you fumble.

love match

You've got an artist's soul, and any guy who chills with you better be cool with spending hours debating a movie or dancing in the rain at midnight. A sensitive and passionate Scorpio will bring you all of the romance you crave.

friend match

You have way to many emotional emergencies, so you should have 911 on speed dial. Thank goodness a level-headed Libra's there when you need someone to lean on. Her advice is always spot-on.

Tissue

If you were a movie, you'd be *Ghost Busters*: all about the supernatural. Artistic, creative, and unique, you're inspired by the unusual side of life, which is why you're more likely to be holding a séance or learning belly dancing than trying out for the soccer team. Your desire to explore the outer limits means you're a risk taker and a boundary pusher—when it comes to pursuing your dreams, you are always willing to go the extra mile.

Olive green

Feng shui

Papua New Guinea

December 25

Successful, Bold, Curious

+/− There's a difference between being a realist and a pessimist, so while it doesn't hurt to keep your feet on the ground, that doesn't mean you have to lose your sense of wonder and appreciation.

love match

Once you spy a unique Pisces with a take-me-or-leave-me 'tude you'll know you've found the One. Just remember that the influence of Neptune on his sign makes him independent, so make sure you give him space when you're in hot pursuit of his heart.

friend match

Sometimes you get so wrapped up in the pursuit of a goal, you forget one of the most important goals: Have fun! Luckily, a Gemini BFF reminds you to loosen up. (One word: "karaoke")

December 26

If you could be a boxer, you'd definitely be champion, because nobody's gonna hold you down. You meet challenges head-on and you're not afraid of anyone or anything. Unsurprisingly, you can often come across as rebellious and you are always finding yourself in conflict with parents, teachers, and flaky frenemies. But you also have the courage to stand up for truth and fairness on occasions when other (weaker) people run for cover.

> YOU DON'T HAVE TO BE DOING THE DOWNWARD DOG TO BREATHE AND RELAX ONCE IN A WHILE.

Sneakers

Swim team

Angelina Jolie

+/− It's a good thing you don't do yoga, because you're totally inflexible. You have your opinions and routines on lock, but you'll never discover new opportunities and friends if you don't learn to lighten up.

friend match

♪ ♫ Your inner circle is tougher to get into than an NYC nightclub. But don't write off a Leo just because she has opinions that differ from yours; once you let her in, she'll stay by your side forever and help you fight even your toughest battles.

love match

You're used to being the dominant one in your relationships, but that might not be so easy with a headstrong Mars-ruled boy. Maybe it's time you let someone else take the lead.

December 27

If life were a department store, you'd be its customer service department: You always want to help out. Deeply concerned with the needs of your family, friends, and even community, you're the first to volunteer at a local animal shelter or rush to your BFF's house when she's dealing with heartbreak.

YOU HAVE A GREAT SENSE OF HUMOR AND ARE GENERALLY OPTIMISTIC AND HAPPY, THOUGH BECAUSE OF YOUR SENSITIVITY TO OTHERS, YOU GET HURT EASILY.

love match

One thing you're definitely not into? Guys who act like they are God's gift to the world. Soon you will be singing your R-E-S-P-E-C-T for a good-natured Sagittarius who understands life's real blessings—like family and friends.

friend match

You are NOT a football (you don't even like the sport!), so don't let yourself get kicked around. Make sure you surround yourself with people who won't take advantage of your kindness, like an equally generous Cancer for whom friendship is golden.

+/− You give so much, you may as well be Santa Claus. But make sure you know who goes on the Naughty list before you start doling out handouts; not everyone is worth your favors or attention.

$ Head of a charity organization

Casual

"Give a Little Bit" —Goo Goo Dolls

Vintage pearl earrings

Collie

Jackie O

December 28

Self-Assured, Sophisticated, Smart

You're just like a classic Chanel quilted bag: Simple as well as sophisticated. You have a solid, grounded energy that carries with it a kind of *je ne sais quoi*; your elegance comes from the fact that you know exactly who you are and what you want. No matter how much you blossom, you never forget your roots, and your earthiness lends you confidence and appeal that make other people gravitate to you.

+/− You love to be appreciated, and you've got plenty of admirers to make you feel special. But sometimes it pays to step off that pedestal and mingle with the common peeps. Holding a pose 24/7 is bound to get boring.

love match

You get so much chocolate on Valentine's Day, you could open up your own candy store. It's cool that you inspire so many crushes, but make sure to hold out for a cool and sophisticated Scorpio who thinks outside of the (chocolate) box.

friend match

You're always down to dole out advice, and you've got a group of girlfriends hanging on your every word. Just make sure you've got your own Dr. Phil for times of trouble, like a loyal and even-tempered Leo who's always willing to lend an ear.

You're just like a duck in
water: Even when you don't try, you always float to the top. Even though you try to stay out of the spotlight, you somehow always find yourself heading up group projects and organizing your friends' social calendars. But it's no accident that people turn to you for guidance: You're strong, sensible, and smart, and you've got a low-key sense of humor that carries you through when other people's expectations are weighing on you.

Talking over coffee

Teen helpline

"The Remedy (I Won't Worry)" —Jason Mraz

December 29

Interesting, Communicative, Commanding

+/− Just like the leader in a game of Simon Says, people do whatever you tell them. But here's another game it pays to know how to play: Sorry. If you mess up, apologize.

love match

Because you're type A, most people assume you're super-serious. But an Aquarius cutie will vibe with your ironic sense of humor, so you'll never have to worry about running out of conversation—or laughs—with him.

friend match

Although you love being in a group, you could use some help when it comes to basic social skills. (Like compromise, and learning to listen to other people's opinions.) A Libra who defines the term "social butterfly" can help.

December 30

You are just like a stop sign: direct, to the point, and if people know what's good for them, they will do what you say. Blessed with a natural talent for taking charge, you've got a commanding presence that makes you seem older  than your age. You're a true queen bee: You want things done right, and you  want them done quickly, and although you can be a generous and good-natured friend, you turn vicious when someone calls your authority into question.

Seashell

Dinner and a movie

Eliza Dushku

+/− You value honesty and don't see the point of beating around the bush, but certain situations call for a little bit of tact. If your BFF's jeans make her look like a sausage casing, keep it under wraps—just let her know that she looks hotter in the peasant skirt.

love match

You're a traditional girl, so you want a guy who will take charge of asking you out. (You wouldn't mind a bouquet of roses, either.) Look for a Leo with an old-school sense of values . . . and a habit of opening doors.

friend match

You just hate mess, so an all-over-the-place Aries drives you crazy with her carelessness and recklessness. But you cannot deny her hilarious schemes will keep you entertained—and keep you from getting too uptight.

December 31

If you were a Disney princess, you would be Belle: all about beauty. (Just no beasts, please!) You spend hours every morning primping in front of the mirror, but people who accuse you of being shallow have got it twisted. You love beauty in all forms, from lyrical poems and classic films to perfect sunsets and amazing couture dresses.

YOU AVOID CONFRONTATION AND ALWAYS SEEK HARMONY AND STABILITY, WHICH MEANS YOU CAN SOMETIMES SEEM SHY.

friend match

It's great that you're such an idealist, but you could use an earthier influence to keep your dreams and plans grounded in reality. A serious and sweet-tempered Taurus will help you find your footing.

Art critic

Diane von Furstenberg

"No More Drama"
—Mary J. Blige

love match

Face it: You've got a serious habit of judging books by their covers. Make sure you don't miss out on a hilarious and fun-loving Aries just because his style's a bit bummy: Beneath those shaggy bangs and the rocker T-shirt, he's a total catch.

+/− You hate mess, chaos, and ugliness and when something doesn't please you—whether it's your friend's chartreuse sweater or a news story on TV—you tend to ignore it. But denial is the ugliest thing of all, so learn how to confront your fears (ugh, angora!) head-on.

No-whip mocha frappuccino

Sangria

Wedding Planner

January 1

Responsible, Organized, Capable

If life were a big math equation, you would be the plus sign. From the fact that those little suckers get tacked onto every A paper you write ("Shoes and Sexism in Shakespearean England"—genius!) to your positive outlook, it all adds up to one thing: You've got it together. In fact, there are only three Cs in your life: Acting Cool, Calm, and Collected. Unfortunately, when it comes to the fourth C—Chilling—you get a big, fat F.

+/− You want to make sure everybody's happy, **but don't let your need to make nice get in the way of getting what you deserve.**

> SOMETIMES IT PAYS TO PUT THE PUH-LEEZE BACK IN PEOPLE PLEASER.

love match

A hot Scorpio overachiever has been driving you crazy with his know-it-all attitude forever. Will the tension make for an explosive relationship or a steady flame? Only one way to find out.

friend match

You need a BFF who's got her act together just like you, so you're not always playing babysitter. (Or worse, cleanup crew.) A confident Leo will balance out your type A tendencies with her creativity and love of fun.

You are like the human equivalent of a KitchenAid Crockpot: You work best when you're under pressure. Whether it's a term paper for social studies or helping your BFF select the perfect outfit for a summer barbecue, you always get the job done right. But staying on 24/7 will make any girl want to blow, so be sure to make time to let off some steam.

Turtle (to slow down!)

Kate Bosworth

"Piece of Me" —Britney Spears

January 2

Reliable, Achieving, Loyal

+/– When you care about someone, you'll do anything to help out. **But you've got worries of your own!** As hard as it may be, sometimes you just have to sign, "Return to Sender," on other people's baggage.

love match

In your case opposites really do attract, and you need a laid-back guy who can laugh with (and at) you when you're freaking out about reorganizing your sock drawer by color. A fun-loving Libra will help keep things light.

friend match

When you're stressing, your Mercury-ruled BFF can help you keep things in perspective. You keep her in line by reminding her that a leg-warmer-and-metallic-tights combo is more repulsive than retro, and she mixes it up by reminding you not to care so much.

322

January 3

You could easily be a lover (as your super-close-knit crew can attest) but you've definitely got some fight in you, too. Whether you're holding court about having tuna casserole for dinner (a no-go) or the importance of going green, you always stand up for what you believe. You aren't afraid to draw a line in the sand, and your friends (and enemies!) feel it: Some people are just plain shut out of your inner circle's cabana.

Your Save the Whales bumper sticker

Debate team

Professional

+/− It is really great to have strong opinions, but make sure you are not talking so loudly you miss what other people are saying. It's not a conversation if only one person's sharing, and you risk missing out on a friend's perspective.

love match

You and a cute Taurus will go head-to-head on everything from school politics to American cheese vs. cheddar. Beneath the constant battling, you're both very similar—and a perfect pair!

friend match

An easygoing air-sign friend will let you take the lead, whether you're insisting on Cherry Coke at the movie theater or calling shotgun in her older sib's car.

January 4

In the great puzzle of life, you're the girl lining up the pieces. An excellent problem solver, your friends know they can count on you to straighten out the Mega-Messes, like what to do when your heel breaks in mid-march or how to decipher your math teacher's mysterious homework assignments. But don't be afraid of not having all of the answers: Sometimes the picture's actually prettier when the edges don't quite line up.

love match

A charming fire sign who is always chatting you up makes your insides go fluttery, but you're not the only girl who's getting a dose of his attention. When it comes to love you're all or nothing, so stick with a loyal (and adorable) Taurus who can keep his eyes on you.

friend match

A sloppy Scorpio friend will drive you crazy with her laissez-fair attitude toward homework and housework. (Read: Her bedroom looks like a natural-disaster area.) But her crazy sense of humor and 24/7 energy will help you loosen up.

Sky blue

ER doctor

Small cottage in Ireland

+/− You're a great girl to have along for a road trip, because you've got the route totally planned out. But sometimes the unpredictable detours are the most fun, so don't shy away from straying off the path.

Surprise picnic in your backyard

Fashion design

Carrie Ann Inaba

January 5

Serious, Resilient, Resourceful

Whenever life hands you lemons, you make organic lemon-infused mint iced tea; when a door closes in your face, you sneak in through the window. Studious, serious, and reliable, you're not exactly a troublemaker, but you can see your way out of any mess without breaking a sweat. (Or smudging your lip gloss.)

+/– Your report card proves how serious you are about your studies. But keep in mind there's one F that's worth having: Fun! Make sure your next extra-credit assignment is a plan to let loose.

love match

Leos are famous for their loyalty and protectiveness, and you definitely need a guy who will stand by you when you're explaining your way out of detention. (It's not your fault the quickest way to first period is through the boy's locker room!)

friend match

You need a friend who'll be your biggest cheerleader, so look to a gung-ho Aries who will happily sing your praises. (Pom-poms optional.) She'll give you that extra push you need to achieve your dreams.

You're just like change for a dollar, because you're always trying to make sense. Understanding the truth about yourself and the world around you is super-important to you, which means you ask, "Why?" more often than the kids you babysit for. By nature an explorer, you're adventurous and courageous and don't shy away from scary situations, whether it's attempting the new roller coaster at Six Flags or asking your crush to dance at the Spring Fling.

Phone

Mint green

FBI Agent

January 6

Faithful, Accepting, Inquisitive

+/− Because you're always reading and asking questions, you have an encyclopedic knowledge of everything from tomato varietals to the mating habits of bees. Sometimes you can slip into being more preacher than friend, so save the lectures for school.

love match

A fellow earth sign might be most compatible in the long-term, but a passionate and inquisitive fire sign will have you asking a new question: "What's love got to do with it?"

friend match

A head-in-the-clouds Pisces friend helps bring out your spiritual and creative sides, and in return your feet-on-the-ground approach keeps her from completely floating away.

January 7

You know that, just like parachutes, minds work best when they're open. You love new people and new ideas, and your creative pursuits are as varied as your fashion choices. (Uptown girl-next-door chic one day, downtown tragic-artist hip the next.) It's cool that you're so open, but as a result you can fall victim to negative vibes from friends and family.

WHEN SOMEONE TRIES TO TAKE THE WIND OUT OF YOUR SAILS, JUST BLOW THEM OFF.

love match

You believe in fate, and you're pretty sure that your destiny involves a certain blue-eyed Leo who always seems to be hanging around. Trust your gut: His honesty and humor make him the kind of guy you're lucky to have on your side.

Activist

Drew Barrymore

"Our Time Now" – Plain White T's

+/− Daydreaming is healthy. Daydreaming in the middle of your math quiz? Not so much. Make sure you check back into the real world every so often, since even you can't imagine your way out of detention.

friend match

A quirky Pisces pal has an appreciation for all things unusual (like old sci-fi movies and browsing thrift stores for original fashion finds), just like you.

You're just like a ten-car pileup, because you're all about making an impact. It's not that you're prone to explosions—you like to keep the drama in check—but whether you're striding down the hallway or kicking butt on the soccer field, it's all about making an impression. You have amazing powers of concentration (you rock standardized tests) and an innate sense of timing, meaning you crack your friends up on the regular.

friend match

Because you both insist on having your way, you and a fall-born BFF have an explosive relationship, with a lot more ins and outs than an episode of *Project Runway.* Friendship shouldn't go out of fashion, so try to work on compromising.

love match

You can be very intimidating, so you need a guy with a strong sense of self to serve as your match. But don't confuse someone who hangs back with someone who's afraid to step up: A quiet, music-loving Scorpio who flies under the radar has more than enough confidence to pair up with you.

High school radio station

Bollywood

Celeb hotspot in Cannes

+/− Your motto is "My way or the highway," but it's a lonely road to travel when you're always insisting there's only one right way.

LEARN TO FORGIVE AND ACCEPT OTHER PEOPLE'S POINT OF VIEW.

Gucci riding boots

Magenta

Dance team captain

January 9

Resilient, Purposeful, Resourceful

If life is like an ice cream sundae, you are the cherry, because you're all about being on top. Ambition is the driving force behind those born on January 9th, and whether you're out to win social chair or want to ensure your friends have the best possible seats at the pep rally, you're all about making sure that you and your people get yours. You're super-motivated and have a way of spotting opportunity before it even has a chance to knock. Just be careful you don't mow down other people on your way to answer the door.

+/− You know what they say about all work and no play: boring. Sometimes you act like Cupid—the boss of everyone else's love life-rather than listening to your own heart.

love match

You might see a funny fire-sign guy in your life as just a friend, but don't underestimate the importance of a good laugh. He'll have you giggling your way to stronger feelings, and your dates will never be boring.

friend match

An always overachieving Saturn-ruled girl might seem like your Number One rival, but you are way more alike than you think. Talk to her as a friend, not a competitor, and find out.

Just like a cobra, you've got no problem waiting until the right moment to strike. (And as your ex-boyfriends know, it's better not to get you angry.) Your friends know they can count on you to be brutally honest, which is why they seek out your (sometimes scathing) advice on everything from boys to bras.

Burgundy

Reality-TV show judge

Iguana

January 10

Tough,
Authoritative,
Realistic

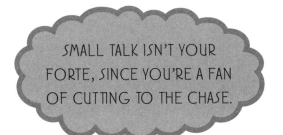

SMALL TALK ISN'T YOUR FORTE, SINCE YOU'RE A FAN OF CUTTING TO THE CHASE.

+/− So maybe you can't drive yet, but you always take the wheel in every situation. Try chilling in the backseat once in a while, and let one of your peeps take charge.

love match

Your love life is the only topic you stay mum about, so even your closest friends won't know that an earth-sign soccer player has your head spinning. But he'll need more encouragement from you than wistful glances, so it's time to put that famous mouth to work for you—and tell him!

friend match

A gullible Venus-ruled friend likes a spoonful of sweet with her dose of reality, and may not understand why you don't ever sugarcoat the truth. She'll help you take the edge off your tongue, and you'll make sure she doesn't get duped by sweet-talking guys or faux Prada bags.

330

January 11

Independent, Capable, Strong-Willed

You're like a standardized test, because you're all about evaluation. You have an opinion about everything (and, let's face it, you're usually right!) and at a party are most likely to be found on the sidelines, scoping out the scene—which is why you can usually spot hookups and breakups before they happen. Super- set in your ideas, you're not the kind of girl to be tempted by peer pressure, and anyone waiting for you to fall in line better forget about it. You're the kind of person who organizes and auctions off all her halloween candy. Just make sure you're attitude isn't taking all the joy out of the little things in life.

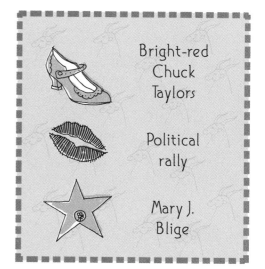

Bright-red Chuck Taylors

Political rally

Mary J. Blige

+/− You're right 99 percent of the time, but nobody's perfect. If you make a mistake, own up to it. You can do anything, including pronouncing the two hardest words in the English language to say: "I'm sorry."

friend match

When your mind's made up, there's no point trying to change it, but that doesn't stop your passionate Libra BFF from debating the merits of Rocky Road vs. Cherry Garcia with you all night long. You love how she stands up for what she believes in!

love match

A sensitive air-sign cutie in your class is intrigued by your take-charge attitude, but intimidated by your intensity. Smile at him once in a while, and he'll see that your bark is way worse than your bite.

You should be a CEO, because you are all about taking care of business. You're the go-to girl for food drives, bake sales, and volunteer time, and you're quick to pick up a new cause. (Save the trees! Go Green!) Unfortunately there's one business you're not so good at—minding your own! Not everyone's as outspoken as you, so be careful not to spill someone else's secrets.

NEVER ONE TO HIDE YOUR FEELINGS, YOU ALWAYS SPEAK YOUR MIND.

friend match

You've got a ton of names in your cell's phone book, but only your Neptune-ruled BFF on speed dial. Her active imagination is the perfect counterpoint for your get-èr-done ways.

LIVESTRONG bracelet

Teen helpline

"A Little Less Conversation" —Elvis Presley

love match

A brown-eyed Aquarius has caught your eye, but his flighty ways and inability to make plans will drive you crazy. Stick with a steady basketball-playing Leo with a killer smile.

+/− The fact that you can talk a mile a minute is charming—you're enthusiastic—but the fact that you have an opinion on everything from the color of your BFF's nails to the best way to eat an ice-cream cone occasionally makes you seem full of yourself. Let someone else get a word in edgewise.

January 13

Maltese

Seventeen magazine's former editor in chief Atoosa Rubenstein

Mod

+/− It's fine to be ambitious, but just remember what they say: The toes you step on today could be connected to the butt you kiss tomorrow. Try not to burn bridges.

Goal-Oriented, Proud, Autonomous

If life were a high-end gym, you'd be the stair climber: You're all about social mobility. You've got places to be and people to see, and you're not afraid to step on the little people to get what you want. You lust after Gucci bags the way some people crave chocolate, and your dream is to become a high-powered attorney or businesswoman. (Good thing you're practicing those argumentative skills with your 'rents now!) You've definitely got your pride, so it can be hard for you to admit any kind of mistake.

love match

You've got a crush on someone new practically every week, a soulful and sincere Mercury-ruled boy might have you singing the praises of coupling off for good.

friend match

When it comes to new people, you can be a little guarded. That's why you need a feisty fire-sign BFF to help bring you out of your shell—when you start to let loose, you can be the life of the party!

You're like a Sony Imax movie screen: all about the big picture. While some people get snagged up on the details, you're able to take a step back and see the whole problem and the whole solution, which makes you an excellent team captain and the perfect leader on group projects. For this reason, you don't shy away from difficult situations—like advanced math classes or malls the day after Thanksgiving. It's not that you're attracted to danger, it's just that you have no fear.

> IN A FILM ABOUT YOUR LIFE, YOUR ATTITUDE WOULD PUT THE RED-CARPET RAVE IN BRAVERY.

Sapphire

Federal judge

Revolution – The Beatles

January 14

Indomitable, Courageous, Organized

+/− When you witness an injustice, it (like someone cutting in front of the snack line!), you're on it before you can say, "Nacho cheese." But some battles aren't yours to fight, or just aren't worth the hassle, so learn to tell the difference.

love match

Nothing drives you crazier than someone who doesn't speak his mind, which is why your heart starts skipping beats when an opinionated and outgoing Taurus waltzes into your English class—and your life.

friend match

Any best friend of yours has to be prepared to cover you when you're headed for a war zone (again). A courageous and faithful Taurus BFF will have your back when you're pleading your No-Grounding case to your 'rents.

January 15

If you were a TV show, you would be *Heroes*; you may not have a secret identity (or a fabulous superhero outfit), but whenever there's a crisis, your friends, parents, and teachers can count on you to step up to the plate. Mom running late and can't pick up your little sis? You'll swoop in on your bike and solve the problem. BFF's boyfriend dumped her on Valentine's Day? You're there with a box of tissues and a pint of ice cream before she can say sniffle. Just remember to pick your battles, as going head-to-head with everybody you meet will just leave you with a headache.

Swiss army knife (a hot pink one, of course!)

Regina King

Youth hostel in Switzerland

+/− Every superhero has a super-weakness, and yours is being too stubborn and refusing to listen to other people's advice.

> KEEP YOUR MIND AND YOUR HEART OPEN.

love match

Every girl knows that boys can be dogs, but don't let one self-centered Sagittarius ruin you on all guys. Just because he was a mutt, doesn't mean that there's not some serious puppy love in your future with a certain cutie born in early August.

friend match

You can't stand any kind of unfairness, and a balance-obsessed Libra is exactly the same way. You'll see eye to eye about almost everything, making her the perfect sidekick.

January 16

You're a glass all-full girl; you can't stand to leave anything half-finished or partially undone. Ruled by the idea of fulfillment, you're extremely dedicated to the activities and projects you pursue but equally obsessed with guarding your close friendships and finding a long-term relationship. (Month-to-month crushes so aren't your thing.) You need lots of positive reinforcement—you practically invented the question, "Does this make my butt look fat?"—and have to work hard to find confidence and happiness on your own. It's true what they say: If you love yourself first, the rest will fall into place (including Mr. Perfect).

friend match

A Scorpio in your close crew is the definition of the word frenemy, always undermining you when you need a leg up. Go ahead and trade up for a sun-ruled Leo who will always be your cheerleader.

love match

Your usual routine is thrown off balance by an explosive Uranus-ruled guy with a penchant for troublemaking.

+/− Being such a hard worker definitely pays off, but be careful of biting off more than you can chew. Running for social chair may sound appealing, but your commitments are stacking up so quickly you're bound to choke.

Walk along the pier

High school principal

Kate Moss

Orange

Pitbull

Zooey
Deschanel

January 17

Independent, Forceful,
Expressive

You could easily be a boxer, because when it comes to getting your way, you are the heavyweight champion of the whole astrological year. Goal-oriented and ultra-direct, you always make your presence felt, whether you are taking control of a group project or strutting—and not walking!—into the cafeteria. Your close friends know better than to argue with you; just like the final chapter of a book, you always get the last word. Just remember, it's a slippery slope from confident to cocky.

$+/-$ You and the Fourth of July have something in common: all about independence. Wanting to do your own thing is one thing, but refusing to play well with others will leave you celebrating every holiday on your lonesome.

PRACTICE
COMPROMISE.

love match

When it comes to romance, you can be the equivalent of a linebacker—intimidating. Good thing a confident and mischievous boy born in early May knows how to push right back.

friend match

You and a Jupiter-ruled friend have been BFFs forever. Why? Your bluntness can be hard to handle, but this level-headed girl doesn't so much as blink when you start on one of your rants.

If you were to be a Disney character, you'd be Peter Pan, because you never want to grow up. You love having fun and being silly just as much as you did as a child, and getting older does not hold that much appeal. (Um . . . responsibility? Some more homework? No thank you.) You crave constant excitement and tend to spend a lot of time in your head, fantasizing about your own private version of Never NeverLand (which just happens to involve a hot boy from your math class). Make sure once in a while you touch down to earth.

$ Preschool teacher

You're awesome at jump roping.

♪ "I'm Like a Bird" —Nelly Furtado

January 18

Imaginative, Naïve, Fun

+/− You tend to run away from anything that's painful (including homework, confrontations, and extra-high heels). In real life it's important to learn how to balance work and fun. Try to get over your fear of all things serious, or everyone will start thinking of you as a joke.

love match

Ironically, though you're fun and playful (and occasionally immature), your best relationship bet is to a totally-together Taurus who acts way older than his age. Opposites attract, and in this case it's all about balance.

friend match

You can be pretty gullible, so you need a trusty earth-sign friend to keep you grounded. When you totally fall for something (an unused iPhone for only $15?), she'll keep you clued in to the joke before you become the punch line.

January 19

You're just like LASIK: all about vision. You've got the true soul of an artist (many famous singers, painters, and writers were born on this day), spending most of your time in your own fantasy world and refusing to compromise your ideals, beliefs, and your desires. Super-intense and ultra-creative, you find it almost impossible to do everyday things like clean your room, do your homework, or listen to your teachers.

YOU OFTEN FIND
YOURSELF AT
ODDS WITH OTHERS.

Oil paints and a canvas, natch

Snorkeling

Janis Joplin

+/− You have got the energy of a fireworks display—but just like fireworks, you have a tendency to burn out quickly. Your moods are constantly shifting (thrilled one minute and devastated the next). Work to create balance and stability in your life.

friend match

Playing well with others isn't your thing, but you and a Gemini friend have similarly artistic temperaments—and a similar tendency to explode when things don't go your way. Oh, well. All that arguing just fuels your creative fire.

love match

Sun-ruled guys have a tendency to think the world revolves around them (big surprise). You're attracted to confident attitudes but won't let yourself be bossed around, so expect a tug-of-war when you try to make it work with a boy born in late April.

You have the same motto as Nike: "Just Do It." If you get the urge to act, you always go for it, whether your gut is telling you to snap up two pairs of the newest must-have jeans or shimmy on the dance floor while everyone else is still standing by the beverage table. No matter how crazy your schedule is or what kind of drama is going down at school, you're confident you can handle whatever comes your way.

YOU HAVE A GREAT SENSE OF HUMOR AND DON'T TAKE YOURSELF—OR LIFE—TOO SERIOUSLY.

friend match

You play cheerleader for a sensitive Pisces friend, and she plays artistic director. Who else would make like a five-year-old and spend a whole afternoon finger painting with you?

Indigo

Day at the beach

Dalmatian

love match

A serious Saturn-ruled cutie may be staying away because he thinks you're superficial. Once he realizes that you just like to have fun, he'll be tempted to loosen up around you—and you may find yourself opening up to him about way more than juicy gossip and the latest lip gloss color.

+/− There is no doubt that people look up to you for your optimism and positivity, but you cannot always take center stage. When your BFF is telling a story, don't interrupt or try to compete with a story of your own; it just makes you seem petty.

Aquarius Girls

are thoughtful and accepting

Aquarius is the third and last air sign of the zodiac. Non-judgmental and non-superficial to the extreme, Aquarius are just like Wikipedia: 100 percent open to what different people bring to the table. They practice a "live and let live" attitude and typically don't seek other people's approval for the decisions they make. This can also make them seem eccentric or difficult to understand.

Motto: "I think, therefore I shop."

Landscape they most resemble: Mountains. Pure, difficult to get to, always reaching for the sky.

Strengths to play on: Rationality, adaptability.

Pitfalls to avoid: Thoughtlessness, flakiness.

Aquarius

January 21 – February 19

Element: Air
Ruler: Uranus

Most likely to be:
Secretly enrolled in a
college-level
philosophy course.

January 21

You are just like an ice cube in water: headed straight for the top. A true trendsetter, if you start rocking wide-leg jeans with a sailor button fly, you can guarantee that everyone in school will start doing the same. Ambitious, competitive and driven, you also know how to kick back and veg when it's time to relax. You're very persuasive so people line up to follow your lead, and you can be friends with just about anybody. (Except for Smelly Boy in your science class.)

Knitting

Emma Bunton
(aka Baby
Spice)

Retro

+/− You know you want to be the best at whatever you do, but you have a hard time settling on any one goal for long. Beware of Dandruff Dilemma— stop drifting!

love match

Whether you like to admit it or not, you're a heartbreaker. Often you don't perceive the effects of your actions on others, so if an Aries guy is way too flaky for you, stop smiling at him and offering homework help. Look for a more driven Sagittarius, whose ambitious energies match your own.

friend match

You often suffer from a serious case of whiplash, always whipping around to watch your friends follow behind you. That's why a confident and outspoken Leo is your ideal BFF. She'll set the pace, not just follow in your footsteps.

January 22

You are just like a mug of steaming hot chocolate: impossible to resist, with a tendency to scorch. Intensely energetic and extremely impulsive, you're a classic wild child: loads of fun. Because you're independent, intuitive, and fearless, though, a ton of friends are willing to take the risk—and get rewarded by your sweetness big time.

THE INTENSITY OF YOUR PERSONALITY CAN
ALSO BURN PEOPLE WHO GET TOO CLOSE.

friend match

A know-it-all Taurus friend can be a little annoying, but when you want to leap before you look, she'll be your eyes and steer you away from the danger zone—like leopard-print tights and the bad boy in your art class.

love match

Your high energy and need for fun mean your idea of a date is definitely not couch time + Sports Center. You need a guy who's as fearless and outgoing as you are, like a super-social Aries.

Hiking gear

Skydiving

"Holiday"
—Weezer

+/− The occasional need to vent is normal; flying off the handle in a rage whenever something doesn't go your way is not. Take some deep breaths the next time you're seeing red, or you'll get blacklisted by your friends and fam.

January 23

Temporary hair dye

Violet

"Me, Myself, and I"
—Vitamin C

Individualistic, Dramatic, Technical

If you were an Olympic sport, you'd be pole-vaulting: bent on reaching new heights, and all about the individual. You have a very distinct style of talking, dressing, and even eating (pasta for breakfast, cereal for dessert), and you're not afraid to hold opinions or beliefs that put you at odds with your classmates—or even your family. Although some of your choices (and, let's face it, outfits) may seem strange to others, you're respected for your fearless and absolute honesty.

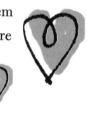

+/− You have a flare for performing makes you a natural in the theater, but you have a tendency to be overdramatic and blow things out of proportion. Save your angst for the stage, and cut your friends—and yourself—a break.

love match

A quiet Cancer may not immediately strike you as the One, but give it time and you'll discover the hidden depths and unusual perspective that you've been looking forward to. Be prepared for *looong* lunchtime convos: You'll both have opinions on everything from cricket (so cool) to karaoke.

friend match

An energetic and ultra-creative Gemini is your perfect best-friend match. Like you, she's got enthusiasm to spare, so when you're looking for someone to help you complete your wall mural (featuring 2,018 Mountain Dew labels), she's your girl.

You could be a statue in a museum, because people are always putting you on a pedestal. Whether it's your friends assuming you've got everything totally together or your teachers fawning over you for being a model student, people admire you for what they perceive to be your perfect life. Truth is, you do give off an aura of perfection, leading some haters to label you an ice queen. But most of the time you feel other people's expectations of you to be a burden.

DON'T BE AFRAID
TO SHOW SOME CRACKS.

Chihuahua

Mischa Barton

Classic

January 24

Admired, Magnetic, Superior

$+/-$ Remember that you're just like a caramel-filled chocolate truffle: Sure, the outside is important, but it's what's inside that really counts. Your cool clothes and perfect hair don't define you; what's really special are the things you like most about yourself.

love match

You often feel like guys only like you because they think you're someone that you're not—flawless and totally together. But a hilarious and laid-back Libra likes you even when your hair isn't perfectly blow-dried, so try sending some loving his way.

friend match

It can be hard for people to truly get to know you, but a sun-ruled BFF makes like heat on M&M's(™): Her warmth makes your hard shell melt. Because she's a Leo, you can trust her with anything from your fave jeans to your deepest secrets.

January 25

If life is a highway, you're the asphalt: totally tough, you're there for every dip, rise, and bump in the road. You feed off chaos, which is why you don't mind family reunions, finals week, or running around from field hockey to sculpture class to choir practice. Talented and energetic, you are never in one place—emotionally or physically—for long. You've had more crushes than a steamroller and more blowouts than a hair salon, but you stay focused on your goals no matter what twists and turns life throws at you.

WHATEVER WILL BE WILL BE.

Stress ball

Fashion magazine editor

Alicia Keys

+/− It's great that you have so much perseverance, but swimming against the current will just leave you exhausted. Every so often you need to relax and go with the flow.

love match

It's extremely hard for you to admit weakness, so even if you're head-over-heels with a floppy-haired Gemini (and his amazing art projects), you're not going to admit it. But if you want the relationship to move forward, you'll have to make the first move—believe it or not, your "hints" are harder to read than *Moby Dick*.

friend match

Even though you are studious and serious, like all Aquarius you love to have a good time. That's why you need a crazy and outgoing Aries to keep you giggling 24/7.

January 26

You're just like Bowling Night: all about the impressive strike. Like the best military strategists, you know when and how to act when you need to get your way—which is, for you, 24/7. When it comes to getting what you want—whether it's a puppy or a pair of new Steve Maddens—your determination has no limits, and there isn't anyone who can beat you in an argument once you get on a roll.

 YOU CHERISH YOUR BELIEFS AND DON'T CARE WHO DISAGREES WITH YOU.

friend match

You play planner for your whole crew, but if you ever get tired of being social director, keep a passionate and creative Scorpio close who will remind you that not everything in life should be predictable.

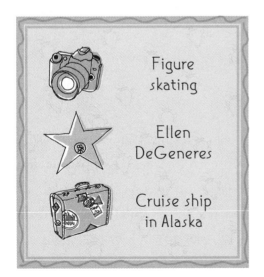

Figure skating

Ellen DeGeneres

Cruise ship in Alaska

love match

You have a tendency to be all work and no play, so to keep things from getting too dull team up with a guy who likes to keep things light, like a Libra. Unlike an Aquarius he won't ever act immature, but he will keep you from becoming a hermit during finals week.

+/− You are quite determined to be a star athlete, stellar student, and devoted daughter. But it's Okay to give yourself a break once in a while! Not everyone can be on 100 percent of the time, and as long as you try your best, everyone will understand if you need time to relax.

January 27

Copper

Foreign-film festival

Angelina Jolie

Bright, Quick, Precocious

You give new meaning to the term *"child star":* wise beyond your years, from an early age you exhibited talents, skills, and emotions remarkable in someone so young. Doing things quickly is big for you: You talk fast, walk fast, and make snap decisions, sometimes without thinking. (Does the decision to TP your math teacher's house on Halloween ring any bells?) Because you're so bright, there's a lot of pressure on you to succeed. Don't be afraid to draw the line, or you just might end up on the cover of *Us Weekly* as the latest has-been.

+/− You have got the brains of someone twice your age but a tendency to act very immature. Some childish pleasures may be fun (such as ice-cream trucks), but when your 'rents want you to grow up and take responsibility for your actions, no tantrums allowed.

love match

Because you're so impulsive, you need someone with more focus and grounding to keep you from making really bad choices. A realistic Capricorn has the presence of mind (and strength of will!) to talk you out of some of your crazier ideas.

friend match

A super-serious moon-ruled friend needs you to crack her up when she's stressing out over her science lab, and you need her shoulder to lean on when life (or your curfew) seems unfair.

If you were a book, you'd be the *Guinness Book of World Records*: your whole raison d'être is pushing limits and mind-boggling achievements. (Now if only you could learn to juggle twenty-seven balls at one time.) You are extremely ambitious but realistic about your abilities, which means that although some of your choices may seem reckless to others, you're actually always in control. Athletic and fearless, you're excellent at sports, but equally good at activities that require mental stamina.

YOU LOVE TRYING OUT NEW THINGS AND TEND TO BOUNCE AROUND FROM ACTIVITY TO ACTIVITY.

Sarah McLachlan

Volunteer work

"Such Great Heights"
—Iron and Wine

January 28

Gutsy,
Strong-Willed,
Driven

+/− Your track record of actually fulfilling commitments is more spotty than a preschooler's napkin. Finish one challenge before you tackle another.

love match

It is no wonder you are attracted to a fearless Aquarius with a reputation for pulling pranks; you're exactly the same way. Once you get together it will be a 24/7 comedy—just make sure it's not called *Dumb and Dumber!*

friend match

Girls just want to have fun, and you and a fellow air sign give new meaning to the term social butterfly. Wherever the two of you go, you're bound to be the life of the party!

January 29

You should be a musical instrument, because you are all about harmony. Though you'll definitely stand up and defend your beliefs—like the cruelty of your school's dress code!—for the most part, you just want everyone to get along. Though practical and accomplished, you also have a passive side that makes it difficult for you to confront challenges head-on and super-easy to procrastinate. And with a ton of friends flocking to you for your take-it-easy vibe, you've got a ton of reasons not to tackle that homework!

YoYo

Oprah Winfrey

Hippie

+/− You're a lover, not a fighter, **but** everyone needs at least a little armor to protect them from everyday abuse. Work on building self-esteem so that other people's opinions—good or bad—don't have so much effect on you.

friend match

Those ruled by the number 2 tend to make great partners, so it's no wonder that both you and a BFF whose birthday falls on the 2nd will be practically joined at the hip, agreeing on everything from TV shows to the best brand of spaghetti sauce. (Classico!)

love match

Like you, a Libra boy will like to keep things laid-back and light, but his studious side will be a good influence when you are tempted to put off your math homework again.

January 30

You could be a dog trainer, because you're all about taking the lead. You have a natural ability to teach, guide, and explain, but you're also a do-as-I-do girl, with a proven knack at inspiring by example. (When you started rocking a bag made of recycled hemp, they suddenly became the new It accessory.) Stress never makes you sweat; you shine during crunch time, so whether you're tackling a big game or a big exam, everyone is impressed by the way you take charge.

TAKE A GAMBLE ON YOUR FRIENDS
ONCE IN A WHILE AND OPEN UP.

friend match

A fun and funny (and occasionally immature) Gemini will keep you from playing the adult too early. Life's too short to be all work and no play, so loosen up and let her bring your silly side out.

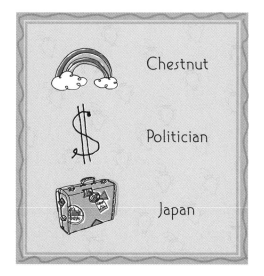

Chestnut

Politician

Japan

love match

Your practical and grounded side is totally tested by an adorable Aries who seems to court trouble wherever he goes. But if anybody can handle his mischievous ways, it's you, so consider letting go—and letting your heart do the thinking for once!

+/− When it comes to many of your thoughts and feelings, you make like a poker player and keep your cards super-close to your chest.

January 31

Shih tzu

Minnie Driver

"Diamonds Are a Girl's Best Friend"
–Marilyn Monroe

Attractive, Admired, Appreciated

Songs and poems should be written about you, because you're the perfect muse. People admire you for your liveliness and sense of humor, and even when you're just dipping into some fries in the cafeteria, you're bound to generate an adoring crowd. You're fun and very social—with so many friends it's easy to always roll with a crowd. Sometimes you feel like nobody really gets you, though, and even though you always get center stage, you often have the sense of just playing a role.

+/– True friendships are a lot like diamonds: forever. Better to have one true friend than ten hangers-on, so pick wisely. It might be time to clean out the closet!

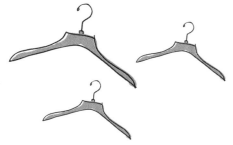

love match

You break hearts left and right but nobody's ever done serious damage to your ticker—or even raised the beat. Expect that to change when a totally down to earth Libra acts immune to your charms and sweeps you off your feet with his casual confidence.

friend match

Loyalty and honesty are very important to you, as you often feel that your life is a little short on both. A Leo friend may not share your love of all things beautiful and glamorous (you'll argue for hours about her flip-flop and jeans standard uniform), but she'll be an important grounding force.

If you were a plant, you'd be an oak tree: strong roots keep you grounded in all kinds of weather (fights between best friends, midterm stress, little sibs), and it's best to avoid bumping heads with you. But just because you have the rootedness of a tree, doesn't mean you're all bark—you've got some bite in you, too. You've got a scathing sense of humor that's always spot-on. Compromising isn't your strong suit, so try to be more flexible. You know what they say—what doesn't bend, breaks.

Red

Talk-show host

German shepherd

February 1

Strong-Willed, Witty, Grounded

+/− Your witty comebacks crack up your friends, but you have to know the time and the place. Ease up on your criticisms and learn to live and let live.

love match

A boy born on the 12th is desperate to go out with you, but his scheming social climbing should have you rolling your eyes. Stick with a loyal Leo boy who has kept the same solid crew since middle school. He'll show the same dedication to you.

friend match

You and your autumn-born BFF have similar temperaments—and a similar tendency to hold onto grudges. But after a falling out, you're going to be the one who apologizes—friendship is way more important than pride.

February 2

Du caviar, s'il vous plaît?

If life is a box of chocolates, you're a champagne-filled Godiva truffle. You are so sophisticated, you could make the Queen of England seem gauche, and your attention to detail (you can spot a faux-Prada bag from a mile off) means you are a perfectionist about everything. Just make sure your snooty attitude doesn't have other people saying, *"non merci."*

IT'S TOUGH FOR YOU TO JUST SPILL YOUR GUTS TO A LOT OF PEOPLE.

Jet-black Porsche

Haute couture

Five-star hotel in Milan

+/− Your perfect meet-and-greet skills leave something to be desired. Even ultra-VIP rooms are meant to be shared, so every so often you might want to give the common people a shot. Pizza and scary movies may not be luxe, but they can be as fun as any four-star evening.

love match

You're in your own world most of the time, which is why you barely notice when a cute Uranus-ruled boy starts flirting with you in the lunch line. Don't judge him just because of his sticker-covered skateboard—you might be surprised by how much you have in common.

friend match

Big sleepover parties aren't exactly your thing. But your Gemini BFF is a different story. You can trust her never to spread your secrets, and her honesty with you—you're the only person who knows she faints at the sight of blood!—helps you open up.

You like to live life the same way you solve math problems . . . guess and check. (Oh—and cross your fingers, hoping for the best!) Carefree and laid-back, you think planning and studying are a snooze, and your friends know you're up for anything, anytime. Your allergy to all things arranged applies to your sense of humor as well: Your friends know and love the outrageous (and sometimes inappropriate) things you say. Just learn the difference between *unexpected* and *unwelcome*—you wouldn't want to accidentally hurt anyone.

love match

Right now you're feeling an animal-loving Aries, but let's face it: Your tastes change more often than a stoplight. All that may change when you meet a Capricorn who's even more indecisive than you. Watch out: Sparks will fly, but he's not the type to settle down.

friend match

Your BFF is ruled by super-serious Saturn, so it is no wonder that she gets frustrated when you are always at least fifteen minutes late. Nevertheless, her organized and practical mind provides the perfect balance to your more relaxed approach to life.

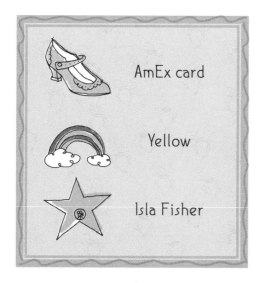

AmEx card

Yellow

Isla Fisher

+/− Make sure your carpe diem approach does not get you in any kind of trouble, like when you fail to prepare yet another bio assignment. Nothing can kill a fly-by-the-seat-of-your-pants attitude like getting hung out to dry.

Amusement park

Musical theater

"Love Today"
—Mika

February 4

Sincere, Lively, Entertaining

If life is a stage, you've got a pretty solid solo act lined up. You're full of energy, and you love the spotlight, which means your friends often play adoring audience to your one-woman show. But you're definitely not mindless entertainment: Loyal to your friends and family and deeply committed to the things you value, you're the human equivalent of raspberry sorbet—totally fresh and good for you, even in large doses.

YOU GET BORED
AFTER TEN SECONDS OF
DOING ANYTHING.

+/— You are dynamic and fun, **but your serial upstaging may leave your besties contemplating some serious backstage backstabbing. Make sure you make time to applaud their talents as well—otherwise the curtain may close prematurely on some friendships.**

love match

Although you're totally charming, you're definitely not the typical giggly girl. A Jupiter-ruled cutie in your class likes you just the way you are and appreciates the fact that you totally ditch the ditzy act.

friend match

A fun-loving Sagittarius is great to have as your BFF, as she's got the energy and the ideas to keep you busy, and whether you're attempting to make your own ice cream or throwing a Frisbee, you're always having a blast.

If certain people wear their hearts on their sleeves, you wear yours on a delicate gold-filigree necklace (with matching bracelet, natch). Effortlessly graceful in everything you do, you even make bearing your heart and soul look easy. You should— you've had plenty of practice! It's great that you're so open about your feelings, but take a lesson from professional poker players: Sometimes it is best not to show your hand too early. (Particularly when you're holding on to the Queen of Hearts!)

Violet

Preschool teacher

Hippie

February 5

Skilful, Demonstrative, Graceful

+/− The fact that you're so open to other people makes you especially vulnerable to getting hurt. Make sure your crushes are worth the life-and-death drama before you let them play Romeo to your Juliet.

love match

You have been secretly pining for a summer-born hottie in your class, but he's got his eyes on someone else. Life's too short for unrequited love! Look for a passionate fire sign who can match the intensity of your feelings.

friend match

You can be quiet, but if anyone tries to mess with your friends, they'll see that you're definitely not weak. Your BFF (whose b-day is in the same month as yours!) returns the favor, and she knows just how to cheer you up when your heart's been broken. (Again!)

February 6

The expression "You can attract more flies with honey than vinegar" holds true for people, too, and you're living proof that staying sweet can mean a big social payoff. People are drawn to you like moths to a flame, and very few ever make their way out of your orbit. Your friends look to you for plans, support, and to be a 24/7 cheerleader. Just make sure your need to please isn't concealing deeper feelings that need to be expressed. Nothing causes a bad taste in your mouth like artificial sugar.

Kleenex

Spirit squad

Labradoodle

+/− From the outside it looks like you have it all, but deep down you worry your friends will bail if they discover your inner dork. News flash: Your true friends love you for you—closet crochet expert and everything—not just for the fact that your disposition is sweeter than Skittles.

love match

A soft-spoken Scorpio has you hoping for a special valentine. But what seems standoffish may just be shyness, so don't be afraid to step up and give him a sign.

friend match

You get a new friend request practically every day on your MySpace page, and your Top 8 is always shifting around. That's because you're ruled by the planet Venus, which makes you extremely magnetic.

Idealistic, Spontaneous, Natural

You like to live life au naturel: from your all-organic hemp-weave T-shirts to your no-stress policy on school (and hairstyles, Ms. Ponytail Princess), you subscribe to the less-is-more philosophy. The only things high maintenance in your life are your principles: You see opportunities for improvement everywhere and are a firm believer in working hard for change. Just not when "work" involves math and "change" involves grades!

☆ · ☆ · ☆ · ☆ · ☆ · ☆ · ☆ · ☆ · ☆ · ☆

friend match

Even though you seem flighty, when it comes to friendships, you're as solid as they come. To you, a BFF really is forever, and you have to know you can trust someone before you open up. A superloyal Pisces has the same idea.

A walk in the park

Head of a nonprofit organization

Drew Barrymore

love match

There's a certain Leo in your class who's got all the girls saying meow. He's way too self-centered and egotistical for you, though. You'll take an oh-so-modest (and oh-so-adorable) Libra guitar player any day.

+/− Living life in the here and now is like a house made entirely from cheeseburgers: fine in theory, but in practice? After a few days, it stinks.

> EVERY SO OFTEN IT'S IMPORTANT TO PLAN AHEAD.

Peach

Teen help line

Spa in the mountains

February 8

Conceptual, Open, Intuitive

You are so in touch with what other people think you could easily have your own psychic hotline. Extraordinarily perceptive when it comes to others, you're equally as clued in to your own feelings, and you always make a point to go with your gut. Your superpowered sensitivity to others is a double-edged gift, however: Make sure your chakras don't get disrupted by negative energy.

+/− Being privy to so much private info puts a heavy burden on you, so make sure you don't blurt out someone else's secret at the wrong time. Just because it is obvious to you that your BFF is fiendishly crushing on a cutie soccer player, does not mean it is common knowledge!

love match

Your usually flawless intuition seems to falter when it comes to your crushes, particularly the sun-ruled guy you have been drooling over forever. Sure, he is superhot, but you don't need a Magic 8-Ball to tell you he's self-centered.
   Outlook not good!

friend match

Your closest peeps know you've got a heart of gold, but you're a little reserved around people you've just met. A fellow Aquarius can help you break the ice super-quickly—after five minutes, it'll be like you've been friends forever.

Opportunity doesn't even have to knock on your door. As soon as you see it rolling down the street, you're already claiming shotgun in its ride. You believe in the power of positive thinking and aren't the type to rely on good luck charms and knocking on wood. You make your own luck—setbacks and disappointments never trip you up. Your motto is: "The sun'll come out tomorrow." And if not, you have been looking for an excuse to rock your rain boots!

Personal assistant

Broadway show

Motivational speaker

February 9

Colorful, Optimistic, Productive

+/− It's great that you're always on the go, but riding so hard just leads to a big old burnout. Take time to chill and refuel. Your friends will appreciate the downtime, and it will leave you totally refreshed.

love match

Your Capricorn crush may not think of you as girlfriend material, but you don't throw yourself a pity party. He'll make an awesome friend, and he knows an easygoing water sign who'll be your perfect match.

friend match

When your moody moon-ruled pal is struggling to get her homework done every morning before class, you can tutor her in math and help her manage her time better. It's worth it. When she's in a good mood, she's the perfect partner in crime.

February 10

Some people march to the beat of their own drummer. You salsa to it. You have a strong sense of self, and your friends look up to you for your confidence as well as charisma. Although you do not care what other people think—you are not afraid to speak your mind, declare your love for old sci-fi movies, or experiment with your fashion choices—you care greatly what they feel. Your BFFs know they can count on you to partner when they need a little spring in their step.

$ Self-help guru

Parakeet

Emma Roberts

+/− You definitely don't shy away from conflict, but all the soap-operatic twists and turns in the world won't stop the constant drama from getting tiring. Learn to back off of arguments before your network rating takes a plummet.

love match

You may be falling for a summer-born daredevil, but there's a problem: He's got his eyes on someone else! Try to broaden your horizons; an adorable Aries will be able to give as good as he gets, and your heated arguments could easily lead to a different kind of spark.

friend match

Your Taurus BFF always looks to you for homework help and emotional support, but what really cements your friendship is the fact that neither of you cares what other people think. Just make sure you don't get stuck hanging out with the same people 24/7—it's important for both of you to bust out of your bubble.

'Tis better to give than to receive, and flush or bust, you've got more than enough wealth to go around. Your gifts are even better than money: super-helpful to anyone in need (like your hopeless-at-homework BF) and full of fun ideas about what to do and where to go, you always leave people a little richer than how you found them. Your friends and family send the love right back at you, and you're totally grateful for it.

friend match

You and your Cancer-born BFF make the perfect pair. Unlike some of your other friends, she's got the inner strength to take care of her own problems, and she actually gives you a chance to rest from your role as resident therapist. Even better, she doesn't take life too seriously, so when the weight of the world's on your shoulders, she always lightens the load.

love match

A Mercury-ruled boy changes his mind so quickly it makes your head spin, so say *hasta la rista,* to his up-and-down attitude. You need someone who has both feet on the ground and both eyes focused on you, so pick a winter-born guy who's looking for serious cuddle time.

$ Personal shopper

Jennifer Aniston

Ski lodge in Aspen

+/− It's great that you're always trying to fix your friend's problems, but remember that sometimes people need to learn to do things for themselves. If they lean on you too heavily, you're bound to fall over, and often the best gift you can give your friends is space to make their own mistakes.

Earplugs

Almond

Christina Ricci

February 12

Protective, Persuasive, Thoughtful

If life were a sandwich, you'd be the turkey and tomato, 'cuz you are always in the middle. Whether you're keeping peace when your best friends go at it or holding court on the superiority of sesame orange chicken vs. kung po beef, your powers of persuasion make you the go-to girl for the final word. Most of the time, you don't mind playing mother hen and laying down the law for your friends. (Let's face it—they're lovable but not the most responsible people in the world!)

+/− It is great that you try to help your friends resolve their issues, but if you feel like you're caught in an endless Ping-Pong ball game—and your head is the ball—you have got to call a time-out before somebody calls a foul.

love match

Once you're done with someone, you're done. A Neptune-ruled boy may have lost a chance when he moved too slow, but consider whether you weren't acting a little bit standoffish. Don't expect him to read your mind. You need to do more than just wish for him to ask you out.

friend match

Your fire-sign friend and her polar opposite winter-born buddy might ask you to take sides in their latest debate as they can count on you to stay neutral. It's not your job to referee, so keep things cool by moving on to other topics.

They say the universe will not end with a bang but a whimper. No worries—if you have anything to say about it, there'll be plenty of explosions before then. Expressive and emotional, you speak your mind (often without thinking). In fact, you have the same carefree attitude when it comes to all your choices. Skinny dipping? Sure! You're up for anything.

Fuchsia

Madonna

Club in Ibiza

A WORLD-CLASS TANTRUM THROWER, YOU KNOW THAT NOTHING LEADS TO A COSMIC MELTDOWN QUITE SO WELL AS PENT UP FEELINGS.

February 13

Spontaneous, Outgoing, Energetic

+/− If you were to take a poll right now, your approval ratings would be through the roof. But what do you like the most about yourself? You're so used to feeding off the energy of other people, you risk losing your grounding.

love match

When you fall for someone, you have a tendency to shout it from the rooftops. But a quiet Virgo will be embarrassed, not flattered, by all the attention, so ease up a little and let him come to you.

friend match

Your water-sign friend is your exact opposite: She keeps her cards superclose to her chest, and is unlikely to let anyone but the inner circle know what she's feeling. Take a lesson from her book. She can teach you a thing or two about privacy.

February 14

If you were a lip gloss shade you'd be coral: to-die-for cute, works well with anybody, and also has just enough of an edge to keep things interesting. You're a true social butterfly, and you love to be the center of attention, particularly when you are cracking up your crew with yet another spot-on observation. (Only you would figure out that your gym teacher's initials spell ICK.) Just make sure you keep it light.

> DISSING OTHER PEOPLE DOESN'T GO WELL WITH ANYBODY'S OUTFIT.

Improv

Entertainment reporter

Mod

+/− Your dry humor is hilarious, but sometimes your sarcastic comments aren't so subtle. Maybe your friend's new do does look like a helmet, but save the jokes for your stand-up routine. Otherwise you'll get booed off stage for good.

love match

The brainy boy born on the 22nd who you've been crushing on has an ego as big as his IQ, so say, "*Au revoir.*" You might be surprised to learn there's a sweet Virgo who's been scoping you out. His goofy exterior conceals hidden depths, so give him a chance.

friend match

You and your earth-sign BFF are the equivalent of sweet-and-sour pork: Her sincerity and sweetness are the perfect balance to your tartness. She's way more serious than you are, but that's a good thing, actually. She can keep you in line when one of your jokes is in danger of going too far.

You're like skinny jeans in 1999: way ahead of your time.

Original and inventive, you think so far outside the box you're up in the stratosphere, and your insatiable curiosity means that when it comes to know-how, you're light years ahead of your peers. That doesn't mean you've got your head in the stars, though. A problem solver through and through, your logic and reasoning skills keep your feet firmly planted on the ground and make you ideal for student government.

friend match

You're more than happy to help your Sagittarius BFF with her homework, but every so often it feels like you're running a free tutoring clinic. Do not let your needs go unnoticed, especially the emotional ones. Speak up if you're feeling used.

love match

A Jupiter-ruled boy has your head spinning, even though you've barely exchanged a word. Pay attention to the small signals he gives, but don't shut yourself off to other options. An outdoorsy Cancer who loves to laugh might be the perfect person to pull you out of your bubble.

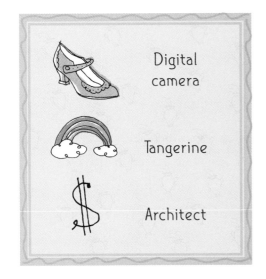

Digital camera

Tangerine

Architect

+/− Your brain is like a computer, always processing info and storing it away for later. But what's the fun without Wi-Fi to keep you connected? Don't live so much in your own little world that you miss out on fun times with those around you.

February 16

Sketch pad and pencil

$ Interior designer

"Let's Dance" —David Bowie

Spirited, Impulsive, Active

Some people look before they leap, but you'd rather jump in with your eyes wide shut. This means you're no stranger to crash landings (like the First Day of School Fashion Disaster of 2008), but it also means you're the queen of getting up, dusting yourself off, and getting back in the saddle. You're allergic to planning, and sitting still gives you the hives. Just remember that sometimes it really is better to be safe than sorry, and breaking certain rules will really give you something to be sick about (like a month's worth of Friday detentions).

+/− Your fave time is the start of a school year, since you're all about new beginnings. But you have a tendency to jump ship when you get bored, leaving you with a string of hobbies and friends you ditched after a month. Try sticking with something a little longer, or risk getting the reputation of a flake.

love match

You can barely decide what to order in a diner, so it's no surprise that you're equally finicky while choosing your guy. But if you think a Gemini is right for you, you're headed for dating disaster. Stick with a steadfast Aries instead.

friend match

You and your best friend *du jour* have no problem, but her sun-ruled ways make her occasionally turn bossy. Before you turn tail and run (as usual) try working through your issues by talking. Her fun and bubbly attitude make her the perfect wing-man (or wing-woman) for you.

If you could be a candy, you'd be an inside-out M&M: soft on the outside, you have a hard center (when people push you, you often surprise them by pushing right back) but still have a tendency to melt. (The biggest trigger that causes you to go gooey? When your friends are hurting—you're extra sensitive to their feelings.) You're not likely to take center stage, preferring to stay in the background, but you have no problem stepping up to the podium when someone steps into your personal space—or tries to step on your personal beliefs.

Yoga

Maltese

Paris Hilton

February 17

Sensitive, Stubborn, Shy

+/− If one of your friends shares her secret, she can count on your lips to stay sealed. But you have a tendency to give everyone in school the silent treatment, and they could mistake your shyness for snobbery. Remember, you can't make new friends by being seen and not heard.

love match

It's true that a lot of the guys in your school are immature, but that doesn't mean every single last one of them is a waste of time. A cutie born on the 12th might change your ideas about romance.

friend match

Your Virgo BFF is practically family, and it pains you whenever you see her weather yet another broken heart. But her outgoing nature and fearlessness can help you step out into the spotlight a little bit more, and you could also take a page out of her book when it comes to the confidence chapter.

February 18

Like a wide lens camera:
You're all about the big picture. You let other people sweat the small stuff. You're too busy making plans for the future and staring off at the horizon to get freaked out by details in the foreground. You're full of original ideas and are hugely ambitious, with goals that tend toward the artistic. Just make sure that all that gazing at the sky doesn't leave you blind to the truth right under your nose. Sometimes the beauty is in the details, and you could be missing out.

Hot-air balloon ride

Fashion designer

Molly Ringwald

+/− You dream of Pulitzer Prizes and Academy Awards, but you might want to finish your English assignment before you begin to plann all those acceptance speeches. Deal with real-life deadlines before you daydream, or you'll end up with a lot of real-life drama.

love match

A winter-born dude thinks you're an ice princess, but you just take time to warm up. Start thawing out, because nothing could be better for you than some quality time with this laid-back, easy going Aquarius.

friend match

Even you need advice once in a while, and your pragmatic pal whose birthday adds up to 8 is just the one to give it to you. The best part about her is that she keeps you from beating yourself up whenever you feel you've failed. If you're your own harshest critic, then she's your biggest cheerleader.

If life is a highway, you're a nine-person Hummer: You know where you're going, you do things big, and people either have to fall in line or risk getting flattened. When you're firing on all cylinders, your family and friends know better than to try to hold you back. (Road kill, anyone?) You're fearless: You love new things, new people, and exploring new interests. The idea of an open road and all of its possibilities totally appeals, and you're the one who motivates your peeps to try a new nail salon, hair color, or pizza spot.

friend match

You and your fall-born friend share one thing in common: a love for adventure. She'd make an amazing travel companion, so go ahead and start planning a postgraduation trip to Paris. Like you, she's comfortable talking to new people, so meeting French boys will be a breeze. *Oh la la!*

Passport

Aqua

Mary-Kate Olsen

love match

You don't have to be coy with the Libra you like, but you don't have to steamroll him, either. Chasing after him every day can get tiring, so make your latest love interest come to you. You don't have to play hard to get, necessarily, but it pays to keep a little bit of the mystery alive.

+/− It is great that you have such passion and energy, and it is even better that you follow your heart. But not everyone who has advice for you is trying to cramp your style, and it wouldn't kill you to listen every once in a while. The best drivers know to follow the rules of the road: breezing by too many *"Caution"* signs without slowing will just lead to an accident.

Pisces Girls
are deeply emotional and spiritual

Represented by two fish, Pisces is the ultimate water sign, which means that just like the ocean, girls born in this period have many hidden depths. Guided by dreams and intuition, they are completely uninterested in staying on the surface of life. Creative and extremely sensitive, they can be excellent friends but also difficult to get along with, and their passion for privacy makes a Keep Out sign look welcoming.

* * * * * * * * * * * * * *

Theme song: "Imagine" (A Life Without Homework)

Fruit they most resemble: Star fruit.
Exotic, sweet, easily bruised.

Strengths to play on: Artistic,
in touch with the universe.

Pitfalls to avoid: Illogical, out
of touch with peers.

Pisces

FEBRUARY 20 — MARCH 20

Element: Water

Ruler: Neptune

Most likely to be: Playing the part of Ophelia in the school's production of *Hamlet*.

February 20

You're like a public relations coordinator for your crew: Sensitive to other people's feelings, you are a master of smoothing out differences and getting everyone on the same team. You are not just a behind-the-scenes wheeler and dealer, though; you've got your very own star power, and are well aware that you never get a second chance at a first impression. Thankfully, you're so dynamic that the only reviews you get are raves.

$$\$$$ Talent agent

Rihanna

Safari in South Africa

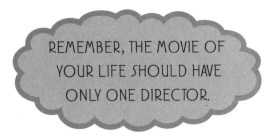

REMEMBER, THE MOVIE OF YOUR LIFE SHOULD HAVE ONLY ONE DIRECTOR.

+/— Your openness means you're great at meeting new people, and you're always ready to make new friends. But having a lot of peeps doesn't mean you have to give into peer pressure. Don't let anyone sway you from your beliefs.

love match

You're a risk taker in lots of arenas: You don't mind gambling on fashion choices, spicy foods, and new people. A certain Scorpio might wish you would take a chance on him. It's actually a pretty safe bet: The Scorpio's quiet intensity can help anchor you and provide comfort when you need it.

friend match

A moon-ruled BFF won't be half as good as you are at getting things done, but if you'll sometimes have to help her when her homework slides, at least you know the exchange won't be one-sided. Her solid values will help you keep your head straight.

February 21

You often wear your heart on your sleeve, which means you won't rub elbows with just anyone. It's important for you to be close to a small group of selects, but when it comes to making it in your inner circle, only super-VIPs get past the velvet rope. Your friends can count on your honesty and sensitivity to their problems, and you apply the same clearheadedness to your own life. On the rare occasions you do misjudge somebody, however, it's easy for you to get hurt.

friend match

A supersensitive fellow Piscean is the perfect complement to you. It takes you forever to open up to someone, but Pisces are known for their ability to listen and not judge, so you'll be able to spill the beans about crushes, insecurities, and your sister's nasty habit of leaving the door open when she uses the bathroom.

Mint green

Ellen Page

Anything that can be paired with a peasant blouse

love match

A boy born on the 10th may show you a little something about chemistry in your science class. Careful: Some combinations are bound to explode. Look for a more stable Capricorn who will stick by your side through even the messiest situations.

+/− Just because you get burned once doesn't mean you shouldn't put your hand back in the fire. Your fear of rejection makes it hard for you to reach out to someone new, but opening up to others is the only way to feed a strong and healthy social life.

$ Political pundit

𝄞 "Miss Independent"
—Kelly Clarkson

Castle in Scotland

February 22

Unselfish, Idealistic, Aloof

Your tendency to give off a frosty vibe doesn't mean you're anti-social, it just means that the opinion of others (good or bad) never makes you sweat. You have firmly fixed beliefs and, although you do not court compliments from other people, and are very attuned to their needs and wants. At the same time, if someone's opinions rub you the wrong way, you can be downright cold. Similarly, you're quick to come down hard on yourself when you think you've failed. Cut yourself (and others) a break now and then.

+/— It is great to have such high standards, but that doesn't give you the right to point out other people's flaws. Focus on yourself and do not worry about what other people are wearing, saying, and doing. It's not your duty to save your classmates from falling victim to their fashion sense (or lack of it).

★★★★★★☆

friend match

No one is easier to talk to than an ultra-supportive Libra BFF, whose sympathy and support can help you keep things in perspective when you feel like you've failed. Add in an energetic Aries who loves to have fun, and you have a trio made in friendship heaven.

love match

Mercury-ruled boys are famous for being notoriously difficult to read, but you actually might find that your totally together act makes a certain Virgo open up to you. If you really want sparks to fly, though, look no further than an adorable Aquarius.

If there is any problem—
feuding friends, sibling drama, or another awful anatomy lab—you will always be the one to step up to the plate. Life is a team sport, and you're the captain: Super-practical and down-to-earth, your friends look to you to play leader. But sometimes your feet-on-the-ground attitude can make you critical of other people's dreams, so learn to lay off the naysaying before your friends call foul. (Sure, becoming a famous actress is a long shot, but it isn't your place to remind your BFF of that every time she's dreaming of Oscars.)

Outdoor concert

Class president

Emily Blunt

February 23

Convincing, Analytical, Pragmatic

+/— Because you're mature and have street smarts to boot, you can sometimes come across as a know-it-all. Don't treat your friends like fan-club members and your conversations like classrooms. No one needs to hear lectures outside of school.

friend match

You're always doling out good advice, but when you need a healthy dose of wisdom, you should turn to a wise-beyond-her-years Cancer. Sometimes you have blinders on when it comes to your own problems, and this way you'll avoid bad haircuts, bad dates, and (most) bad decisions.

love match

You're a good girl, but your tastes run to the bad boys. Take a chance on that winter-born brooder, but avoid the truant Taurus who's always hanging out in the restroom during class. Best case scenario: He's trouble.

February 24

If what goes around really does come around, you have got a lifetime of good works headed right back at you. Whether you are spearheading your school's food drive or babysitting your little bro gratis, you are racking up brownie points with the universe quicker than you can say, "Karma." Just make sure that your focus on do-gooding does not mean you skip out on your duties to yourself.

IT'S OKAY TO BE SELFISH EVERY ONCE IN A WHILE.

+/− You would give the Paul Frank T-shirt off your back if someone needed it. However, there is a fine line between being generous and getting walked on doormat-style, so unless you like getting trampled, sometimes you've got to draw the line.

friend match

When it comes to social scenes, you're always tempted to hang back. But a Saturn-ruled BFF is all about fun, fun, fun, and she'll make sure you don't think of yet another reason not to go on your class trip to the water park.

love match

You may try to overlook a floppy-haired Aquarius because you seem to think you have nothing in common: He's all about parties, sports, and having fun. But he's got a sensitive understanding of the world that will surprise you, and his laid-back attitude might do you good.

If you were a bumper sticker, your message would be
"'Tis better to give than to receive." Even though you're still waiting for your phone to blow up with a message from your higher calling (green issues? Education reform?), you can't stress about how to curl your eyelashes correctly when you know there are people in the world trying to figure out how to eat. It's great that you're so dedicated to others, but once in a while it's okay to take pleasure in the petty details. A new sundress will make you feel great, so once in a while get on the receiving end of some of your charity.

friend match

You might think a certain Scorpio is all about makeup and malls, but her ability to enjoy the moment is a skill you definitely need. Make sure you're not isolating yourself from the people who can bring you to a happier place. You're only young once!

The New York Times

Ruby

"Waiting on the World to Change"
—John Mayer

love match

An air sign you've been crushing on may seem less than thrilled with the attention. Like many Gemini, he finds it difficult to make up his mind, which spells disaster when combined with your sensitivity to others' feelings. You need a guy with the fluidity of a water sign, like a Cancer.

+/− You are so dedicated to your ideals, you get frustrated when things don't go exactly how you want them to—especially if someone else sabotages your plans. Learn to let go before your reputation for giving morphs into a reputation for giving grief.

Music critic

Corinne Bailey Rae

Sporty

February 26

Serious, Critical, Stimulating

You are much better than a hypnotist: You're seriously expert at getting people to do what you say. You have an intuitive sense of what makes people tick, and you use this to your own advantage. (You're the only one in the world who could motivate your mama out of her PJs and into the park for some Saturday a.m. Pilates.) Just make sure you work your magic for good, not evil. Just because you know which buttons to press doesn't mean you can play people like pianos, and you don't want your people calling bogus on your skills.

+/− Your perceptive ways mean you see people's faults super-clearly. Be careful, because your criticism hits harder than you know, and you don't need to point out other people's problems. Power down that radar and turn your attention to the one person you can really control 24/7: You.

love match

You're not a girl prone to PDA—or even DA! But you can't expect your crush to read your mind; you're going to have to give the boy a hint. July-born boys are extremely perceptive, so you might get a little bit closer to ESP bliss with a Cancer.

friend match

A sensitive fire-sign friend will see right through your tough girl act and help you learn to express your feelings, not repress them. Nobody can be a power player 24/7, and you need to let her help you loosen up.

Actions speak louder than words, and yours are screaming. A mover and shaker, your understanding of the world around you—from MP3 players to your mom's up-and-down moods—means you know how to get things done. All that mojo makes people want to be around you (you can't blame them for wanting to coast on your vibe), but it also means you're extremely demanding of other people. Before you act up because somebody dropped the ball, remind yourself that nobody's perfect. Your harsh words sting more than you realise.

Bluetooth headset

Black Lab

Sarah Jessica Parker

February 27

* * * * * * * * *

Magnetic, Capable, Worldly

+/− Though in some ways you're a walking encyclopedia, your entry on "Self-Awareness" is seriously sparse. You've got a big blind spot when it comes to what you want, which can lead to problems in your personal relationships. Take some time to fill in the blanks, or you'll end up filing a lot of data under "Bad News" and "Breakups."

love match

You've got the patience of an alarm clock that's already ringing. You get tired of people (especially guys!) after only a few weeks, so that sensitive Sagittarius poet who recently caught your eye is as good as gone. You need someone who keeps things as fresh as you do, like a volatile (but exciting) Mercury-ruled Virgo.

friend match

You've got a ton of friends (you've got five separate people to see this weekend alone!), but only an ultra-perceptive Pisces can really get to know all of your dirty little secrets. This might seem scary, but keep her close; her unfailing vision can help you see yourself more clearly.

February 28

It's a shame you weren't born on the Fourth of July, because you're all about fireworks. You're very emotional and have a tendency toward extremes—you either *looove* it or hate it—and have more energy than a lit fuse and a powder keg. Your enthusiasm is contagious when you are at the center of a group. (Whether you're kicking off the dancing at spring homecoming or launching your school's first ever Pajama Day.)

Cheerleading

Ali Larter

Vegas, anyone?

+/− When it comes to listening to other people, you go temporarily deaf. You don't like anybody standing in the way of your good time, but some of your stunts are just plain reckless. Be careful; you're playing with fire.

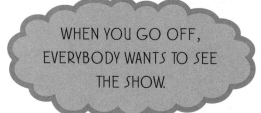

WHEN YOU GO OFF, EVERYBODY WANTS TO SEE THE SHOW.

love match

A July-born dude's got a serious thing for you, and it's no surprise. After all, you're charming, funny, and you've got the biggest smile on your face. But he's the equivalent of Pop-Tarts for breakfast: All sugar, no substance. If you're looking for something with a little more staying power, look no further than a loyal Leo.

friend match

If your crush doesn't give you a second glance, it's easy for you to turn it into a disaster of cosmic proportions. That's why you need an earth-sign friend to bring you back down to the ground. No need for drama.

☆ ☆ ☆ ☆ ☆

February 29

You have got the exclusive on the world's most VIP birthday, and it's no surprise: Starting with your once-every-four-years DOB, everything about you is special. You do things your own way and in your own time (spaghetti Bolognese for breakfast, anyone?), and though you're quick to laugh at yourself, your acceptance of others means you never make a joke at someone else's expense. And though you may not get to throw down for your b-day as much as everyone else, your joyful attitude means spending time with you is a 24/7 fiesta.

friend match

A spring-born BFF knows everything about you, from your favorite condiment (salsa) to your favorite month (August). Her sign is ruled by renewal and regrowth, and when you're together it feels just like the playdates you had when you were five. Keep the friendship strong and stay forever young.

Lilac

Prom committee

"L.O.V.E."
—Ashlee Simpson

love match

You know you are a special girl, so you are picky when it comes to love. But an Aquarius who usually flies under the radar might change your mind about relationships. He will be able to see how truly special you are.

+/− It's understandable that you don't want to share all of your dirty laundry with the world, but shoving all of it in the back of a closet will just lead to a big, smelly mess. Your quirks make you unique, so don't be afraid to flaunt your fabulousness and don't be so concerned about what other people think.

Amethyst

Art-gallery owner

Retro

March 1

* * * * * * * * * * * *

Artistic, Changeable, Ambitious

If beauty is in the eye of the beholder, you've got killer looks. You see beauty everywhere—an empty field in the morning, a steaming cup of chamomile tea, a new Prada bag (face it, that's art)—and are drawn to creative pursuits. But just because you're more likely to be scoping out the art scene than brushing up on science stats doesn't mean you're a flake. You can be both disciplined and practical, and when you want something you always keep your eye on the prize.

+/− It's great that you're always reaching for the stars, but you have to understand that bumping your head along the way is just part of the process. You have a tendency to get discouraged when things don't go your way, **but don't let doubts drag you down. You'll never get where you're going weighed down by so much negativity.**

* * * * * * * * * * * * * * * * * *

friend match

A Capricorn BFF might think you've got your head in the clouds, but don't let her rain on your parade. By nature she's sensible and down-to-earth; she can help you stay grounded, and you can help her dream big.

love match

One day you're batting your eyelashes at the air-sign hottie in your French class, and the next minute you're leaving without so much as an *au revoir.* The truth is you won't be ready to settle down until you meet a smoldering fire sign who's just as creative as you are.

You ought to be mafiosa, because you're all about loyalty. Your friends are like *familia*; you would do anything for them. You apply the same unwavering commitment to all of your projects: When you start something, you'll put in 100 percent of your time and energy into making sure it goes perfectly (whether it's creating the world's best lasagna for your BFF's sleepover, or even redecorating your bedroom). But not everyone you meet is going to be worthy of your all-the-time allegiance, and even though you have a hard time letting go, when people cross the line you have to learn to say *ciao*.

Collie

"You've Got a Friend"
—James Taylor

Beach in Miami

March 2

* * * * * * * * * *

Loyal, Imaginative, Persevering

+/— You like to keep your friends close—super-close—and have a hard time when your peeps disagree with you or don't include you in all of their plans. But nobody likes static cling, so learn to let go and allow some distance between you and your BFFs . . . or your friendships will soon be swimming with the fishes.

friend match

A supersensitive water-sign BFF will have you scrapping 24/7 on her behalf. It's fine to want to stick up for your friends, but you might be better paired with an outspoken Leo who is more than happy to defend herself.

love match

When it comes to a certain studious Scorpio, you wear your heart on your sleeve. But the fluidity that rules his sign makes him resistant to overt signs of affection, so if you want to really catch his eye, back off and let him do the chasing.

March 3

Your motto is "intelligent design": You are both imaginative and practical (you can not only imagine the perfect open-back summer sundress, you can actually sew it), which means you usually find a way to get what you want. You're equally good in science and art and can swing with a broad social scene, from the mathletes to the cheer-tators. But in some ways you're ultra-private; although you're always mapping out plans (for a new bedroom decor or an all-in-one toothbrush, fork, flosser, and chapstick). You have a tendency to get lost in your mental landscape.

School event

Student council

Jessica Biel

+/− It's great that you're consumed with whatever you do, but you can't expect your friends and family to play adoring population to your head-of-state. Make time for their interests. Relationships are like democracies, and unless you want a revolt on your hands, you have got to back off from playing Mussolini.

friend match

A faithful Taurus BFF will stick by you, no matter how many times she has to rescue you from the drama of your own life. Just make sure your cell's turned on when she's going through a crisis of her own.

love match

There is no astrological equation to help you choose between a cello-playing Capricorn and a fastball-throwing fire sign. One will lead to an intense and explosive relationship, and the other will help stabilize you over the long-term.

They say it's better to be alone than in bad company, and you'd almost always prefer the company of a good book, a movie, or a sketch pad. Independent and self-directed, you don't mind rolling solo and find it freeing to be away from the crush of the crowd. That doesn't mean you go Quasimodo, though; a few close friends keep you connected to the world outside your bedroom. Just make sure you're not putting too much pressure on a narrow social pipeline. Take a lesson from the trees: If you want to grow, you have to branch out.

friend match

You have a tendency to withdraw, but a fun-loving Aries can help break you out of your shell. Her natural sociability helps put you at ease in large groups, but her sensitivity to your feelings will guarantee that when you feel ready to flee, she will help you make a getaway.

Lit mag

Chef

Jeans and a
sweatshirt

love match

You'd much rather a curly-haired air-sign crush drop you a message on MySpace than tell you to your face that he likes you. Unfortunately, air signs are notoriously impatient. If you want someone who doesn't mind taking it slow, look for a shy but oh-so-adorable Scorpio.

+/− Do not let fears about new situations and people keep you from following your dreams. You may be a wallflower naturally, but you'll bloom much quicker if you are willing to step into the spotlight every once in a while.

March 5

Aspirin.
All that stress—
headaches,
headaches,
headaches!

Maroon

Eva Mendes

Expressive, Polished, Incisive

You are living proof that still waters run deep: Nobody would ever guess from the calmness of your exterior how stormy those seas can be. You're an expert at keeping it together 90 percent of the time—not letting school stress or friendship drama take the wind out of your sails—but it's definitely not all smooth sailing with you.

+/— You often live life in extremes: Your highs are extra high and your lows are rock bottom. But all of the ups-and-downs will make you seasick after a while, so it's important for you to surround yourself by people who balance you out.

PASSIONATE AND EXPLOSIVE, YOUR TEMPER IS LEGENDARY AND YOUR MOODS TEND TO CHANGE FASTER THAN YOU CAN SAY, "STORM CLOUD."

love match

You're ruled by Mercury, which means you change your mind all the time. A quiet earth sign and a daredevil Cancer are both competing for your attention, but no one will capture your heart until an intense Aquarius sweeps you off your feet.

friend match

You and a Scorpio BFF will be at each other's throats more often than a necklace. You need friends to calm you down when you're ready to explode, not add fuel to the fire. An-impossible-to-ruffle Libra is a better bet.

All that glitters isn't gold, but you'll take it anyway—diamonds, silver, rhinestones—you've got more glitter than a Claire's boutique. Some people may think you are shallow because you are drawn to beautiful things; you are deeply romantic and love to fall in love with the world around you. But you have a tendency to see people as good only because you want them to be. You have to learn to distinguish between the real deal and cheap imitations—otherwise you're just chasing after fool's gold.

Compact mirror

Dinner at a waterfront restaurant

Grace Kelly

March 6

Aesthetic, Attentive, Devoted

+/− You've got a great eye for what looks good, but a huge blind spot when it comes to all that lies beneath the surface. Not everything (and everybody!) worthwhile has a shiny happy coating, so try digging deeper.

love match

You love eye candy, but a gorgeous Gemini might have little more than surface charm. His dual nature could have you melting one minute and melting down another. Don't write off a studious Virgo in your science class just because he flies under the radar—he's a diamond in the rough.

friend match

You and your best friend are both ruled by Venus, so you're both shopping addicts and can spend hours making each other over. Try reaching out to a deep-thinking Aquarius who will help you see there's more to life than looking good.

March 7

If you were a painting, you'd definitely be a Picasso (no, not because you have three heads): You're all about the abstract. You're always trying to give meaning to the world around you and can't stop asking questions like why and how. There's no doubt that your interests pull you in a different direction than most of your classmates, but don't stress—most geniuses have to break away from the norm. (Just ask Pablo.) But all of that alone time can make anybody go through a blue period, so make sure you reach out to family and friends.

Museum

$

Children's book author

★ Jenna Fischer

+/− You should be proud of the fact that you march to the beat of your own drummer, but sometimes you just end up feeling as if no one understands you. You can't expect ESP from your friends and family, so if something's on your mind, say it. It doesn't take a psychic to know you will never feel connected otherwise.

love match

A sensitive fellow water sign will play the perfect muse (yes, boys can be muses, too!) to your artistic efforts. But be careful that your relationship does not get too unstructured and chaotic. You'd actually be better paired with a technical thinker like a Gemini.

friend match

A Saturn-ruled pal has her feet firmly planted on the ground, so even though it might feel like she's always teasing you for having your head in the clouds, you play an important role in her life. You help her dream bigger and teach her not to care what others think.

March 8

Sometimes you feel like the only blue M&M of the bunch:
Like you just don't belong. You have very strong opinions and often find yourself in conflict with the people around you (like when you absolutely insisted your BFF's party be an outdoor barbecue, not an indoor dance party). However, your strength of will and your understanding of other people mean you also have the ability to win people over to your side. You prefer the company of a few close friends to a big crowd, and the friends who do make it in the inner circle stick to you like melted chocolate to the hand.

friend match

A Leo BFF is the girl to turn to when you feel it's you against the world. Strongly ruled by intuition, the Leo understands you when you feel as though everyone else just plain isn't listening.

love match

A certain green-eyed guy in your science class is drawn to you as though you were a magnet. His ruling planet, Neptune, is in line with yours. But a Mercury-ruled boy might be better able to keep up with your mischievous sense of humor.

Artist

Kat Von D

"Right to
Be Wrong"
—Joss Stone

+/− There is no shame in going against the grain, but sometimes your attitude can just plain rub people the wrong way. Try to consider other people's points of view before speaking and acting out, or else your reputation will be more sour than sweet.

March 9

Bronze

Peer counselor

Brittany Snow

Perceptive, Visionary, Conceptual

You have a tendency to get lost in your own universe sometimes, but you're no space cadet. The truth is you see way more of what's going on than most and have an accurate and sensitive perception of the world around you. Unlike people who take things at face value, you'll always trust your instincts—and your sixth sense is always dead-on. Just be careful about biting off more than you can chew. You've got more hangers-on than a closet, and all of those responsibilities would make anyone a mess.

+/− You have got a lot of people leaning on you but still have trouble feeling like your friends really get you. Make sure the support flows both ways.

FRIENDSHIPS, LIKE FREEWAYS, WORK BEST WHEN THEY'RE TWO-WAY.

love match

It's important for you to keep your options open, as any relationship with you tends to get intense very fast, particularly if you pair up with fellow water signs like Scorpios and Cancers. A Capricorn class clown with an outrageous sense of humor might win you over.

friend match

An Aquarius BFF distinguishes herself from the rest of your group: When you're together, she tends to play leader. This is not a bad thing. Every so often it's nice to snooze in the backseat, so go ahead and let her take the wheel.

Socrates said, "Know thyself," and though you don't get down with dead Greek guys as a rule, at least in this instance you agree. (The all-toga wardrobe? Not so much.) You are just as likely to be turning your gaze inward as outward, and keeping a journal or blogging are both ways that you try to express your deepest thoughts. Just because you are a budding philosopher does not mean you are self-centered, though; you follow the Golden Rule and do good unto others, too.

Tarot cards

Carrie Underwood

Classic

March 10

* * * * * * * * *

Sensitive, Empathic, Soulful

+/− It's great that you're so focused on the spiritual realm, but don't let it stop you from making everyday decisions. The meaning of your dreams might be an interesting topic for your next blog post, but the F on your social studies paper means only one thing—a grounding—so make sure you get some studying time in.

love match

A tall Sagittarius boy might need a little more encouragement than you're comfortable giving right now. Make sure you're not unconsciously discouraging the people who will be right for you. A smile will be more than enough invitation to the soulful Pisces who is your perfect match.

friend match

A moon-ruled girl is there when you want to discuss your deepest dreams, and when you feel the need for silly. Bust out a game of Twister or your little bro's Guitar Hero; you can't live in your own head all the time.

March 11

It's no wonder your friends don't want to play Monopoly with you: You're always a step ahead of the game. You rock the trends long before others jump on the bandwagon (you were cutting up your own T-shirts since you could hold scissors), and you've got so much jump on the news you could start your own channel. You have a deep fear of being left behind, but ironically have trouble letting go of the past. Don't let it make you paranoid about giving up people and activities whose dates may have expired: Hanging on to old drama will spoil anybody's outlook.

Navy blue

Basset hound

Vineyard in California

+/− You like to have control over everything around you, but nobody likes to play handmaiden to your queen. Let your friends plan a party or pick your Friday-night-eats spot for a change; otherwise you might find yourself dethroned.

love match

A Jupiter-ruled jock may be about much more than weightlifting and repetitions (which is good, because you know about as much about sports as a fish knows about climbing Mount Everest). And a scorching hot Aquarius is bound to make a lasting impression on you.

friend match

A Pisces friend of yours isn't stuck up; she's shy. You can teach her a thing or two about being outgoing—you exude confidence—and she'll be there to support your many metamorphoses (from schoolgirl chic to goth girl to, yes, even cheerleader).

March 12

Nobody's gonna break your stride and can't nobody hold you down: When you hit a bump in the road, you just leap straight over it. Your friends admire your courage and persistence. On the rare occasions when you totally wipe out (the third-grade talent show debacle still makes you cringe), you're the queen of picking yourself up and dusting off. Your comeback act means no matter what great things you achieve in your life, there will always be an encore.

friend match

Your MySpace Top 8 is always changing, but a sweet, sensible Sagittarius might be the one constant in your ever-revolving group of friends. You two are like candy-covered apples: A perfect balance of sweet and tart.

love match

A Leo's good looks will have your head spinning, but a match between a water and fire sign will fizzle out before it can even spark. A Uranus-ruled air-sign boy, however, will build you up when you need support and mellow you out when you need some R & R.

Your level-headed BFF

Hockey game

Actress

+/− It's great that you dive headfirst into everything, but sometimes the old saying really does apply: You've got to look before you leap. Certain situations and people will spell bad news no matter what language you're speaking, so rely on your more cautious friends to steer you clear of the obvious pitfalls.

March 13

Yoga mat

Advice columnist

Stray cat

+/− It is awesome that you have such a roll-with-the-punches attitude. But that doesn't mean you should play the martyr and let yourself get beat up. If something's really bothering you, speak up, and maybe you can figure out how to change it.

Accepting, Courageous, Intuitive

If you could be a bumper sticker you would say, "Everything happens for a reason." No matter what happens in life, you are convinced it is meant to be, and your Zen attitude helps you turn even the twistiest roads into straight paths to success. You come blessed with so much intuition it's like you're the 411 from the future; you can't stop yourself from making predictions (cargo pants will definitely make a comeback), and you're usually right.

MAKE SURE THAT YOU DON'T COME ACROSS AS
A KNOW-IT-ALL; AFTER ALL, NOBODY LIKES A TALKING HEAD.

love match

A blond Venus-ruled boy and you are like a black-and-white cookie: Both halves are totally different, but neither one works as well alone as it does with the other. But he's not the most perceptive when it comes to subtle signals, so you'll need to do more than smile to communicate your interest.

friend match

You and an Aries BFF are so attuned to each other's feelings, it's like you have ESP. Unfortunately, you also have the same taste in boys, so watch out for clashes in the romance department.

Both you and Einstein have something in common (thank God it's not the hair): for you, it's all relative. You know that the view depends on where you're standing, and you shy away from absolutes. (Your favorite word is *"possibly."*) Opinion essays are hard for you because you see both sides of every issue, and you do well at parties because you relate easily to many different kinds of people, from the football fanatics to the drama-ramas. In fact, you find that you shine the strongest when other people are fanning the flames.

☆•☆•☆•☆•☆•☆

Magic 8-Ball

Baby blue

Musician

March 14

• • • • • • • • • • • • •

Flexible, Independent, Patient

+/− It's great that you can see multiple view points, but every so often it's important to take a stand. You don't want to be wishy-washy about everything (like what movie to see or whether breaking into school to go streaking is a bad idea—it is!), or eventually you'll get hung out to dry.

love match

An outgoing summer-born guy may be your very own American Idol, but a fun-driven Sagittarius is just the thing you need to keep you singing a love song.

friend match

Your Mercury-influenced ways make you wary of settling into deep friendships with just anyone. You'd much rather wait until you find a true BFF, like a straight-shooting Virgo who has an opinion about everything.

March 15

You are always reaching for the stars, but that does not mean you're spacey. Ambitious and competitive, you want to stay on top of everything you do, so whether you're pulling an all-nighter to perfect your bio project or sporting a pair of 4-inch wedge heels, you're always reaching higher. You'll gladly take on difficult assignments and aren't afraid of failure. Just make sure to take care of your friendships, too.

> YOU KNOW WHAT THEY SAY: IT'S LONELY AT THE TOP!

School newspaper

Eva Longoria

Casual chic

+/− A little bit of competitiveness is a good thing, but getting green with envy when things go well for others is definitely not cool. Your BFF's successes don't make yours any less impressive, so stop clinging so tightly to the top of the pyramid before jealousy sends your mood into a plummet.

love match

There's an element of Pisces ruled by playfulness, which means it's easy for you to fall into a buddy-buddy routine with an easygoing Aquarius. In order for the connection to move beyond friendship, you'll have to show that you're looking for more than a barrel of laughs.

friend match

You and an earth-sign friend have an identical sense of humor, and you're always scheming pranks and practical jokes. (Like putting red hair dye in your sister's conditioner—at least it wasn't permanent.) But for a shoulder to cry on when the going gets tough, look for a sensitive air sign.

March 16

If you were a piece of clothing, you'd be the perfect pair of jeans (fess up, you've got seven pairs): Totally practical, infinitely versatile, and everybody's best friend. It's not that you don't dream big—you do—but you always take practical steps to accomplish your goals, and you're much more likely to be doing than dreaming. In general, you're self-confident, but you have to be sure that in your quest to be everybody's BFF you don't give up what you want. Selling out will never be in style—not even when paired with the perfect denim.

friend match

Try not to be affected by other people's jealousy. Find a supportive and loyal Taurus friend who will let you be the shining star and love you for it!

Chocolate brown

Sporty

Lauren Graham

love match

You always find yourself attracted to the fire signs: A skateboarding Sagittarius is your latest love interest. (Unfortunately, he'll turn out to be a wipeout.) You need an air sign who floats through life effortlessly to help you over all the little bumps in the road.

+/− You take your lesson from *Project Runway*: When you set out to do something, you make it work. But when you get discouraged, you have a tendency to cut out, rather than see the project through. Quitting is always last season, so hold tight to your commitments and make sure to see them through.

March 17

* * * * * * * * * *

Flexible, Expressive, Enthusiastic

If you ever got a tattoo (as if your mom wouldn't kill you), it would have to be a butterfly. You're all about taking flight, flitting around to multiple activities (from ballet to snowboarding to photography) and from social group to social group. In fact, you hate to feel penned in by any one crowd; hanging out with the same friends all the time makes you feel like your wings have been clipped. Your tendency to get bored easily makes it difficult for other people to keep up, which means you're often in danger of flying solo.

Coral

Goldfish

"Breakaway"
–Kelly Clarkson

+/– It's one thing to try new things; it's another to never followthrough on old plans. All that jumping around is making you flakier than snow, so learn to honor your commitments (if you say you're going to be at your friend's b-day party, be there), before all of your peeps leave you out in the cold.

- - - - - - - - - - - -

love match

You change your mind about your crushes more often than you change your underwear: First a Jupiter-ruled martial artist, then a Taurus soccer player, then an Aries artist. Your heart heals fast and moves quickly, but a Cancer with bright blue eyes may be the one to change your runaround ways.

friend match

A fire-sign friend will be able to keep up with you as you cruise from interest to interest, but a loyal Leo will demand more of your time and energy than you're willing to spare. Keep in mind: You could learn a thing or two from her dedication and dependability.

In your personal entourage, you are always the one playing agent. Whether you are brokering a clothing barter between your two BFFs (her white dress for three of her colored bangles) or negotiating entrée into your fave restaurant on Friday night, you're always pulling the strings. When you know what you want, you'll go after it aggressively (the near fistfight at Nordstrom's over the last size 4 bebe dress ringing any bells?) but can be patient when the situation requires it. And, like any good agent, you know how to seal the deal: When you start something, you finish it.

iPhone

Dancing at the hottest club in town

Vanessa Williams

March 18

* * * * * * * * * *

Intuitive, Powerful, Diplomatic

+/− All of your wheeling and dealing on other people's behalf means you easily lose sight of personal values. Compromise is the key but not when it comes to your principles. If you're not comfortable doing something (like letting your lab partner take credit for your work), stand up for yourself.

friend match

Typically, Pisces and Libras aren't compatible, but March 18 ladies are strongly influenced by Mars and fire, meaning you and your air-sign BFF make an unstoppable pair. Nobody says no to you two, as both of your parents know.

love match

A fellow Pisces might have your head spinning. Careful: He's got more game than a basketball court, and may have you crying foul before long. Stick to a true-to-his-word Aries.

March 19

If slow and steady wins the race, your future holds a lot of blue ribbons. You'll climb every mountain—and face down every frenemy, French test, and freaky teacher—in your effort to succeed. You're not naïve (despite what your parents seem to think, you know exactly how the world works), but your openness and optimism occasionally make you seem younger than you are. Your rivals shouldn't be fooled by your ray-of-sunshine exterior, though. When it comes to going the distance, you're all business.

SLOW DOWN AND HAVE SOME FUN!

Manolo Blahnik stilettos

District attorney

Chic hotel in London

+/− No one can ever accuse you of being lazy. But all work and no play spells social disaster, so be realistic about how much you can accomplish. Heading up the pep rally committee, cocaptaining the soccer team, as well as taking three advanced classes, may seem like a good idea, but you're way too young to get caught in the rat race.

love match

Your practical side wishes that romance were more like an equation: Flirtation + digits = lasting relationship. But it's okay to let formulas go by the wayside, so let yourself get swept away by a magnetic and intense Scorpio.

friend match

You're right on the Pisces-Aries cusp, which means you have got a one-track mind that's hard to derail. That's why you need a perceptive Virgo BFF to let you know if something's not such a hot idea (like cutting off all your hair and bleaching it—not a good look for you).

Logical, Sensitive, Versatile

March 20

You're worse than a book of Sudoku: It takes forever to figure you out. Because you were born on the last day of winter, you're heavily influenced by the idea of change. Multitalented and versatile, you've got more paths available to you than a maze. You're deeply romantic and sensitive to other people's feelings, making you a loyal friend. But it can be tough for you to let go, so just make sure you're not hanging on to a bunch of dead-end relationships.

friend match

You and a moon-ruled BFF are solstice sisters, both born on the very edge of two seasons. (This explains the way you seem to be able to communicate without speaking.) A light-hearted Gemini can keep you from getting too intense.

love match

A studious Sagittarius won't mind the challenge of getting to know you. He's an expert at puzzles and has the patience to put the pieces together.

YOU'LL NEVER KNOW WHICH ROAD IS RIGHT UNLESS YOU START WALKING, AND TRUST YOUR FAMILY AND FRIENDS TO GIVE YOU THE BIRD'S EYE VIEW.

Purple

Soccer

Your BFF's car . . . Road trip!

+/− Because you have so many options available to you, it's almost impossible for you to make choices—even the small ones. (Whole-wheat bagel or toasted? Sesame or poppy seed? Butter or cream cheese?)

THE PLANETS: A QUICK TOUR!

The Sun gives life to our solar system and represents tremendous creativity and power. It symbolizes the outward drive of the ego, striving toward unique individual expression. Those ruled by the sign of Leo and the number 1 are forthright, demanding and lend much-needed energy to others.

The Moon stirs the depths of the oceans and regulates the tides as well as human emotions. Reflective in nature, the Moon symbolizes the world of dreams. Those ruled by the number 2 and the sign of Cancer tend to be feeling types who work well with others in group projects.

Mercury is the small, speedy planet closest to the sun. Named for the winged messenger, Mercury rules Gemini and Virgo (as well as the number 5) and symbolizes quick thought and communication. Mercurians are detail-oriented and full of vivacity and impulse. True players—in more ways than one—they're drawn to games and puzzles.

Venus represents a love of beauty, whether of a sensuous or a more idealistic nature. Those born under the signs of Taurus and Libra, as well as those whose number is 6 are all bathed in this warm and rich energy. The goddess Venus is associated with desire and attraction—her son was Cupid!

Mars was the god of war, which is emphasized by the reddish appearance of the planet. Originally Mars ruled the signs Aires and Scorpio, but now Scorpio has passed to Pluto. Martian energy is aggressive, adventurous, highly motivated to succeed, and in general unstoppable!

Jupiter is the largest planet in our solar system. The jovial, optimistic, and lucky qualities of this massive planet are associated with Sagittarians and those ruled by the number 3. Jupiter was king of the gods—so jupiterian people are very positive, wise, dynamic, and constructive about solving problems.

Saturn is represented as dark and cold, a fatal force. However, it has a deeper meaning of structure and of taking responsibility for one's actions. Capricorns and those ruled by the number 8 believe in law and have strong personal values.

Uranus is the ruler of Aquarius and the number 4. This planet symbolizes strongly individualistic and at times rebellious energies. The movements of the planet Uranus are erratic, so Uranian types are spontaneous and impulsive—and they hate doing things the "normal" way.

Neptune was the king of the sea in classical mythology. Neptunian people are profound but difficult to pin down. Fantasy-rich, the minds of Pisces and those ruled by the number 7 often are attracted to highly imaginative goals. They exert an irresistibly magnetic influence and are known for dissolving barriers.

Pluto was the dark god of the underworld and lends hot, volcanic energies to those born under the sign of Scorpio. Plutonic areas are traditionally those of money, power, and sexuality. The planet Pluto represents fate—but fate is not set in stone! Pluto's power can be harnessed to achieve amazing transformations.

Acknowledgments

· ·

With extreme gratitude for the significant written contributions by Laura Schechter.
Thanks also for the terrific research and input by Marissa Grossman.

· ·